IN LOVE WITH DAYLIGHT

DAYLIGHT

A Memoir of Recovery

WILFRID SHEED

SIMON & SCHUSTER

NEW YORK   LONDON   TORONTO   SYDNEY   TOKYO   SINGAPORE

SIMON & SCHUSTER
Rockefeller Center
1230 Avenue of the Americas
New York, NY 10020

SIMON & SCHUSTER and colophon are registered trademarks
of Simon & Schuster Inc.

Designed by Levavi and Levavi

Manufactured in the United States of America

1   3   5   7   9   10   8   6   4   2

Library of Congress Cataloging-in-Publication Data

Sheed, Wilfrid.
In love with daylight : a memoir of recovery / Wilfred Sheed.
p.   cm.
1. Sheed, Wilfrid—Biography.   2. Authors, English—20th century—
Biography.   3. Depression, Mental—Patients—Biography.
4. Recovering addicts—Biography.   5. Cancer—Patients—Biography.
6. Polio—Patients—Biography.   I. Title.
PR6069.H396Z469   1995
823'.914—dc20
[B]   94-42001
                                                                        CIP

ISBN 0-671-79215-6

To Dr. K., Dr. X., and most especially
my old friend Dr. T.

CONTENTS

INTRODUCTION

This book was not, I'm relieved to say, exactly written over my dead body—only against my unflagging resistance. I've never been the least interested in the nuts and bolts of sickness and health. In fact, even when I've been so ill myself that there's been no avoiding them, my position has always been "Just tell me what I'm supposed to do, and who do you like in the World Series?" or the Oscars, or any damn thing that doesn't require thermometers and blood tests every half hour. A few brief but intense rendezvous in hospitals have also left me with an abiding hatred of the color white, and when I finally leave this planet, I can only hope that any doctors and nurses in the area will be gaily caparisoned in all the colors of the rainbow, with a roaring fire playing on the tapestries. Surely that isn't too much to ask.

So how did this book happen? Innocently enough, and extremely circuitously. In the fall of 1989, the late magazine *Lear's* asked me to contribute to a symposium on the meaning of the word *spiritual*, which is the kind of request that usually has the word *wastebasket* written all over it. For people who try to do this stuff for a living, symposiums are strictly amateur night and a chance to be shown up by Jane Fonda or Hulk Hogan or some other muffin-headed celebrity on a roll; who but an actor can work up a full head of seriousness in three hundred words any-how?

On the other hand, I had a soft spot for *Lear's,* which had several friends on it and gave great parties, and for once, I also had something to say on the subject, and I thought, "Just this once—and I promise never to do it again," and wrote the fol-lowing.

Last year I was hit by a barrage of ailments that reintro-duced me to the joys of recuperation, a pleasure I'd almost forgotten about since I was hit by polio, the A-bomb of diseases, at the end of World War II. (Hiroshima happened the same year: fortunately my life has not kept up this pace.)

The spiritual life becomes very simple when you're sick. You pray to get better, and if and when you do, you don't need to be told to be grateful about it: it gushes out of you. And you discover, in the same giddy rush, that just being alive, even on a no-frills basis, is astoundingly good: and this remains, for me, the primal insight. G. K. Chesterton once said that if a person were to fall into the waters of forgetfulness and come out on the other side, he would think he had arrived in paradise. But all you need to do is spend a couple of months on your back, or return home from a war and come downstairs to have breakfast in your own house (I'm told by veterans that just having a bath-room to yourself can seem like going to heaven).

So my private proofs for God, or whatever, begin with this: the sheer capacity for happiness, and one's sense, when it happens, that this is correct and normal and not some freak of nature. When health returns, it feels like coming home, with everything just as you left it: and the other thing, the bad news—the broken leg or even the mental breakdown—feels like the freak. But now you are back where you belong, in harmony with the universe. And from this I deduce with some conviction that the universe is *essentially* a good place to be, despite appear-ances, and that if it means anything, it means well.

The trick of course is to stay on its good side, and this would take, has taken, hundreds of books to discuss. Let me just say quickly: concentration, kindness, and in my own case the Catholic tradition—there has to be *some* tradition—which gives me a sense of companionship over the centuries. To which I would add, by way of illustration, that the two most intense and unqualified pleasures I have had in the last year have been respectively the marriage of a son and the birth, courtesy of one of my daughters, of a grandchild. The universe's wishes can be devious beyond exasperation at times, but I like to think that it has its simple pleasures too. And on days like that, even the God of Job can be sensed to smile for a second.

Beyond that I can only hope that if, in the biblical phrase, one lives out one's days "in the eye of God," or at least someplace in the neighborhood, one will someday come to see old age and death as equally natural and simply the next thing to do.

I honestly don't know if this thought will help me then, but it helps me now.

And that, I trusted, was that. It was in truth a blissfully happy time in my life, and I was delighted to tell *someone* about it, but certainly not to make a big production out of it. After all, what was the message? The Secret of Happiness is to get sick, or break a leg, or come back from the dead, or perhaps to imagine that you've done these things and hope for the best. Then, shortly after that, someone else asked me to take part in a symposium about the meaning of God, and I remember jotting down something like this: "If a certain general hadn't ruined the phrase forever, I would say that 'God is the light at the end of the tunnel,' and maybe the light in the tunnel as well, if you're a saint"—but this one I *didn't* send in. It was basically the same thought anyhow, a celebration of waking up from a bad night and falling head over heels in love with daylight, and I felt the public had had enough of my wisdom on this subject, and I had certainly had enough of dispensing it.

However, my soon-to-be friend Phyllis Theroux wrote me a letter after the *Lear's* piece asking permission to reprint and circulate it in her Virginia neighborhood; and a while later, after we'd met in person, the same lady suggested, so casually that I doubt she remembers it, that I expand the piece into a book someday.

A thousand times no! My response was a lot more emphatic than her request. There was no way of expanding this particular material without reaching back into the world of sickness that I had just so cheerfully left; and furthermore, if I couldn't read a whole book about health matters without alternately flinching and falling asleep, how on earth was I going to write one?

On the other side of the ledger was a dawning realization that every time the subject came up in conversation, I had something to say about it that the others hadn't heard before and wanted very much to hear now, just in case it applied to them. Everyone has a tryst with sickness someday, or expects to with various degrees of apprehension, so anyone who has visited that country becomes an automatic object of curiosity. How does it look? How did he take it? How would *I* take it?

Insofar as I had learned anything new at all in the land of sickness, it gradually occurred to me that maybe I had no choice. Whether you've witnessed a crime, or discovered a pothole or a cure for insomnia, you simply have to skip your next appointment and testify—especially if you believe you have some honest-to-God, non-sugar-coated good news to report. What we had here, in other words, was the literary equivalent of a subpoena in the hands of a surly witness from whom much of this book had to be dragged.

And, as it turned out, I was not to be let off lightly with a novel either. My first instinct, like that of a child who has to confess to something embarrassing, was to make up a fictitious character to whom the whole thing *really* happened. But in matters of sickness and death, you have to put up or shut up; you have to level. Did this happen or didn't it? does it actually feel like this, or are you just guessing? If you don't know for sure, the experts will move in quick as a blink and sweep your testimony into the dispose-all, and replace it with the old, outsiders' version, and you might as well have skipped the whole trial.

So stripped (for now—the novel comes next) of the armor of fiction, I toyed for all of five seconds or so with the possibility of writing impersonal nonfiction. Just the facts, ma'am. On the first day, patient complained of such-and-such and noticed so-and-so, a soreness of the this and a swelling of the that. But what you really remember is the moment when the wallpaper began to drive you crazy, especially combined with the doctor's cough: sickness becomes personal immediately. And that's the part people want to hear about. The symptoms they can get from a textbook. What they want right now is to walk for just a day or an hour in your pajamas or hospital gown and listen in on your thoughts and take your measure. Are you some kind of a hero (hell no, in my case), and does one need to be? Proof of ordinariness will be much appreciated, so never mind your usual airs and graces. Every pirouette takes you further away from the people you're talking to. So I've tried to keep those to a minimum, confining myself simply to what each sickness *feels* like, and what recovery *feels* like, whoever you are.

The centerpiece of my testimony actually comes at the psychological moment when you throw away the hospital gown, either because you're cured—in which case, bingo! no complications, and no book—or because you're as cured as you're going to be, and must get back into life somehow, ready or not, in which case, also bingo, but a library's worth of complications.

What distinguishes the only three illnesses I've ever had (if you subtract measles, age six) is that all three are generally deemed incurable, and that each has caused me to lose something quite irreplaceable, something I would have sworn I couldn't live without. The first of my Big Three, polio, cost me, for instance, the world of games, around which my whole world turned: when I wasn't playing them, I was thinking about them and planning a long, happy future with them. ("We're going to Zanzibar this summer!" "Swell—what do they play there? cricket or baseball?") The second, addiction-depression, deprived me of not just the sleeping pills that brought it on but the whole congenial drinking life, from wine tastings to bar-bellyings to motor trips through France (who could bear to send back all those wine lists?) to, finally, the best part of all, the solid-gold time spent with friends in the small hours, when for a long moment, held like a note of music, you understand each other *perfectly*. In short, it cost me nothing less than the best minutes of the day and the best years of my life. Or so it seemed at the time. Giving up booze felt at first like nothing so much as sitting in a great art gallery and watching the paintings being removed one by one until there was nothing left up there but bare white walls.

. . . White again, the color of death as far as I'm concerned, and back to the hospital for number three, cancer. So far the jury is still out on this one, and long may it remain so, but the Big C, as they call it in show biz, has already left a wintery calling card: without giving away too much of what passes for a plot in here, I'll just say that C. has made some mean little inroads into the joy of eating, that last redoubt of the sensual man. But as I quickly learned, cancer, even more than polio, has a disarming way of bargaining downward, beginning with your whole estate and then letting you keep the game warden's cottage or the badminton court; and by the time it has tried to frighten you to death and threatened to take away your very existence, you'd be amazed at how little you're willing to settle for.

But *how* little? This is theme No. 2 of what follows. A fellow I know lost a whole leg to cancer, and was happier afterward than he'd ever been before, simply because he was alive and the enemy was gone. So one might start the bidding with that. The long, wary truces of cancer that might end at any moment with a call to arms, or might, contrariwise, last forever, send you a command invitation to speculate over and over about precisely why you're putting yourself through all this and whether it's worth it. Is there a point at which life is no longer better than death? Since I've never regarded myself as any kind of Candide or Lemuel Pitkin, who insists on looking on the bright side as life whittles away at his arms, legs, and senses, I'm sure that there must *be* such a point—some moment when you're ready to fold what's left of your hand and say enough is enough. But in spite of some quite serious whittling, I've never even come close to that point myself.

Quite the reverse. After each of my "unbearable, insupportable" losses, I have felt not only undiminished and unready to die, but quite goofily elated, as I tried to describe in *Lear's*. As it happens, shortly after writing that ode, or squawk, to joy, I came across a sublime illustration of the mood I'd been talking about in the form of an old, old movie short, built around Johnny Mercer's splendid song "GI Jive," showing an average sort of Sad Sack barely surviving the horrors of army life in World War II and plunging at last into the joys of peace. In the final scene, the war has just ended and our hero capers around a deserted Times Square in civilian clothes, fairly bursting with happiness. *That* was how I had felt after each of my illnesses, even though I wasn't exactly dancing by the end, but leaning, like some black-comic character, on a pair of canes, sipping Diet Coke to keep my mouth from turning to dust, and wondering where the cancer would strike next. If the war is over for now and the bombing has stopped, that's simply how you feel, whatever the damage.

At least, that's how I felt—and by chance, how every survivor I know seems to have felt too. (Have you ever heard of a crippled athlete who did *not* have a great heart?) When I was a kid, religious folk would say things like "God only seems to send polio to people who are strong enough to take it," but experience has since told me that the folk had it exactly backward. To judge only from the polio veterans I've known, God has made just about everybody strong enough to take it, so affliction can land where it likes. All landing fields are fully equipped. I have yet to meet a victim of this plague who has not made a *perfect* adjustment to it, and then some—Exhibit A being Franklin Roosevelt, whose gargantuan, cartoonlike self-assurance saw us through war and depression as if they were just more pool exercises. Indeed, for relative cockiness, the only group I can think of to compare with our alumni would be some of the blind people I've met, although their adjustment must be infinitely trickier than ours and I wouldn't presume to speak for them. (Here and throughout I should emphasize that there is absolutely nothing scientific about what follows—just a patient's-eye view and a lifetime of observation. As Ross Perot would say, "You can talk when it's yo' turn.")

Numerous people who have had to care for critically injured patients have testified, as polio nurses once did, to how amazingly quickly the patient's spirit seems to take over and begin to pull *them* through, as if it were a new presence in the room, preternaturally strong and self-assured. At this time of maximum dither and uncertainty, "it" knows exactly what's needed around here.

But although the phenomenon happens often enough to be considered (by me, anyway) a fact of nature, you can't set your watch by it: the positive reaction to one's plight may occur instantly—or it may take what seems like forever, if the patient's imagination hits a depressive groove and gets stuck. So you obviously can't say to him, "Okay, start pulling us through this." And you equally can't say, "So he or she has got a great spirit—don't they all?" It's a miracle every time one of these comebacks, or mini-resurrections, happens—but they do happen again and again, and in the rare case when they don't, I would guess that something else is eating the particular subject besides his paralysis or whatever. Afflictions have an uncanny ability to clean up after themselves, and even leave you laughing, but they obviously can't guarantee to root out deep-seated psychological glitches—although they have a pretty good record with those too.

Perhaps the hardest glitches for nature to cope with are those caused by any feel-good chemicals that may have been brought in to help out. The great James Thurber, for instance, was never reconciled to his blindness, partly because it led him in the course of it through countless painful eye operations, each of which must have raised and dashed his hopes brutally, but partly also because he seems to have tried to drink his way out of trouble, and it simply can't be done: booze is like an exit door painted on the wall for which alcoholics and other optimists manage to fall every time. There is no sadder specimen on heaven or earth than an old drunk around two in the morning after he's just hit the wall for the thousandth time, and it doesn't matter *how* good or bad his eyesight is or how many operations he's had.

Which brings me to Illness No. 2, addiction-depression, the

centerpiece of this book, though it didn't start out that way. This particular section just grew and grew, at the slight expense of the others, because (a) so much of this complaint seems to take place in one's head, and not in some obscure corner of the body, and (b) because it must surely be the only disease ever devised for which the preferred and only medicine is talking. But although addiction has been damn near talked to death by now, in print among other places, I found, when I needed it, that most of the talk was not only completely wrongheaded but curiously undescriptive as to detail, and not written for the likes of me or possibly you. During the whole time I was under this particular cloud, I would have sold my soul cheerfully (if I could have done anything cheerfully) just to hear from someone else who had passed this way and could tell me what was actually happening to me and what to expect next. But among all the thousands of inspirational and pseudoscientific words I could find on the subject, not one came close either to describing what I was going through, or suggesting anything useful to do about it except go to meetings and talk, talk, talk, which is the water I swim in anyway. So I've had to write it myself, scene for scene—all the things I would like to have read back then.

Fortunately, my chore has been lightened somewhat by the subsequent publication of William Styron's excellent *Darkness Visible,* which renders the pit of depression exactly as I found it, thus freeing me to some extent to pick up where that book left off, with the final run for daylight, of which giddy experience addiction actually provides not one but two—a phony but delightful one which they call a "pink cloud" and the real thing, which rolls up sometime later.

These two breakthroughs, the facsimile and the genuine, give one an unparalleled opportunity to isolate the purely manic aspect of recovery from the solid coin, the ephemeral glee from the lasting peace. But unfortunately neither of these new dawns, true or false, can be appreciated without a long look at the night they're reacting to—the night that defines them and makes them look so good. A book about health is perforce a book about sickness, and in the matter of artificially induced depressions, there seems to be an almost exact equation between down and up, as if one could with a mighty effort turn the minus sign next to one's melancholy into a plus and watch one's spirits rise like mercury—just in time, in my case, to take on Illness No. 3.

No two of these things are identical, and one finds that the cards have been shuffled again for cancer. The usual pattern of remission and recurrence of this illness lends a stop-start quality to any elation you may feel over its high points. Every cheer comes with an asterisk, but so does every groan, as the will to live keeps pounding back. And there's a certain excitement to be had just from living on the edge: you are more fully alive than you have ever been, and getting more out of each day. If the will to live can't have quantity it will have quality, seizing on one great year in exchange for ten or twenty dull ones.

Sad to say, there is so much cancer going round these days that there's not much other hard news left to report on it. What makes my own case unusual and germane to this book is that the cancer is focused on my tongue, the organ with which in a roundabout sense I earn my living, and with which I also enjoy sinfully much of the living I make: in other words, I like to eat, almost as much as I once liked to drink; and between mouthfuls I like to talk, and after mouthfuls occasionally to sing too, in a low growl that is all my own. So if *that* were carted away, it wouldn't leave me with a hell of a lot. I could write a great book about *loss*, but what I'd spend the proceeds on I can't imagine.

Since much of this has been happening as I write this book, I've left a few pages of this part in journal form: it's a daily sort of illness, a soap opera, and you don't just make one big adjustment to it but hundreds of little ones that add up to a big one.

But some adjustments seem to explode out of nowhere and change your life just like that. My late friend Anatole Broyard reported being suffused with an unearthly euphoria when he first got wind of his cancer, along with a curious sense of superiority to average mortals, who never get to see their lives as clearly as he now saw his. Civilian readers I talked to about Broyard's epiphany couldn't make head or tail of it, but it made perfect good sense to me. Although I had never greeted my own bad news in that particular way, it was certainly in the realm of possibility. It's just that Anatole received his apocalypse a little earlier than most, and was spared the dark night that usually precedes it.

For most of us, there's no avoiding the fact that learning you've got cancer can be a gruesome experience, especially if your system is depressed at the time anyway, as mine was; but even with your heart wedged deep in your boots, the speed of mental adjustment can be quite uncanny, and the number of people I've known who've lived and died anywhere from serenely to downright happily with cancer defies normal imagining, almost as Broyard's essay did.

I guess the revelation for me was to find that a good death *doesn't* defy imagining at all, once you've had cancer yourself for even a little while. With that thunderclap event, a certain initiation seems to occur and mysteries are cleared up—but there's a limit to how much you can share this with people who haven't been there. As the reaction to Anatole Broyard's piece indicates, people have a built-in resistance to good news about things like cancer and polio because they want to believe it so much that they don't trust themselves. Which is why, contrary to my most fervent wishes, such a book as this *has* to be personal. The sugar coating of pain is such an industry in America that you have to be twice as convincing as usual when you want to sell *real* sugar. And this means that you can't say you heard about it from someone else, or read it in a government report.

To take at least some of the curse off the personal aspect, and retain a fig leaf of privacy, I've adopted certain ground rules for what follows. But first let me state briefly why I think it's a curse to begin with, starting with the most selfish reason. For a novelist, writing about one's life has always seemed like a terrible waste of material, the veritable blowing up of a gold mine. And for anyone in the pontificating business, it always seems like bad luck to invite questions such as "Who *cares* what you think?" and "What's so important about *your* life?" too often. Vanity can make chumps of us all, and unless you're an unmarried, childless, friendless orphan, it can also embarrass the hell out of your loved ones. And this is Reason No. 2. Every memoirist holds his friends and family hostage, wittingly or no, and while Poppa is making that fearless confession for the ages, Junior is most likely thinking of moving abroad and changing his name.

So here are the rules.

My parents, wife, and children will barely be mentioned—if you assume that they acted perfectly throughout, you won't be far enough wrong to matter. In the case of doctors and such, I have fudged their identities slightly by making all of them male; most of them were anyway, and to specify the few who weren't by gender would have threatened the general anonymity. (The other possibility, that of reassigning the sexes randomly, struck me as plain silly and disorienting, like hearing Bob Hope's voice come out of Dorothy Lamour in *The Road to Morocco*.) So imagine them as you will, and as they sound, bearing in mind that a ratio of two quite bad ones to one quite good holds up surprisingly well for both sexes.

To disguise the hapless Happy Valley, I have for starters removed all its features, architectural, topographical, and anthropological, and in case that isn't enough, I've stressed and overstressed the fogginess of my perceptions while I was there. But if anyone thinks he can spot it anyway, let me further add that this part of the story took place a good six years ago, since which time every single aspect of Happy Valley may have changed, including its very existence: what abides is the point of view I heard there, which still echoes through popular magazines and advice columns, and books about recovery too, and which seems to me not so much wrong (though it usually is) as completely unreal. Although there is much talk these days about getting in touch with one's body and one's emotions, people in the ambit of addiction seem to learn very little from either, but to be totally at the mercy of received opinions and abstract definitions. Yet in real life, the physical experience of polio taught me more about coping with addiction/depression than all the outside opinions I heard put together, as the two illnesses would later combine to help me make more sense of cancer. The irony is that the people who insist hardest that addiction is a disease are the ones most likely to discuss it in a physical vacuum and treat it like a virtual outer-body experience.

In contrast to Happy Valley, the nameless cancer hospital in my third section definitely *does* still exist and deserves much warmer words in retrospect than it gets in the text. In my journal I was trying to convey once again the patient's-eye view, this time of doctors and nurses, which view tends to be liverish and adversarial in even the best of hospitals. One is not at one's best right now, or in any mood to hand out gold medals. But if you used my particular hospital or my particular doctor (whose blushes I will spare), gold medals would hardly seem good enough for either of them. It's a lot easier to fight an illness when you don't have to fight the doctor as well.

Finally, the "I" character, aka me; I wish I could say, as novelists in law courts are wont to do, that he is a composite. But this is true only in the sense that we are all composites: otherwise it's pretty much me, all right, what there is of me. The character is not so much a composite as a reduction. The sick person who says he doesn't feel quite himself today has it exactly right. Sickness is like a hostile takeover in which the part of your mind which hurts manages completely to dominate and silence the rest of you. And recovery might be defined for present purposes as the triumphant return of the rest of the self, with horns tooting and drums rolling, and the demotion of pain to its usual place sulking in the corner. Whether or not you've heard the last of this miserable creature, it will no longer call the tunes or define you, to yourself or anyone else, if you can help it.

And here the story ends, with Lazarus throwing off his winding sheet, or the GI jumping on his uniform, and dancing or wheeling his chair wildly through the streets, wishing this moment could last forever. It does last quite a while, and I've let the camera linger on it, to remind myself more than anyone of how *real* the happiness was, and how ordinary and available the materials were: the street in the movie is ordinary, the GI's first civilian suit is ridiculously ordinary. The whole scene is just around the corner.

So why aren't we all out dancing right now? Well, there are complications. Once one's old self has moved back in, new stories will start up, and some of them will probably be sad ones. For reasons dating back at least to the Garden of Eden, the greatest happiness imaginable wears off with sickening speed and suddenly isn't good enough for us. A religious person might point out that we weren't put on earth to dance all day anyway, although some returners from Hell come awfully close to it. A friend of mine who spent four years in the Pacific Theater of the Absurd in World War II, flinching from trees that might or might not contain Japanese soldiers and jumping out of his skin every time a twig snapped, told me that he could hardly look at his suburban lawn of an evening without wanting to kiss it. "Life can't *get* dull enough for me," he said.

This would be an extreme case: if you go down far enough you might conceivably stay up forever, which is something for depression cases to look forward to, if they can still look forward to anything in that condition. But for the run of mankind, the dancing does have to stop sometime, and you are left with nothing but an unbelievably good memory.

Which, as I said in *Lear's*, I've been living off ever since.

1.

POLIO

In terms of simple profit and loss, polio was both the best and worst of illnesses. What I lost from it, by the time the smoke had cleared and the fever had cooled, was the use of one and a half legs—make that one and two-thirds by this time—and all the things I could have done with a full complement down there: ballroom dancing, tightrope walking, the list goes on and on. What I gained, some of it anyway, is the subject of this chapter.

Although there is no sadder sight in nature than a sick child, sight and reality don't always match, and in the matter of polio (and maybe other major diseases too), I found that the earlier you caught it the better. At borderline fourteen, the age when I got mine, the spirit seems to knit as fast as a young athlete's bones, and one's adjustment is so smooth and swift that it seems like a natural function, the way Nature itself would handle it for us if we didn't *think* so much, and worry, and drag the future into it. Not that kids don't think and worry too, but they're not stopped in their tracks by thought, the way adults are, or at least not for long, because their tracks are so swift.

On the minus side, I also believe that children have more trouble with pain than they will later because they can't see to the end of it or around it or remember enough good stuff from before it came. But there was very little pain connected with polio, except the pain of loss, and that I remember breezing past so buoyantly that it plays back to me now like a boy's adventure story. "Huck Finn Gets Polio"—if the phrase makes you jump, well, that's the difference between being sick and *reading* about sickness. The reader has to be solemn, if he has any heart at all, but the patient doesn't. And I only wish I could waltz through a head cold these days as blithely as I skipped past the mighty scourge of the forties.

The other advantage of being what my friend Jill Krementz might call "a very young invalid" is that you can't help learning things at those ages. Just as the laziest of kids learns to speak English—a daunting feat, quite beyond many industrious adults—so did I, the laziest of teenagers, learn more useful lessons from polio than from any single thing that has happened to me, without precisely being aware of learning any of them.

I have in fact written glancingly about the experience twice before, and each time reviewers accused me of holding something back, as if polio *must* have been a shattering experience whether I admitted it or not. They know best, of course. But more recently, Edmund Wilson's last volume of diaries came out and I found Wilson describing me as looking "unconsciously" like one who has suffered, and I felt obliged to open the case once again.

Whatever it was Wilson saw, "unconsciously" is certainly the right word for it. Speaking now strictly consciously, I'd say that polio seemed much more like a vacation from the pains of growing up than an addition to them. It's a common fallacy, to which even great critics may not be immune, to suppose that if you see am unhappy-looking blind man he must be unhappy about his blindness. In fact, it ranks high among the gripes of the handicapped that the rest of our rich inner lives gets shortchanged like this. If Bessie Smith had had a wooden leg, critics would no doubt have assumed that her great blues songs were all based on missing limbs. The possibility that a deaf-mute might actually be frowning over the Death of God, or the annual collapse of the Red Sox, is not even considered. Who is this guy trying to kid?

Yet I didn't feel certain that Wilson was altogether wrong. When I tried to read Geoffrey Ward's biography of Franklin Roosevelt a few years ago, I found myself hopelessly stalled at the part where polio strikes—these people in the book *didn't know what was happening,* and waiting for them to find out suddenly seemed unbearable. More recently, a friend with a much worse case than mine sent me a memoir of his own induction into our little fraternity, and the same thing happened, only more so. This was a *friend,* and I knew him, and I wanted to shout something encouraging to his young self, although nothing I said could have helped him to handle it better than he in fact did. But I knew that something unspeakable was about to happen to this man, and I just couldn't go on reading.

So why did my memory keep insisting that my first days with the illness were so carefree? There was something eerie about the tranquillity of my polio album, as if I'd been given some form of Twilight Sleep during the siege that had removed all the bad parts from my mind retroactively, although not, if Edmund Wilson was right, from my face. But if so, the drug must have been mighty effective, because I've been over this ground again and again and I can't find more than a couple of fairly bad moments, each of them over in a twinkling and replaced by good ones.

And it's not as if my vision of the period was clouded, quite the opposite—my memory is clear as glass. I don't even have to shut my eyes to see my mother's strained expression, for instance, at the ground-floor window of my first hospital (visitors were not allowed in the room the first few days), and can even make out the figure if not quite the face of the buxom nurse who blushingly handed me a washrag one day and announced that there were certain parts of the body I would have to wash for myself—thrilling talk at that age and in those days.

But perhaps my sharpest memory of all is of writhing on my bed a few weeks *before* I got polio, grappling with the possibility of someday catching it myself. We'd just been given our new rooms at school for the fall, which makes the scene all the more vivid since I was still seeing it for the first time, and the day was unseasonably hot, and for a moment or two I was next thing to scared out of my wits. I couldn't take it, that's all, I'd go crazy if I got polio and had to give up baseball, and of course, football—and *walking,* which I'd almost forgotten about. And I'm sure that if someone had chosen that moment to show me a picture of myself as I would look a year or two hence, crawling spindle-shanked, my face an apparent mask of pain, over an ice-cold floor to get to the bathroom in the middle of the night, I'd have gone crazy on the spot.

Yet if this vision of the future had come with a sound track, and the contorted mouthings of the kid on the floor had been audible, I would probably have heard something along these lines: "I—would—have—to—say that this is one ridiculous place to put a bathroom . . . and (mutter, mutter) the seat'll probably be even colder than the floor, if I know my English houses . . . haven't these people ever heard of *rugs?* Maybe they think they're bad for your character. (Whine and snarl.)" The first night I had to crawl to the john after my family returned to England in 1946 would, I now realize, have provided the perfect setting for a primal scream of rage at my situation if there was ever going to be one, since half of me was in Dreamland and the other was wide awake and sore as a boil about it. Yet although the scene would be enacted again and again on three continents (American bathrooms are best), I can recall no thought more profound than that of getting back to bed as fast as possible before that, too, got cold again. Somewhere, probably in my sleep, I had absorbed the certainty that self-pity was simply not in my best interest: I could bay at the moon all I wanted, and rail at fate and curse God, but all I'd be doing was making myself miserable.

So just like that, I gave it up, before I had even tried it. There was no conscious decision about this or any special virtue in it: *none* of us felt sorry for himself, that I ever heard of. Polio victims didn't cry because (a) we were too busy trying to get better and (b) what was in it for us?

Even at my worst moment, which came about six months into the course, when I caught a glimpse of my new legs in a full-length mirror down in Warm Springs, Georgia, and was reminded, before I could get my guard up, of pictures I'd recently seen of concentration camp victims, my first thought was that it would take a *lot* of exercise to put the meat back on those bones.

The thing was, I never doubted I would get cured, and the sight of my skinny legs (which I, being of a squeamish disposition, might still be bothered by—if I saw them on somebody else) only doubled my determination to "get on with it," as my mother would say. And there was a healing euphoria just in that: we were *doing* something, we were *going* places. Every day another muscle, and on to Berlin in the morning.

In fact, I would leave the famous Warm Springs polio farm after a mere five weeks because I wasn't sure they shared my Churchillian enthusiasm for the blood, sweat, and tears of this thing. It was a sleepy kind of place, where you didn't expect much of *any* kind of thing to happen. Some folks was old and some folks had the poliomyelitis, but they'd all probably be dead before you could even say "My dog and my hog took a walk," i.e., about half an hour in Georgia talk.

But looking back at it, I think maybe the worst of it was not really the sleepy atmosphere or comatose staff of Warm Springs, but the sheer number of other patients. The place was full of *polio* victims, for pity's sake, and who needed that? Many years afterward, my latest brace maker and I were talking about the characteristic cockiness and self-reliance of polio veterans, and he said, "Well, that was certainly true of your generation, but I'm not so sure about this one," and he went on to surmise that the Great Depression might have injected some starch into our spines, and this may indeed have had something to do with it. Hard times breed tough people, and even us sissies didn't assume that happiness is a birthright, if anyone is crazy enough to think so now.

But retracing my own steps all the way to Warm Springs, I find another less obvious explanation for our particular style. Before going to Roosevelt's place, I had enjoyed the luxury of being one of a kind, the only case of polio anyone knew and therefore the resident expert on the subject. Nobody else could tell *me* how to cope with this strange illness, they could only watch in admiration, which, this being America, God bless it, was stated, and wildly overstated, loud and often: "Boy, you've shown me a lot of guts . . . you've got some kind of heart in there." Shucks, guys. I knew I wasn't that great, and later my system would rebel violently against this fluff, and well-meaning words like *pluck* and *spirit* would send me howling from the room. But during those first delicate months, I'm happy to admit that being considered a lionhearted hero did permanent wonders for my morale. I wasn't a polio victim: I was a polio fighter, and a damn good one.

Until I got to Warm Springs, that is. There I was just another face in the crowd and another anonymous pair of legs to be pumped by the leg pumper on duty at the swimming pool that day. To hell with that. I wanted my pedestal back right now! . . . But here I have to be careful because I once invented a fictional character 90% unlike myself and dispatched him to Warm Springs to get another angle on it, and he was a proud son-of-a-bitch who might have wanted a pedestal even without the polio.

But sticking strictly to memory, I think I can say with certainty that my old self and my fictional one alike would have gone straight up the wall at the merest suggestion of an encounter session with other polio cases. What do I need *them* for? Is there supposed to be something *wrong* with me? The whole notion that I was now part of some kind of special group and was somehow troubled about it and needed counseling would have unleashed a tirade, born of equal parts fear and defiance, to make the windows rattle all the way to Atlanta. I can handle this myself, thank you very much.

So maybe part of the edge my generation had was that deep down they left you alone, which is not such a terrible place to be as people sometimes paint it, when you have good friends on the other levels of consciousness. At any rate, you're going to have to face being on your own sometime, and I was glad to do so early on, while people were still fussing over me, rather than later, on some cold street corner after the last bus has left and the passing drivers seem to suspect one of carrying a gun in one's cane.

So that was another lesson I learned without being aware of it. At Warm Springs I had felt slowed down by the sheer number of people involved. A polio patient is by necessity an activist who travels fastest alone. He can do more than most sick people to improve himself—in my case, by bending and straightening my good leg against the physiotherapist's palm until we were both ready to drop, and striving to turn my one, equally good, foot right and left against the same object, long after the functionaries at Warm Springs would have packed it in for the day; and the small triumphs that are almost guaranteed in the early stages were of the kind that caused Roman emperors to close the city for parades and Wall Street to bury itself in ticker tape. Hey, I can sit up without help—well, almost. Well, I did it once. And as my stomach and back muscles came back, the adrenaline just flowed and flowed, building as it were a carapace of adrenaline that has never left me. I was the Tarzan of the wheelchair set.

"It's no use trying to get polio victims to enlist in handicapped causes," someone in the business once told me, "because you guys don't think you *are* handicapped." Precisely. The period when I might have been learning to adjust to the word was so packed with small accomplishments that it was impossible not to feel like one of the world's winners ever afterward.

But a second and more sobering lesson comes as a rider to this one, which is that there are limits against which it is finally useless to hurl oneself; you *can't* do everything. When the football player Dennis Byrd recently made a splendid partial recovery from a paralyzing injury, there was much feckless babble in the media about how his spirit had done it. "If you knew Dennis, you never would have doubted it," said one simple fellow, to the indignant roars of the paralyzed community: if you really want to make us mad, just keep talking like that. If spirit was all it took, you could roll the nation's wheelchairs into the sea right now. And the blind would see and the deaf hear. We all have big hearts. It goes with the territory.

The Byrd episode was typical, in several senses, of the world I was now entering, the world of the permanently handicapped (lightweight division). The recovered athlete always, and quite properly, thanks God for his cure—to the muffled indignation, one imagines, of the doctors and nurses in charge, who have probably performed prodigies of redemptive medicine for this ingrate, and to the dry amusement of handicapped readers, who might like to remind our hero to say another word of thanks to the sports fans who bought the tickets that paid for the doctors and the billion-dollar equipment that the rest of us couldn't afford.

But the athlete was right the first time—the decision as to who gets spared and who doesn't is finally in the lap of the gods, or the roll of the dice, or whichever Higher Power you use. Undoubtedly your own cooperation is necessary, in the sense of the old saying that a nickel and a winning personality will buy you a ride on the Staten Island ferry. Your own cooperation is needed to get you as far as the water, but the nickel that takes you across comes from on high, or from wherever you think winning lottery tickets come from, and all the effort in the world won't improve your chances of sailing today.

So long as this is understood, it is always a pleasure, tinged with envy, maybe, but not ruined by it, to see a brother like Mr. Byrd make it across the Great Divide, and I can't imagine anyone begrudging the man praise for a job obviously well done. Athletes seem to rise to their new physical challenges almost as if they welcomed them after the rote rituals of their sport. The real and valuable message they have to offer is that on this particular ferry, you have to row like hell even after they let you on board, and it's good for people to be prepared for this.

That said, we can only laugh that we may not cry over the sheer quantity of bubbleheaded public gush that attends these cases: "Watch it walk, watch it talk," as they used to say at Warm Springs, where I learned at least *one* useful thing, which is that one of the perks attached to our own stock of hard, and hard-won, truths is a license to make jokes about them as black and sick as the law allows. Only healthy people say that handicaps are not a fit subject for laughter: they are a *perfect* subject for laughter; they are God's own banana peels. So if you hear someone cackling at the back of the movie house as the coach tells the one-legged veteran that he can so be an all-American wide receiver, look for one of our gang. As the Fat Man in *The*

Maltese Falcon put it, "We must have our little joke." The pill
of knowledge that was once so hard to swallow has become a
gourmet dish, and when I heard Damon Runyon's famous saying "The Race is not always to the Swift nor the Battle to the
Strong, but that's the way they're betting"—well, that tasted as
delicious as only a sour apple can. A diet of unpalatable truths
does wonders for the system, and the handicapped people I've
known have all seemed uncommonly well adjusted, in a prickly
sort of way.

And while we're betting, I'd also like to wager a couple of
bob that whoever coined the various euphemisms for our assorted conditions was not him or herself handicapped. "Physically challenged," indeed! We were challenged and we lost,
baby, and that's all she wrote. There's nothing bitter or twisted
about it, unless our natures are so inclined anyway, but on the
contrary, a great sense of liberation. The truth does occasionally
set you free after all, and we can say things like that because
we've been there, we've looked the worst in the eye and lived.
(Which doesn't always mean *you* can say things like that. Like
other minorities, we prefer to make our own jokes, and yours
had better be pretty damn funny.)

But looking the worst in the eye is not, I should add quickly,
something you should rush into. In the matter of getting used to
things, the golden rule is always to let your body go first, dragging your mind behind it. If you try to jump the gun and resign
yourself to things like sickness and death before your body is
ready for them, the images will simply annihilate you. Nobody
ever got used to blindness, or living in a wheelchair, or crawling
to the bathroom, in his mind; yet when the time comes, the
body often moves amazingly fast, handing out instructions as it
goes on how to handle the latest disaster, like the next clue in a
game. Your task is to keep your mind occupied between clues,
keeping the truth or at least the words at bay until your body
has learned the next moves. If, for instance, I'd been told at the
beginning exactly how far I'd get with my exercises and where
I'd end up, I might indeed have felt like a cripple and quite
bowed down by it; but I was able to convince myself that I was

going all the way until my body was ready to tell me otherwise, and until I'd learned slowly for myself, pushing against that unyielding hand, that this is where you get off.

As a matter of fact, for years I believed that my own smooth adjustment to my losses was entirely the consequence of the religious faith I'd inherited from two excessively endowed parents and had since supplemented with my own snappy work as an altar boy and choir virtuoso (it's my book, and I can describe my singing anyhow I like). Indeed, a firm belief in miracles and the power of prayer, and a trusting nature, did treat me to three and a half years of unbridled optimism, at the end of which I was so used to polio that I could barely remember what life had felt like without it (although even today I still occasionally walk and run perfectly in my dreams, along with playing the piano and talking fluent French). Faith had more than done the trick for me, and I guess a truly pious person would say that my prayers had been answered that way; but that's the kind of faith you only get to use once, and I gradually lost interest in praying for anything, because I couldn't think of a grown-up way to do it. I'd had my wish from the Good Fairy, and I wasn't going back for more.

Only much later did it dawn on me that I needn't have subjected religion to this intolerable stress and that a lot of people had adjusted just as well as I had without believing in prayers or miracles at all. And it was only then that I finally learned the most useful lesson of all—that the real miracle was in the way the body-and-soul comedy team was assembled in the first place. "There are no atheists in foxholes" was what they said in World War II, and in the same gut sense of the word, that Goodness and Wholeness are overpowering forces in themselves, there were no atheists in the polio ward either, because at that moment, whatever life remains in you rallies spontaneously like a volunteer army in a city under siege, and suddenly every last cell and corpuscle is at the barricades, and Faith is very much part of the ensemble: I'll think of *some*thing; *some*one will think of something. "Where there's life, there's hope" is a rather simple thought to end up with at the end of such a bloody war as this one. But it's good to know that yet another major truism checks out, as Runyon might say, at the ticket window.

The natural lease on this degree of exuberant animal faith seems to be roughly two years for polio, and that also seems by good chance to be enough. During that time you can keep racking up small victories, not matching the early spectacular ones in my case—the mighty battles of the back and stomach, both of which regions had been feared lost, and the prolonged fighting over the use of my right leg, a trophy that came out of the war almost as spindly as ever, but blessedly functional—but solid enough in the way of small toe wigglings and knee flexings to keep the psychological momentum going. For weeks, the big issue hung in the balance—would I need a brace for the right leg too, and be condemned thereafter to walk with a waddle, or could I con the Universe into letting me use my very own leg once again, and walking with *half* a waddle, a ruptured duck for sure?

The physiotherapist was noncommittal. "Keep pushing," she said sternly, and by the Nine Gods of Rome I pushed, until I was ready at last to give it a try. The brace maker stuck stiff brown paper under each leg and traced them both to be on the safe side, as you might measure sick twins for matching coffins "just in case," but the man only actually made one brace, and I remember feeling alternately elated and embattled about this, depending on which leg I thought about. The good one was safe, yeah! The bad one was going to be trussed up for a while—but don't worry, we'll get you out of there somehow, old man.

And, hey, I was standing now, a thousand feet tall, and taking stiff little steps like a mummy on his first day out of the tomb, and *wobbling*—man, this was tough! But great! Again, the life in you surges forward against the doubts—will I ever be able to do *any* of this? We're dealing with reality now, not some dream of trotting, fully healed, onto a ball field. Gravity is awfully strong, is it not? And my powerful inclination to pitch forward with every move would later remind my father of Hegel's definition of walking as "a series of attempts to fall down, constantly arrested." My own picture of it has me perched on a steep hill, safe so long as I didn't move a muscle but in danger of starting a rockslide if I so much as twitched. It still makes me sweat to think about it.

But I pushed off somehow, and quickly too, before the fear could congeal into an invisible wall with spikes on it, and made it across the room, some other how, in a thousand short strides, a Chinese sort of journey, to a mixed sound of bated breath and muted encouragement. "That's it . . . that's the boy." At some point, either that day or the next, I tried to lengthen my stride just a measly inch or so, and went careering immediately into a downward spin. But strong hands (whose? St. Michael's, no doubt, or one of those guys I'd been praying to) braced and "trued" me, and I returned to my mincing ways.

"That was great," murmured the chorus. "You did just fine . . . much better than I expected." Hard to believe, but absolutely necessary if I was going to have something nice to sleep on, to help ward off the doubts which I now picture dancing round my head all night like Hieronymous Bosch devils—and okay, let's get started again. This was a war, all right, no mistake about that, and maybe it was the traces of that ancient war that Edmund Wilson saw on me; before your body can present you with a smiling *fait accompli*, it has fought long and hard for its life and yours, and the happiest of war veterans still looks like a war veteran; a scar is still a scar, and the body knows what it knows. And even a merry-andrew like John F. Kennedy is deemed fit to govern because he carried this authority about him.

But who can say what Wilson saw? Nineteen forty-five was such a time of elation, with the war outside winding down slowly—the big one, that is, old WWII itself—and myself cranking up rapidly, that the good memories simply overwhelm any bad ones. Since walking is mostly a matter of technique, and since crutches can cover for any number of technical mistakes, there was no way I wasn't going to improve *fast*, at the kind of speed that makes people on roller coasters giggle, and in no time I was swinging giddily around the room, and down the hall, and finally, wonder of wonders, out onto the street, where the breeze felt fresher than anything that had ever come in through my window. If you'd told me just six months before that the height of happiness would soon consist of leaning on a pair of crutches and inhaling deeply, I'd have woken up screaming.

. . . As I would now too if I was told polio was going to drop in on a child of mine, or a friend, or even on a character in a book I was reading; because I'm back on the outside again, and it looks just awful from out here, no matter how much you know. The grace to fight these things is granted to you only so long as you need it, like a voucher good for just one dance. Once you leave the floor, you are merely another concerned civilian, and my sympathy for someone else in my old boat would, I think, be almost as intense as if I'd never heard of polio.

Well—maybe they wouldn't handle it as well as I did . . . but they would, I'm practically certain, because, as indicated in the introduction, every cripple I've ever known has handled it well, as if the illness did indeed carry its own antidote. Which doesn't, to repeat, make the victims any less heroic. It's just that there is a great deal of heroism latent in human beings as such, and activating it is an enormous pleasure for oneself when it happens and an enormous relief to onlookers as well, who are trapped in their outsideness and can see nothing but the kid hobbling or the blind man groping.

But long before I found myself swaying on my new crutches that first day out and exulting in the warm gray wetness of it all (although cold bright dryness would have done just as well: any old weather is better than none when you've been locked in bed awhile), I had realized for sure that the people watching had been having a much worse time of it than I had. As early as my mother's first visit to the hospital, I had known, without putting it in so many words, that it was now up to me to cheer up the Healthy of this world if I wanted a decent conversation with them—and if I didn't want them to drag me down with their compassion, which can weigh a ton. And now, while she and my other well-wishers stood watching eagerly, it was payoff time for all of us. They'd had a terrible winter and I'd had an exciting one, but I was the hero today regardless, and it was no use telling them that there really was nothing to it, because that would have made me seem all the braver, and I was already over the limit.

Yet although my courage obviously passed belief, I was also

their representative out there: if I could do it, maybe there was hope for them too, in whatever straits Fate had in mind for them; but again they would have said something like "If we only had your heart!" And that sort of talk was to be avoided, because I was beginning to believe them.

I mean, what did *I* know? Maybe I *was* special. I hadn't been to Warm Springs yet and met all the other "special" people, and right now I was still king of the hill and cock of the walk. If the payoff for my friends as I stood there that day was gratifying, the prize for me was like unto the winning ticket in the Irish Sweepstakes. And much of the pleasure came from simple vanity, which had grown almost as much as I had in bed (I'd added several inches to my height, which made standing all the weirder). In the very earliest days of this saga, before the word *polio* had even reached my ears and mind and I was aware only of a killer fever, I had fallen instinctively into a style that it would take me another forty years to articulate, in the following magic words: "If you can't feel good, you can at least look good."

I believe my original motive for "looking good" was simply to reassure other people and maybe myself (though I wasn't aware of needing it), but later, I'd wound up convincing myself that I must be a hell of a fellow to create such a fine impression. It was a great investment. For the slight extra effort it takes to twist a snarl into a smile, I had turned into the all-time perfect patient, absolutely tops in my field. Not that I had planned any of it, but that first day on crutches I suddenly had it all, I felt good, *and,* to judge from the faces around me, I looked good too. And the fact that I was missing the use of one and two-thirds legs seemed like a small price for such bliss, especially since the loss was, I knew for a fact, temporary.

But if any question remains as to how someone in this condition could even *think* he was happy, I can only appeal to the master truth that awaits one at the end of all those journeys— that is, when even the small triumphs are over and you realize to your surprise that you've actually lost the war after all—which is that God, or the Great Whoever, has been so lavish in His gifts that you can lose some absolutely priceless ones, the equivalent of whole kingdoms, and still be indecently rich; a George Shearing or Ray Charles may get as much happiness as a man can hold from music alone, while a Cézanne or Vermeer gets the same amount from sight. The potential sources of pleasure are actually much too opulent for our jerky, got-to-keep-moving attention spans to exhaust, and most people go to their graves without fully exploiting, or sometimes even discovering, at least one of them. How much more, for instance, might I have gotten out of music if I'd been trapped in the dark with it like a blind man?

Well, pray God I never have to find out. Each of these dozens of gifts becomes, as you think about it, the indispensable one, without which life would not be worth living, and I can't imagine music making up for the loss of sight. So Ray Charles seems just as superhuman to me as I apparently seemed to my friends that day. Rolling the film back to that moment, I find my cup running over with the joys of self-satisfaction alone, which were reasonably well deserved to that point and which fitted in so rapturously with the universal happiness of 1945 that for the next six months, I could have been living in Paradise. Everything about the first year of a handicap is as clean and uncomplicated as The Last Good War seemed to be, as it raced to a close in Europe matching me step for step and laugh for laugh, as if the whole world were experiencing on a larger scale the joys of recovery from a very large sickness.

But self-satisfaction is dangerous material, and it would be misleading to suggest that nothing but virtue and a serene flow of moral superiority comes out of things like polio. I could swear that Dr. Johnson once said, "It is difficult for an invalid not to be a scoundrel," though I've never been able to trace the quotation. At any rate, he should have said it, because it's abundantly true. In fact, I was just about to enter the zone of temptation myself, with the fever gone and self-consciousness moving in, and have lived there ever since. If I had to boil the first phase of it down to a single sentence, it would be "What do you do with yourself when your fifteen minutes of fame is up?" Anyone who has spent time with either babies or old people will tell you that the craving for attention is the most demanding and enduring of human needs—so much so that artists commonly yearn, and millionaires make plans, to go on receiving it even after they're dead. So imagine the plight of the cripple who realizes one fine day that the often overwhelming attention he's getting right now is the most he's ever going to see. Nothing ages faster than this year's disaster victim, and once the bystanders have drawn whatever inspiration and reassurance they're going to get from him, their faces will vanish one by one from the bedside and the limelight will be switched sharply to someone else.

Part of you is probably relieved by this, and part of you is not. First, the relief—the kind of attention I'd been getting had begun to seem suffocating the moment I got better, like a warm blanket on a hot day, and incidentally would give me serious and most useful doubts about the value of public attention ever after. The day I was taken home from the hospital, I was startled to find, everywhere my stretcher went, strange faces gaping down at me from all sides, presumably just because I was there; and ever since, I've never been able to look at the bright-eyed crowds at movie premieres without thinking of ambulances and of how any anonymous citizen being bundled into one would upstage Elizabeth Taylor herself. But in either case, the central figure is simply providing food for people's curiosity, and curiosity will eat practically anything.

Even when you know it's all nonsense, however, it's tough coming down from being a saint, a spiritual superstar—and not just coming down to the next floor either but all the way to the basement—because if you're not superior, you're inferior, just another "handicapped person," who henceforth has to whine to be heard. And I guess if you're one of Dr. Johnson's scoundrels, or one of the villainous cripples who populate fiction if nowhere else, you might well decide not to take the elevator at all, but to hold on to people's attention, never mind the quality of it, and live forever off the remains of your credit as a martyr, meanwhile using all the insights into human nature and the slight contempt for it that you picked up lying on your back. The alternative to using people is to feel abandoned by them—which may be why I made the hero of my novel a politician.

But this, as I say, is usually fiction; in real life, the handi-capped tend, in my small experience, to be quite well pleased with themselves if they have simply met their own demands and standards; your standards, dearly though they may love you, really don't concern them much anymore. The healing ma-chinery, working on its own schedule, has made them not only ready for some good clean abandonment by now but eager for it. At a certain point it dawns on the neophyte cripple that even his near and dear aren't quite with it anymore; they haven't kept pace with him or learned the things he's learned, and it's time to say his thank-yous and be on his way. He still has a job to do, and the sympathy that once was so genuinely helpful now seems kind of dumb—these people don't really *know*, do they?—and, in the nicest possible way, kind of a nuisance too.

In certain respects, he is now tough as nails: the second-stage invalid has, in D. H. Lawrence's phrase, "come through"; he has outgrown the need for attention, and he has learned almost everything he needs to know about coping with his condition. But the wisdom of illness is quite specialized, it is coded only to tell you about itself, and the survivor may be in for some rude shocks from other directions, as I would soon be finding.

My first witness is actually more a newspaper account of a person than a real one. Jim Abbott, the famous baseball pitcher, has fashioned out of his life a picture-book guide to dealing with a specific handicap and has frequently been treated as a picture-book character by the outside world for his pains. Mr. Abbott was born without part of his left arm and has been obliged ever since to endure a lifetime of sentimental applause and bottom-line discouragement. "Isn't it wonderful that he can pitch in Little League. So what's he going to do with himself now that he's retired from baseball?" Every stage of his journey has been considered the end of the line: high school, college, "Amateur Athlete of the Year"—but at every stage his achievement has carried the slight taint of affirmative action. Isn't he wonderful, considering . . . until, that is, he does the impossible and makes the Big Leagues, where condescension ceases—and Abbott han-dles that very well too, even the most onerous aspect of all, the one you *don't* learn about in your first year at this school, that of being "a role model," identified everywhere he goes with his handicap: not Abbott the great pitcher, but Abbott the great *one-armed* pitcher. Although the man must have been listening to this stuff from the age of seven, he plays his part day in and day out with a good-humored resignation that, believe me, is tough to pull off and almost impossible to keep up.

A hero, from any point of view—but then, in the heat of a pennant race and in the madness of New York, he is blindsided by something he's actually been spared more of than most people: criticism, cold, harsh criticism that doesn't even mention his arm or his courage, but treats him as just another lily-livered incompetent in a city that never sleeps (who would dare to?) and Abbott explodes, not magisterially, as one might expect, but like a hurt child—or at least that's how it sounds in the press.

If the report was accurate, I know exactly how he felt. A handicapped child grows up, almost inevitably, hard on one side and soft on the other, as the forces of niceness strive to "make it up" to him for his losses, until he often winds up being overpaid. During my first year of polio I received enough spoiling to last a lifetime, so that a great deal of the character that I laboriously built up each day with my physiotherapist was washed away by nightfall in the waves of kindness that came bombing in for the rest of the time. I wanted a subscription to *Life* magazine? Done. *Look* too? *The Sporting News?* Anything else? (The good part was that I got bored with magazines even faster than normal and began reading books as well.)

Since I virtually owed it to society to feel good, and display it as widely as possible, I had for six months at least, the equivalent of a moral pass in the pursuit of happiness. And although my circumstances, and the strong advisability of keeping God on my side, restrained me from the wilder forms of swinging, there was nothing to stop me from becoming a connoisseur of the small self-indulgence, cultivated without guilt and with everyone pitching in to help. No demands could possibly be made on someone who'd been through what I ostensibly had; if he can still enjoy it, for God's sake, let him do it, eat it, or sleep late just dreaming about it.

The misunderstanding upon which my moral ruin was based

was that I was never more than a moment away from brooding as wretchedly about my condition as my family probably was, and must be constantly headed off from this. But only once do I remember taking direct and villainous advantage of this misunderstanding, and that was when a member of my entourage complained mildly about the unrelenting tedium of emptying bedpans. "You think *you've* got it tough?" I said, and was hit by remorse immediately. The truth was that emptying bedpans *is* awful, and I was living the life of Riley, and that from now on playing the self-pity card would be the sin of sins for me, the one I must avoid at all costs or go straight to Hell (unless, of course, it's a question of catching the last plane out of Saigon or the last ticket to a great musical; then a little extra limping can't hurt—or help either, I should add).

But there are a lot of less obvious sins you can fall or slide into, and it was during this period that I first really got to know my *bête noire*, sloth (we'd actually met before, but only to say hello; now it moved in, pillows, cushions, and all). Since this is not, I believe, a generic problem for the handicapped, it suggests a larger truth, namely that in any crisis, your strengths get stronger and your weaknesses weaker as you try to cope, and what might be a minor defect sometimes flares into a major one and you become almost overnight a coward or a libertine or, in my case, a world-class sluggard.

The safety catch on most sins that keeps their devotees from practicing them to their heart's content is, of course, the expense, financial, spiritual, or both: they usually cost money and you always feel lousy about them; and this goes double for sloth. Later, when I was trying obligingly to come up with reasons for drinking *quite* so much as I did (see chapter after next), one of the few valid ones I could think of, outside of the sheer pleasure of the activity, was that it made laziness feel good—or, if one wants to be superanalytical about it, made it feel as good as it had felt way back when I lay sprawled on my bed and knew that I had something good coming to me: the world owed me one, and this was how I chose to be paid, leafing through magazines and thinking deep thoughts. Clearly, a good drinking man was in the works.

The next year I would be jerked to my senses, as if by a red-faced sergeant, when I arrived in an English boarding school and found how much *work* would henceforth be expected of me, polio or no polio. My first report card summed up the situation better than it knew when it said that Sheed's intellectual development seemed to be somewhat ahead of his emotional development, by which they probably meant that mature boys don't look as if they're going to cry every time they're handed more homework. But that was me now—tough-minded as could be and able to face hard truths as fast as you could throw them, but tender as a baby when asked to do an honest day's work.

This had its funny side, and I soon became a master of the educational shortcut. But what was less funny was the sense of spiritual paralysis that sometimes went with it. Shortly after breakfast on certain days I would feel a giant torpor creeping like Novocain through my system, and if I didn't move fast, I could lose a whole day to it, then and now. Thus I learned that stoicism is not the same thing as character, and that being able to take punishment is only half the deal: you're supposed to *do* a little something as well. Up to this point, I had been applauded for doing absolutely nothing—so why spoil it? But the applause was getting thinner now and perfunctory, and would soon cease altogether. And it's possible I didn't like this.

The authorities, I gathered, ascribed my manifest gloom to the aftermath of polio, and once again they were probably a little bit right, but in a much more complicated way than they could have supposed. It seems like a sick joke to suggest that one should have to pay with a hangover for the euphoria of convalescence, but such is the cost accounting of the goddess with the scales, and this particular euphoria had run up quite a bill. No sooner was I out of doors once in that spring of 1945 than I was out again, slugging softballs from my wheelchair and racing the same vehicle along the empty streets of wartime, practicing U-turns on a dime. Sometime in May, I returned to my old school in triumph, King God for a day, and spoke in some debate they were having there about the United Nations, yes or no? or World Peace, is it good for America? and got a five-minute ovation for my pains—hey, the speech wasn't *that* good.

I remember an ominous twinge of annoyance that they weren't applauding my speech at all, and then another twinge when the school paper ran a smarmy editorial afterwards about my pluck and what a great guy I'd always been (funny, I'd never noticed they felt like that). But my father said something like "Face it, my boy, you're enjoying yourself enormously—as indeed you have every right to." And I was indeed enjoying myself, sucking every last ounce from this honey of a year, far and away my best one on earth so far.

And when the party ended, I wasn't worried about polio, I was already used to it: there was still a cure out there someplace, but I was in no great hurry for it. And meanwhile, I was hopping around like a monkey, graduating from two canes to one and swatting cricket balls with a certain rigid elegance, courtesy of my stiff left leg, happy in action now and miserable at rest.

My chief problem by the end of Year One was that convalescence wasn't fun any more but flatter than the state of Florida. Laziness, when it checked in now, didn't feel good at all but rotten through and through, informing me that it was time to get things moving again. Forget the applause, forget the quiet-hero bit. This might be called the awkward phase of handicaps, as you go from being tops in your field and the best little patient in history to being the new boy in class and as bored and restless as an actor between roles. Recently an old friend with a much worse case than mine called me up from Arizona to chat about this and that, and in passing said that he felt in some ways he'd had it easier than me because he'd never left the convalescent nest but had been surrounded all his life by caretakers and loved ones, and the reliable straps and harnesses of home, whereas I had had to get back into life and slug it out.

Unlike the masters at my English school, my friend Michael did know what he was talking about: a nest is a fine and private place, whatever shape you're in, and being told that one is *just* well enough to leave it can cause exquisitely mixed feelings: couldn't I just wait here until my cure arrives? The stork should be along with it any minute.

But of course Michael was imagining himself, in *his* condition, trying to make it in the outside world, and not imagining me. I would have gone crazy in a nest and in fact would not be happy again until I was all the way out, as far from sickrooms and melting glances as my rickety legs would carry me. Driving from Phoenix to Amarillo a few years later and bellowing the songs from *South Pacific* into the desert silence, or hitchhiking with a backpack from Sydney to Melbourne to Adelaide a few years after that—this, or its humbler equivalent, even if it's only flexing your fingers for the first time, is happiness for a polio patient. After that, let's hear no more talk about handicaps.

Yet every now and then, for long afterwards, I would fancy I heard the siren song of the sickroom calling me to rest, and I came down with a lifetime of colds and suspected flus during Year Two, particularly during the examination season. And as late as my early thirties, I would write a heartfelt story about a man who can't bring himself to get out of bed for years on end. It was a private thing—most polio veterans are anything but lazy—and maybe I would have heard it even if there had never *been* a sickroom. The great insoluble in one's life, and question for a rainy day, is how one might have turned out if life had taken its normal course; I might, for just one instance, have been less hardheaded about certain physical realities but more so about the realities of sports, concerning which I continued to consider myself a superstar at bay until I blessedly ceased caring a few years later.

Then there's the question of daydreaming, a practice to which I was already deeply committed and would have pursued wantonly anyhow, in the regular classrooms and offices of life, but which takes on a particular urgency when you're in the grip of an allegedly incurable disease. "Tell me something nice!" you command your imagination, though perhaps not in so many words. "Go out and find me some good news." And just like that, a luxury becomes a necessity: it's now daydream or die, and the imagination sets off each day in search of new stories and rosy scenarios and medical breakthroughs that haven't been utterly disproved yet, fantasies with the cellophane still on them. And some days you believe all of them and other days none. There is a cure for absolutely everything that ails you just around the corner, which is only fair, because the flaming worst is also just around the corner. The whole of *Paradise Lost* and *Re-gained* will eventually be fought out in the mind of a sick person, but what my three illnesses have taught me that I would never even have guessed otherwise is that some of the worst defeats occur before you get the sickness, and that the victories begin almost immediately afterwards. Yet the imagining self can give you a bad day at any point and, either way, always seem to be either far ahead or behind the rest of you at accepting the new regime, bouncing in with impossibly good news one day and inconceivably bad the next, as optimism and regret war for your attention.

Although the laziness was all my own, I imagine my con-frères had their own equally personal scorecards of wins and losses, of lessons learned and temptations succumbed to in those first few months. As the dust settles on one's final status, how-ever, all handicapped persons (except scoundrels) suddenly find themselves faced as one with the same task, in equal parts in-vigorating and exasperating, but at least a task, a purpose in life—and the task is simply to make the world, and ourselves, forget for as long and often as possible that there has ever been anything wrong with us: to be, in other words, "great pitchers," and not just "great one-armed pitchers."

Of this two-headed assignment, making oneself forget is the easy one, the part that is practically done for you; you find a routine within the realm of the possible, and you strip-mine it for concealed pleasures and for the small amount of happiness it takes to fill a human container. I remember, for instance, no greater joy than that of hobbling down to a hotel restaurant for the first time to eat breakfast (and I *still* get a bang out of it). There was nothing sentimental about it. I wasn't thinking "Isn't it wonderful I'm able to do this?" Eating a good breakfast with a fresh crossword puzzle in front of you is simply a hell of a pleasant thing to be doing that most people don't bother to enjoy, because they think playing polo or chasing butterflies is better. Bless them. I once asked a rock-climbing friend if he could tell me where exactly the kicker came in his sport, the precise moment when one can pause and say "I'm happy right now!" and he hadn't the faintest idea. We breakfast eaters know these things, while men of action frequently don't have time to think about it.

So fooling, and satisfying, yourself is child's play, as I would discover again later in this book, when once again I would fear losing something, lose it anyway, and go on about my business. At that point I had begun to wonder if I hadn't simply invented a happy childhood to comfort me in early senility and an impossibly rosy sickness—but no, it really works that way. You get used to things incredibly quickly, and are ransacking the horizon for new pleasures almost before the old ones are out the door.

What takes a while to get used to is other people. "Other people" have always just walked in the door: they are like the first faces you saw at the bedside, and they haven't got the word yet that you don't need constant help anymore. And their sheer man-eating considerateness conveys the message that you haven't fooled *them,* your handicap still sticks out a mile, and you still have to be interrupted with assistance every time you move, before normal discourse can resume. ("You weren't very nice to that man. He was only trying to help" are the first words I expect to find on my tombstone when I fly over.)

Americans spend a deal of time worrying about their sensitiveness and polishing it to a fine glow, but this is like a tennis player working on his one good stroke. What we should be worried about is, as usual with us, overdoing it. If there's one thing that makes handicapped flesh crawl, it's the approach of a "sensitive" person, planning to make a meal of one. Jean-Paul Sartre once postulated a leper who couldn't bear to be kissed, but that touchy fellow could be any of us. Imagine for a moment what it is like to spend your life being helped; then visualize the effort this particular person has made not to *need* help—and honor it. And leave him in peace.

Unless, that is, he obviously needs help. God knows, I'm not suggesting a massive wave of indifference, only of common sense. You can figure that a blind person knows how to walk down a street, or a one-legged one how to get out of a car, without the assistance you probably don't know to provide anyway (an average person's idea of being useful is to grab the victim's arm, a move calculated to disorient blind people and send lame ones toppling to the sidewalk: you could hardly do worse if you tackled them around the knees). A handicap is just a series of inconveniences to add to the normal inconveniences of life, and in no time one is handling them just as automatically—until some damn fool tries to get to Heaven by helping one with them.

Coping with the outside world might be called Phase Three, and it's easily the longest, but it's also the one you can do the most about, which makes a nice change. The seasoned gimp knows he can't hope to straighten out the whole public and get them to shape up: they are just part of the situation, and situations are meant to be exploited, not cried over, as every scoundrel knows. A turning point in my own life came the day I was gravely escorted to a seat on a French train reserved for "les blessés dans la guerre." I was old enough to be a war veteran now, never mind what war, and possibly even a hero, and perhaps I subconsciously cultivated a pained look on the spot, acquired in Korea or the Foreign Legion, so I could get *more* train seats, and perhaps that's what Edmund Wilson thought he saw that day. One night in the West End saloon in Manhattan, a friend of mine who knows his military history helped me to fashion an eye-popping army career that bought us both drinks all night, and you need a pained look for that kind of work.

The larger lesson this time was that a limping child is a sad sight, but a limping adult is all in a day's work—especially if he's reduced his limp to the status of sprained ankle or minor skiing accident. By the age of sixteen, my old blatantly handicapped self had all but vanished, not to reappear for some forty years, when I would learn a footnote to the above great truths—that two canes equal a handicap, one does not. Just a short time ago, I began to figure a second prop couldn't do me any harm on the cracked sidewalks of New York, and just like that people began opening doors for me again like clockwork and worrying about where I'd like to sit: would I prefer a hard chair or a soft one, etc., which is all quite welcome at the age of fifty-five and up, when being handicapped really *is* all in a day's work and almost everyone you know has something wrong with him/her, but is not so welcome when you're a teenager trying to keep up with a gang.

What my new two-cane status did most was remind me, almost mellowly, of all the odd bits of psychic luggage I'd picked up during those first packed months of polio. You would have to be very unlucky indeed to experience any illness on that scale and not encounter a great deal of kindness, and a great deal of intelligent sympathy as well. Some people are so good at that kind of thing that you find yourself marveling—how did he know I wanted that? how could she be so wise? Like great French waiters, the Naturals never crowd the customer, but you never have to go looking for them either. And they even have perfect taste in sick jokes.

Those heavenly visitors and many others only slightly less gifted can play hell with your misanthropy. It's almost impossible to despise the human race so long as these people are in it. However, don't despair—you don't have to quit hating people altogether. Leaving a theater one rainy night, I could have sworn the next taxi was mine until I found myself almost trampled into the mud by a lady otherwise well known for her charitable activities. Not tonight, buster, was the message. But then—rain, a light mist, a threat of snow, just about anything will deter the average do-gooder on his appointed rounds. Often the self-same people who festoon you with the most help when there's nothing better to do are the ones whose eyes glaze over fastest, like supermarket customers, when their own interests are at stake. Self-assertion in good works easily converts to plain old self-assertion when the chips are down. Which at least hands you a good laugh as you stand watching the cab pull way.

Again, this is nothing to cry about. God gave us canes or crutches or wheelchairs for a reason: every one of these is a potential weapon in the right hands. And if you can't deploy them in time, you can always play your trump card and lie down in front of the enemy's car, or stage a fit—okay, you don't really do these things, but you think about them. By the time I returned to the United States from England at age sixteen (and returned again to England at seventeen, etc.—it's a long story) the whole business of recovery had become increasingly like a the whole business of recovery had become increasingly like a game in which one is constantly challenged to come up with ingenious ways to do things: if I grab this rail here and swing over to that chair there—or maybe I could just slide along the wall here, and—would it be out of the question simply to dive under the table at that point and leave on my hands and knees? (My able-bodied father claimed he once did leave a dinner party that way, but I've never seen the right layout for it.) And the substitution of people for objects only makes it more interesting: suddenly you have living furniture to maneuver around, sofas engrossed in conversation, smug-looking armchairs that don't know where, to stick to first things first, the taxis hang out. Sometimes you feel like grabbing a cab for the sheer sport of it even when you don't need one, while grabbing one for somebody else is like pitching a no-hitter.

In other words, I felt good again, ridiculously so at times, as if Nature, in a rare fit of extravagance, had forgotten when to stop pouring. Having given you all the gumption you need to fight polio, it adds enough for good measure to fight the Minotaur and the Medusa as well. But, lest it be supposed that becoming handicapped is a delight from beginning to end, it should be repeated that there was a very tough year of transition, complicated by adolescence, English food, etc., as I evolved from a model patient to an in-your-face cab grabber. So addiction is not the only disease to come with two dawns—a rosy flush, followed by a slump, followed by a festival of lights. And it's not the only one to take its time. As I recently learned all over again—even when you *know* you're going to get used to something eventually, you still have to get used to it. You can't skip the paperwork and the waiting completely, even when you can see across to the other side and hear the trumpets sounding. But it's incomparably better knowing than not knowing.

Once you are used to your new condition, your imagination becomes free once again to rest or amuse itself; you stop scanning the skies for miracles, and life returns to an agreeably small scale of operations. The really big news in my second year, for instance, was the chance discovery of a power serve in Ping-

Pong that automatically elevated my game and my confidence several notches. Opponents would start out tapping the ball back and would end up blasting with all their might.

On that and several other fronts, I had taken the arts of concealment to such dizzy new heights that I was genuinely surprised now by offers to help: where had I gone wrong this time? If I stumbled, I had learned to stare balefully at a nonexistent pothole until the others could almost see it too, and if I outright fell, I was up so fast it seemed like an optical illusion. Or so I hoped. The truth is I was probably always a lot more handicapped than I let on, either to myself or others. My knacks were all geared to the same end, a massive cover-up, a downright Watergate of the nerves and muscles, in order to pass inspection. As Bernard Shaw says of duchesses, if people treat you like one, you *are* one; and I worked on my walking as assiduously as Eliza Doolittle worked on her talking: not just to do it better, which is hard, but to fool people, which is surprisingly easy. And I would receive my reward for all this spit and polish when someone I knew slightly would exclaim on, let's say, our third meeting, "What's the matter—did you hurt your leg?" It was like smuggling the Hope diamond past smiling Customs officials.

But I was like a regiment trained to parade better than fight, and when the so-called post-polio syndrome hit me in my mid-fifties, it weakened the whole physical apparatus just enough to call my bluff on all fronts at once—and no one could have been more surprised than I to realize quite how much I'd been faking it for all these years. If these charades are to work, Bernard Shaw's duchesses have to bamboozle themselves just as thoroughly as the public, and I was deeply shocked to find I could no longer turn my hip in the general direction of a softball without falling on my fanny or execute a power serve without clutching the table.

It was clearly time to take stock. But since I'd convinced myself there was nothing wrong with me to date, there didn't appear to be much stock to take and right up to the year of infamy, 1988–89, I'd have had trouble naming a single important thing I'd learned specifically from polio, except that it's not such a big deal as it looks, but better get your immunization shots anyway. *Immediately.*

It was only when a new affliction rolled up that I began to think about this subject in any kind of depth, and behold, here was the stock I'd been looking for, all the old polio lessons, half buried in dust, but in good condition, as if they'd been waiting for another illness to come along. "I've been here before," I remember thinking. "I know how to *do* this." I already had, as they say, an "attitude" toward whatever came next, loaded and cocked, as soon as I felt up to it. (The first lesson of any illness is, of course, that sick is sick, and that at a certain pitch of it, you can't do anything about it at all but hang in there.) And I knew that my old attitude from polio days was the best one, therapeutic blather notwithstanding, and the one that would eventually pull me through. *When* I felt up to it. If your illness consists, as my next one would, precisely of *not* "feeling up to it"—well, turn the page for instructions.

Many pages, in fact. Unfortunately, attitudes can't usually be defined, only demonstrated, and in this case, rediscovered. But two aspects of the polio attitude would prove so immediately useful that it's worth squeezing them into some kind of words, these being (1) an awed respect for the authority of the body and (2) a thoroughgoing skepticism about those who trade in its upkeep.

The two outstanding distinctions of polio as a teacher are that it was and is incurable, and hence mysterious, but that it is also quite decisive and unequivocal. Nobody ever told a patient of this illness that it was all in his mind. Something definitely happened, Mr. Jones, although we *still* don't know what it is.

Which did not keep certain doctors from calling themselves specialists and not being flung into jail for it, and from charging three times as much as other doctors not to cure their patients. Even in the prevailing welter of ignorance there was a definite pecking order, somewhere near the top of which must have perched one particular chap my parents sent me to see at presumably sacrificial cost to themselves but who, when I got there, consigned the actual inspection of my carcass to an assistant, confining himself to a few bracing and excruciatingly phony words on my way out about "coming along famously" and "coping wonderfully."

I have never felt so cheated, but I shouldn't have, because in the worlds I would be entering these many years later, of mental and physical malfunction, nothing would prove handier than a "show me" attitude toward doctors and paradoctors. Although I have been blessed over the years with the acquaintance of several splendid ones (along with some clinkers), I've never quite shaken the conviction born that day on Park Avenue that doctors are primarily confidence men, in a sometimes good and sometimes bad sense, and that the medical map is still full of unknown seas and dark continents concerning which they will undoubtedly think of *something* to say, because the Wizard of Oz can never be stumped, but concerning which their guess may actually not be a great deal better than yours. The silver-haired charlatan who almost ran my parents into debt that day would have been the last to tell one how little he actually knew about polio. In fact, he probably wouldn't even have got his assistant to tell one. So it was up to me to figure it out for myself— excellent mental training, as time would tell.

The skepticism conceived in Warm Springs, where they did nothing for us at all, and nurtured in offices like the above, would one day prove my last line of defense against a new breed of charlatans, and my first line of attack as well when that particular tide turned.

Perhaps the clearest signal I would receive between my private wars that there had been a changing of the guard among the nation's quacks came many years later when some persistent backaches of my wife's were variously and confidently diagnosed as being either "all in her mind" or the result of a congenital, and of course incurable, malformation of the spine. "Operate anyway," she insisted, and lo, the tiniest of pinched nerves showed up guiltily between two vertebrae, to be summarily removed. And the backaches ceased.

Never mind for now the quality of the doctors involved: no doubt one could have found better ones. But not more instructive ones. "It's all in your mind," I learned from these men, usually means "we're still working on it," while "psychosomatic" seems to be Greek for "search me." The American weakness for spiritual and self-help explanations is a book-length subject in itself—Christian Science remains our defining religion and pragmatism our philosophy—but enough for now to say I'm glad I had an illness that inoculated me so thoroughly against it that I don't even believe *dreams* are all in your mind.

No doubt, if polio could conceivably be considered psychosomatic, it would have been—in fact, I did hear some loose talk about "the polio type" that came close to suggesting "a polio personality." But by and large, this most starkly physical of afflictions provides no such happy hunting ground for the mind-over-matter brigade as my other two diseases would—either cancer, with its mysterious mutations and remissions, or addiction, with its audacious claims to *be*, yes, indeed, a disease, but one with its own quite unique rules and prescriptions. In each case, a Heaven- or Hell-sent opportunity to learn how reality actually works is blown, as it is with crippled athletes, and replaced with the usually childlike dreams of transcendence and the all-important self. "They said it was cancer, but I know he died of a broken heart." No. He died of cancer, all right. And there is nothing he or you could have done about it, except grow in wisdom and strength. After fighting like hell, of course.

But now it's necessary to imagine the whole world spinning round more times than I care to count, and me perforce spinning along with it, forgetting some things with every spin and learning others, absorbing in sum a million experiences that had nothing whatever to do with polio; and then spinning some more, until it's all jumbled together and bound loosely into a regular middle-aged man, who is about to encounter the ultimate "all in your mind" sickness, the one that is so metaphysical that its practitioners are not even trained to practice earth medicine.

If so *many* things hadn't happened between times, undoubtedly I would have dismissed the whole addiction-disease fandango with a sneer, and learned nothing from it. But when it came, I was in no shape to dismiss anything. For roughly fifteen precious months, I would be as vulnerable and open to suggestion—and possible exploitation—as a child with polio, a condition writers over thirty usually have to reconstruct painfully and erratically from memory. And the joke was, I felt too lousy when it happened even to take notes or make rudimentary sense of my thoughts.

So I've had to reconstruct it painfully and erratically from memory.

2.

RING OUT THE OLD ILLNESS, DRAG IN THE NEW

They never did learn very much about polio, if you'll recall, except how to prevent it, and I was surprised at the force of my irritation the day I first read about Dr. Jonas Salk and his famous vaccine. I could have sworn I knew better than that by this time—knew, for instance, that I wasn't going to get my legs back now, whatever anyone discovered; the switchboard in my spine had been dismantled years ago—and knew from observation that a lot of two-legged people were absolutely miserable. In fact, none of the numerous get-happy books of the period even mentioned legs, so far as I know. Yet here I was flinging the overseas edition of *Time* magazine against the wall of my Oxford sitting room so hard that the staples flew out. What had *taken* the man so long? Was it those three-hour lunches again? Fabulous adjustment, my foot. One gleam of light under the door, and I was back where I began, pounding the sky with my fists and howling for a cure.

Well, this was *really* the end, baby. There'd be no more research now for sure, and no more gleams under the door, or hopes so small and crazy that I hid them even from myself. It was a small loss and a huge one at the same time, but I guess what griped me most wasn't my own totally hypothetical loss as the spectacle of all those people smiling and cheering as the last boat pulled out, as if they'd actually won something. I guess the message for the poor wretches left on the dock was "never again," but it was hard to say, because they didn't even seem to be looking in our direction any more. We were *last* year's cover story now.

So what else was new? There's a certain satisfaction in a conclusion, even a bad one, and slamming the book shut on polio probably made more sense by now than keeping it open a crack. Santa Claus has to leave sometime. And nothing had really changed. The pubs were opening in half an hour, or it was time for tea, or for some other giddy English pleasure. Compared with the earthquakes of the past, the Salk affair barely registered a tremor, and my guilty joy at discovering you don't have to *work* very hard at Oxford resumed full blast as the magazine hit the wall.

As fate would have it, that very year or thereabouts, polio would go out and try to make things up to me by rendering me extravagantly unfit for the Korean War (anything for a pal), and whether my 5-A status in two countries saved my life or not, it did wonders for my perspective: I was *alive* and would probably remain so for a very long time, as polio whisked me away from one danger after another like an anxious mother.

Simply being allowed to live is a gift whose value has fluctuated constantly ever since. In good times, it has seemed like the least one could ask, but then a Vietnam comes along, or a worldwide plague, and it again becomes a pearl beyond price. The cries of AIDS victims for help from *some*where, *any*where, contain a note of sheer despair that I've never heard from the most physically disabled of my friends, not because AIDS hurts (pain is the least of it) but because it kills, and life itself turns out to be infinitely more desirable than mere arms and legs, or just about anything I've had occasion to consider.

At any rate, there was still more than enough death in the air of Europe ca. 1950 to make just being alive shine with an incomparable splendor. It's a sorry thing to measure one's blessings by counting other people's and finding that one's own pile is slightly bigger, but it's what one does, and a tutor of mine who'd lost his senses of taste and smell in the war, and couldn't bend his right leg to sit down, made me feel like a—very sympathetic—Hercules (and I trust I did the same for him).

You can never separate the world of illness from the larger world for long, and I remember similar infusions of sadness mixed with strength as I half strode, half limped through the streets of Mainz in Germany right after leaving Oxford in 1954. This town had truly been leveled, bombed to smithereens—who knows? possibly by mistake; it was the age of the snafu—and here I was, alive in the ruins, in manifestly better shape than Mainz, Coventry, Nagasaki, or scores of other sturdy-looking cities that had recently bustled with life. No wonder my generation carries its handicaps so lightly. Our mental landscapes are dotted with fields of white crosses to remind us of our luck.

This sense of narrow escape would still be on hand to offer wry consolations when, years later, I came once more up against that hardest of life's mysteries to accept, the well and truly incurable disease, nature's perfect crime. Compared with most of war's random victims, I had actually been given a pretty fair shake: attention *had* been paid to polio, money *had* been spent, but all I had learned for my pains was that while a billion-dollar lab has a better shot at finding the answers than a philosopher in a bathtub does, there's no point getting mad if it fails. Mysteries don't yield to high pressure. Wishing *doesn't* make it so. Rich people die, too.

Useful truths to take into the long night ahead. So far, I'd only had one mystery disease. I still had two to go.

Nothing could better testify to the insolent inscrutability of the human body than cancer—so much so that when an old polio hand learns he has it, it seems almost like coming home. In life as in art, the deepest mysteries are often the simplest. The Mona Lisa's smile consists of no more than a few everyday brushstrokes, while polio is just a virus and cancer simply a name for some nonconforming cells. Surely a few million dollars should bring these babies into line and straighten out their thinking in no time?

But you already know the answer to that one. For over a century, brilliant scientists, armed to the teeth with grants and absolutely tiptop equipment, have been hurling themselves at cancer, which still sits there like Muhammad Ali's chin, daring all comers to hit it if they can. Well, the next dollar *might* do the trick, and Lord knows we have to keep shoveling them in just in case. But meanwhile, you still have no choice except to enter or re-enter the curious world of illness with its bedpans and boredom and endless blood samples, while the Big Picture of cancer or whatever shrinks inevitably to a small one, and what looked so profoundly tragic from outside seems more like a bad practical joke that you just have to live with hour by hour. Everything that happens in a hospital is a routine, from the nurse taking your blood pressure to the priest administering the last rites, behind a makeshift curtain, to the guy in the next bed. The people who work in a hospital have to see things this way or go crazy, and some of this self-induced anesthesia mercifully rubs off on the patient. "What are you in for this time? polio? cancer?"

It was in this sense that I felt I'd come home. The visitors round the bed looked exactly the same as before, which is to say melodramatic. You have the odd feeling that they are taking this thing too seriously because they *don't* have to live with it. They can go home after this and freshen up for the next bout of sympathy. Too much. You can't keep up, and on the whole, find you almost prefer kidding around with the staff, who know that sickness is a routine and death is a routine, and that you and they and your visitors too are all under equal sentence of it—so what's the big deal? And what's for dinner tonight? (Not again—I don't believe it!)

But before I could renew my studies in this field, I was obliged to wade through the purely man-made swamp of addiction-depression, which might sourly be described as history playing itself out as farce the *first* time. Cancer really is a mystery, but it was never clear to me why addiction of the sort I experienced had to be one too, or at least as much of one as everyone made out. Surely certain measurable things happen to the nervous system and the metabolism that can best be countered in certain specific ways with certain loosely predictable results, no?

If such knowledge exists—and I'm not absolutely sure it does, brain chemistry being yet another of life's puzzles—it is not considered suitable for the ears of the patients, who are all assumed to be in the grip of a sinister psychological condition (in earlier times it would have been called a spell or curse) that automatically distorts what it hears and turns it into what it *wants* to hear. The name of this condition, curse, spell is Denial—and don't pretend you don't have it, either.

So I still don't know much more about the plague that would hit me next than my ancestors knew about the King's Evil or King Tut's Revenge. Although I seemed to have enough physical symptoms to fashion several illnesses out of and would proceed to ask every expert in sight (there's a unique density of experts in this field) precisely what was causing them and when the pain might conceivably end, all I learned for my curiosity was that I obviously had an incurable personality disorder and must go to meetings immediately, and forever. Thus mystery was answered with mystery, and if a real illness hadn't come along, or at least the threat of one, I might be battling the clouds and fog to this day.

3

HALCYON DAYS AND ATIVAN NIGHTS

This is the point in the movie where the male characters suddenly turn gray at the temples and the women look sort of powdery, but everyone's basic features are allowed to remain intact for the rest of the reel. In other words, thirty years of rude good health seemed to pass in a flash, and while the post-polio euphoria did not last anything like that long, it seemed to leave a certain undercoat of well-being that henceforth kept out the worst depressions and left me bobbing up and down with the rest of the human race while the afternoon Devil, my imaginary playmate of childhood, lay safely buried in the backyard.

On the other hand, it had also left me with an unholy taste for toasting my good luck, and attempting to feel better than good night after hilarious night—once you're tasted perfection in this field, it's hard not to keep going back for more—which began to catch up with me sometime in my mid-fifties, trussing me up eventually in one of those banal contemporary tangles of booze and pills, "the disease of the stars." There was certainly nothing unique about it. Doctors prescribed the pills like candy, and they worked much better than candy, and we took and took and were off on a magic carpet ride that came without landing gear. And almost overnight the skies over New York and Los Angeles were filled with "incurable personality disorders"—the actuarial probability of which I would now question heavily, though I had no quarrel with it at the time: like most people in my profession, I couldn't have mounted much of a case for my own sanity at the best of times, and this was suddenly as far from being the best of times as it's possible to get.

How the pills began, I'm damned if I can even remember. I had always made something of a fetish of getting a good night's sleep, on the debatable assumptions that the kind of writing I do requires a reasonable amount of energy, and that energy comes entirely from sleep, so I began taking the occasional sleeping pill long before anything like hard-core insomnia had set in. The seduction of it was not that it relieved any stress that I was aware of, unless the boredom of counting sheep or ballplayers whose names begin with a B counts as stress, but that I seemed to get such great results each time. One Librium was worth at least a thousand sheep, plus a self-satisfied lunch to celebrate afterward. Later there was usually a manuscript waiting to be read for the book club where I worked, and a manuscript doesn't care if you've had a martini and a glass of wine for lunch or even if you have to read the same sentence three times. It was the most indulgent of work partners, and four or five hours would pass in a dream until it was time for the usual evening festivities, made possible by the cheap vintage wine and affordable scotch of the seventies. At those prices, you felt you'd actually be losing money if you didn't get a little bit buzzed each night.

But never much more than that unless I ran into one of those night-shift drinkers like Willie "North Toward Home" Morris who don't start until eleven P.M. Drunkenness is one of the most *uncomfortable* (as opposed to painful, like hangovers) sensations known to man, equivalent to sitting around in wet clothes during the early stages of vertigo, and I wanted no part of it then or ever. But in those days I could stop drinking on a dime, and float up to bed on a passing cloud, and, more often than not, grab a pill around three or four in the morning to round out a perfect day and start on another.

In other words, it was an eerily stable and middle-class drinking life, drastically different from my previous life in Manhattan, where every day had been an original. Prior to 1973, the year we moved to outer Long Island, I had never held a steady job for more than a minute or so, or brought home a reasonable-sized paycheck or, wonder of wonders, huddled in the lee of medical coverage. Fortunately, I remembered the wonderfully self-justifying phrase of Flaubert when he found himself in a similar predicament: "I live like a lamb that I may write like a lion"; so *that's* what I was doing. And after a few obligatory roars at the desk, I could turn into a country squire without guilt and feel, truth to tell, mighty relieved not to have to live by my wits for a while.

Maybe I relaxed too much. But it seemed more than worth it. Several salubrious years seemed to pass without any change at all, the sleeping, the working, the drinking, all remaining at par, no more, no less. Even my friends seemed to stay the same age. In fact, nothing in the picture seemed to move, except the pills, ever so gradually tightening their grip; and, more significantly perhaps, the pages on the calendar. I was approaching fifty, an age when the most perfect of human structures starts to buckle a little and changes demand to be made even in the habits of a lifetime.

The pills certainly seemed to think so. After taking them on and off for several years, I found one night, and then the next, that if I *didn't* take one now, the insomnia became serious indeed. And thus I learned, as drinkers have been learning since the dawn of time, that booze was now playing for the other team and that this finest of God's gifts has a mean streak and a killer instinct. Having once put one to sleep with lullabies, it switches without warning to keeping one awake with acid rock. A friend of mine had recently been forced onto the wagon by racking, wild-eyed insomnia; not the boring, gentle stuff I was used to but a nerve-jangling, sweat-soaked nightmare.

So far as I could see, that fate was still some distance up the road from me, and besides, the man drank brandy. Nevertheless, it was scary, and I had other scares from other friends who had recently shown, or were now in the act of showing, how quickly that last stretch of road can be negotiated between mastery and collapse, youth and old age. Maybe the traveler is the last to know, but checking weight for age for liquid capacity, I too might have been approaching the point where you either get off the bus slowly and with some dignity on your own or wait for the crash.

It's nice to think that I might have done the smart thing and started to cut down on my consumption of this and that. A few friends had done it already, with varying degrees of ease. It was, I supposed, no harder, or easier, than admitting to other physical losses. It seemed only yesterday that you could do a hundred push-ups, too, or dance all night. The big retreat was on, on all fronts, and for whatever comfort it was worth, drinking was far from being the only thing we couldn't do as well as we used to.

However, it's one thing to give up hauling yourself around a dance floor, and another to stop raising your glass a few inches, and no doubt I would have been hard to convince—maybe impossibly so. Some people are constitutionally incapable of getting off before the crash, and these, for want of a better word, we call alcoholics; but many more would like to stay on just a *little* bit longer and get a little bit closer before they decide. A lot depends on how much fun you're having, and I was still having the maximum, little realizing that what had seemed like an early warning from my "night-night, there-there" pills was more like a last call.

Well, little realizing most of the time. Rummaging for memories, I suddenly come upon a picture of myself lying on my bed in something like a trance. I've just upped the ante with a real sleeping pill, as opposed to a namby-pamby tranquilizer, and seem to have gone temporarily catatonic, neither awake nor asleep but quite immobile all the way to my eyelids, and quite speechless, like a fairy-tale character under a curse. It only lasted a few minutes. Just long enough to scare my wife into calling a doctor (who simply said, "This sounds serious" before rolling over), and to reduce the subject to the kind of jibbering breakdown where he decides to join the priesthood immediately, or the French Foreign Legion. After a couple of such nights, it would have taken no willpower to speak of, and certainly no "programs," for me to change my ways from top to bottom: blind panic would do.

But the episode did not repeat itself, and I hadn't yet learned that in this game every warning shot has to be taken with total seriousness, however isolated. And before it could happen again, the ultimate good-news, bad-news pill had entered my life, an innocent-looking little number called Ativan, which I was assured by a local doctor was absolutely nonaddictive and altogether wonderful.

And wonderful indeed it was. Ativan turned out to be a perfect little Jeeves among pills, tactful and anonymous, tucking one into bed every night and slippering out of the room without leaving a trace. Ativan has no aftereffects or side effects, or even during-effects to speak of—except the one it's paid for. It doesn't even make you feel good, like its fast-track brothers Halcion and the addict's delight Percodan, or logy the next day, like the heavy-footed members of the sleeping pill family.

All it does is guarantee you a vintage night's sleep and a clear head the next morning, whether you deserve one or not. Alone among the barbiturates of my acquaintance, Ativan didn't seem to care *how* much you drank or smoked: Jeeves would take care of everything after you'd passed out (not that I ever quite managed to do that, but it was a challenge). No doubt Ativan would discreetly hand me a bill for all this someday—the setup was surely too good to last forever—but that eventuality seemed a million years away as one sailed into each bright day of work and play.

Before this begins to sound like an ad for some pharmaceutical company, I'd better jump ahead of my story for a moment to add that Ativan, like all the others, keeps scrupulous tabs on every one of those great nights of yours, and the bill can be a whopper, quite beyond your means. And it won't be handed to you discreetly either, but slammed in your face. Suddenly it isn't Jeeves you're looking at at all but the greasiest monster in butler's clothing that the fens of your imagination can generate.

Nevertheless, I can't, as AA members tend to do, deny that the good times were good. For seven years or so, I had myself a sweetheart contract with this ridiculous little pill, and I'd be loath to hand those years back, if only in terms of all the manuscript I'd have to do over. One's work feels, at least, wonderfully relaxed the next morning (although it probably reads about the same as before), and one's timing seems *mellow*, like a Teddy Wilson piano solo. "Ah yes! that's it, that's the sound I want. Son of a *bitch*!" I remember sitting on the porch one summer afternoon after such a morning, and what with friends playing a raucous game of croquet on the lawn and an evening of fun to come, thinking, "I am a genuinely happy man"—and adding, with my next heartbeat, that this will surely end someday, and I hope I can take the end gracefully. But in any event, it will have been worth it.

The bill for such days is *enormous*, part of the price being remembering them perfectly, but with all the warmth suddenly gone. And whether you still think it was worth it after you've paid up is a matter of temperament, and also a matter of how good your days are now that it's over. But again, that's jumping ahead.

Zooming the lens back to that period, I'd have to admit that Ativan played fair, in the sense that Agatha Christie played fair, scattering clues in my path that I might easily have picked up if I'd wanted to. Quite early on, I began to sense that my relationship to booze had changed slightly. The lunchtime drink was not altogether optional anymore but quite pressing, in a polite sort of way ("when you're quite ready"). At the same time, pills of this group tend gradually to numb the libido, so that booze moves up gradually on the charts past other pleasures until it becomes the high point of the day. *Gradually.* This was the thing that made the clues difficult: their slowness in declaring themselves. And meanwhile life in general seemed so wonderfully good that you thought you were enjoying it all equally. But you weren't.

Ativan's next clue was not hidden at all, but it didn't seem so all-fired serious either. I had just flown back from Washington after a couple of jolly days with the subject of my next book, Clare Boothe Luce, and I'd left my pills on the plane, and suddenly found myself staring at what my mother's contemporaries used to call a "white night"—a night where sleep didn't even seem a possibility.

No big deal. I was "up" from the trip, and further up still

from being in New York, the world's insomnia capital, and well rested from a thousand pills, or about three years' worth, which I'd taken to popping as absentmindedly as one brushes one's teeth—although never more than one a night so far; and after a soak in the tub I did catch a little sleep of a fretful sort and felt drowsily snappy at lunch the next day, and that was that.

The next visitation was nothing like so ambiguous, and for at least three years after it happened, it would return to haunt me as starkly as any of the nightmare memories I would ever hear at an AA meeting, although it was quite different in kind.

The ambience was a far cry from the standard grubby men's room in back of a saloon with one's head stuck in the toilet. It was more like an endless showing of the movie *2001* in a Quaker meetinghouse. Again I had left my pills behind, this time in an Australian hotel room, so I had already spent a sleepless day-night in what seemed like thirteen hours of unbroken sunlight flying from Sydney to San Francisco. When we arrived, it was too late to pick up a prescription for anything, and our hosts were too healthy to need any kind of pills, so I had a couple of drinks with these dear good friends until I felt superficially sleepy enough to hope for the best, and lurched upstairs, feigning drowsiness to myself.

As they say in the comic strips, *brroing!*—my eyelids flew open, to whatever sound eyelids make, and simply stayed that way: trying to shut them again was like sitting on a suitcase to close it and watching it spring open again, so I reached for a book instead and read it—the life of Moe Berg, as it happens, the polymath ballplayer—and finished it and reached for another, a merry book about the saloons of San Francisco—which in my current state reeked to me of stale beer and Lysol. This night was whiter than white and the sheer brute wakefulness made even reading seem strenuous and unpleasant. Moe Berg was obviously an interesting man, and the book was fine, but I didn't enjoy a minute of it, and I don't want to hear another word about Moe Berg to this day. The saloons were places I would have loved once, but the wit of the barflies sounded quite desperate, like patients screaming in straitjackets.

I finally gave up and put on my brace and trundled downstairs, where for the first and only time in this story I had a sip of dawn vodka, and amazingly it did the trick, calming everything and bringing it to life simultaneously as booze used to, but also leaving me feeling sinful and a little apprehensive. At my wildest I could never stand the thought of drinking in the morning, but this wasn't morning, I told myself, it was eighteen o'clock at night.

I realized, though, for the first time, the interchangeability of booze and pills and understood in a flash the reason I craved a lunchtime drink these days. It was simply because last night's Ativan had started to wear off by then and I had to take *something*, and the craving didn't care which it was, as long as it was sedative. "Name your poison" suddenly had a real meaning for me: it was already the only choice I had.

Or was it? If I'd been able to walk away at *that* point, I would truly have had it all. That's to say, I would have had almost all that I was going to get of the good life, and still have missed the worst of the crash. "Quit while you're ahead." Incongruously, my mind wanders back to Muhammad Ali, about whom, by coincidence, I'd agreed to write a book the last time I'd been in this house. The Great One had talked with obsessive admiration of the few fighters who had retired in time—Gene Tunney, and precious few others—who had left the ring with a spring in their step and all their marbles in place.

But Ali hadn't been able to swing it, and neither, it seemed, would I. As Ali himself might have agreed, you always feel either too good to quit or in too far to turn back. And today was already a beauty, and definitely not a day to quit. Parked regally on the sofa in that fine old San Francisco living room, and reading a marvelous article by Roger Angell on the subject of big-league catchers, I felt the strength flooding unmistakably back in. Morning has always seemed the perfect time of day, so long as it keeps quiet, and today was no exception. Proof, if proof were needed, was right here in this wonderful magazine. Where the Moe Berg book had seemed so bleak and unrewarding, I suddenly found myself reading maybe the greatest and richest piece of work I'd ever seen anywhere or by anyone, worth three stars and a rebel yell.

And with that false dawn, I probably lost my last chance. As we all met for breakfast I felt like a model of sallow good cheer, and by lunch I was sparking on all of such cylinders as my particular model comes with and felt good for at least another hundred thousand miles. That was March 1984, but by the time I finally sputtered into the shop in February 1988, the sparks were all gone and the rest of the good life was only good for scrap metal.

4.

ATIVAN DAYS
AND HALCION NIGHTS

Clare Boothe Luce used to say, in her whimsical way, that back in the thirties, when booze came roaring out of the closet, the only difference between the alcoholics and the others was that the alcoholics had better constitutions. And by this half truth of a definition I certainly qualified.

By normal standards, I was in terrible shape that night in San Francisco; and if I'd felt commensurately lousy for long enough, I would have *had* to do something—namely (and I knew in my heart this was so) cut off all supplies of chemicals entering my system, including the cute one, the one that was so much fun at parties. So where did that fatal surge of life come from? Four years later, when I finally turned my liver over for inspection, it turned out to be clean as a whistle and fresh as a baby's. In fact, everything underneath the shattered fretwork of nerves was purring along like a dynamo and ready for more. It seemed almost a shame to leave the party with such a magnificent infrastructure still to be ruined.

But the Lord giveth and taketh away, as advertised and with a vengeance. That same constitution and those surges of life would be my salvation someday—but if it hadn't been for them, I wouldn't have *needed* salvation. Only they could have dug me in so deep, and only they could have dug me out again. Some joke, boss.

The first two years after my little San Francisco earthquake were almost as pleasant as usual, but with the slight difference that my iron control over booze had begun to loosen slightly. From time to time I would go skidding past the finish line and find myself having to fake sobriety almost harder than it was worth. Although just about any imitation was good enough to fool my fellow drinkers, clever teetotalers were too much like hard work, and I no longer stopped to joust with them on the way out. By then, I was so busy practicing saying "Good evening, officer. What brings you out so late?" that I was afraid I'd say it to my host by mistake.

And even if I stopped in what used to be time, I'd sometimes find myself on the wrong side of the great divide anyway and clambering back gracelessly. They'd shortened the track on me without warning, and although I could still discuss Sartre with the best of them, I didn't feel a damn lot like doing it after midnight or so, by which time an occasional word might come out funny. (Try saying "existential angst" yourself some night.) God knows, I could still pass for cold sober in a hard-drinking society, and in fact, looking around as I enunciated my too-perfect good-byes, I usually seemed in better shape than most anybody else my age. So I wasn't plumbing the depths yet, but simply joining the middle-aged branch of the human race, with its receding gums and hairlines and diminishing capacities for absolutely everything: the Age of Wisdom, as Ortega calls it, and not much else.

Moreover, I was still middle-aged only on a part-time basis. The worst of lushes experiences the occasional reprieve, the magical evening when it all comes back to him and he can play the harpsichord again—which incidentally helps a little to explain the phenomenon known as alcoholic denial. It's not true that you can't control your drinking—for three nights a year, you can control it perfectly. For the next two years, my own ratio was much better than that, and the good nights still far outnumbered the bad ones, so that, cocking an eye at my own peers, I judged myself to be sitting reasonably pretty. On my fiftieth birthday four years or so earlier, I had found myself repeating with some satisfaction the words of Winston Churchill, that mother of bad examples, that "I believe I have taken more from alcohol than alcohol has taken from me," and I felt I could say them still, if a bit more shakily, as late as March 1986.

But there was a difference, and I suppose I knew it, between me and Churchill and most of my fellow rumpots. Alcohol might have taken a few things off them here and there—a brain cell or two, an ounce of ambition, a little something in the complexion—but it hadn't robbed them of sleep. The difference between me and them was entirely the sleeping pills, which, in collaboration with brother alcohol, had begun to call the tunes more and more imperiously.

It took me a disastrous while to recognize precisely what was happening here—and when I did, I would inevitably have to face charges of denial myself, for blaming the pills too much and letting alcohol, the blonde with the blue eyes, off the hook.

If anything, it was the other way around. As an average hagridden Judeo-Christian, I was always ready to accept that the thing I enjoyed most, namely the booze, must be to blame. And why not? Since no one ever "craved" a pill like Ativan the way one craves a drink, and since doctors I barely knew routinely renewed my prescriptions for these pills without a word about side effects, I had no trouble with the proposition that what I had was a mild sleeping disorder, compounded by incipient alcoholism, and no denial about it. Truth to tell, I'd been expecting it ever since college and had only wondered what was keeping it. My own definition of alcoholism had always been "anyone who drinks as much as he did in college," and I was certainly close to that level now. So I was hung by my own definition. And besides, the roll call of great alcoholic writers was so distinguished that who could mind joining it? It was the kind of list you lie your way onto, not off of.

So it was only later that I began to question the rather abstruse and abstract matter of alcoholism. Right now, I was just curious to know how far I would go with this condition before the end, and how bad that end would be when it came, and I got my answers to both questions in a breathtaking rush. After moving up on the victim with mealy-mouthed caution for thirty years or more, addiction turns up the speed at the last moment, pouncing and tying him up hand and foot, body and soul, in nothing flat. After a last-minute remission in Barbados, where everything seemed to flow back together the old way, with sleeping, writing, and casual, take-it-or-leave-it drinking forming a single stream (if I could have kept traveling, I might conceivably have outraced trouble forever), the booze-and-pills gang seemed to be waiting for me at the airport, as if they couldn't waste another minute to get down to business; and in an astonishingly short time, I found myself a high-security prisoner in their private chemical factory, feeling as if I needed a drink every couple of hours after the night's narcosis of pills had worn off by lunchtime, and unable to go anywhere where I couldn't get one.

This was, of course, intolerable, and it didn't take much character to do something about it, because it was also hellishly uncomfortable. Drunkenness is, as noted, disagreeable at the best of times, but this wasn't even that good: if you could get a decent half hour out of it, you were lucky, after which it was just plain dingy, in steadily increasing increments. Did people really live like this? To this day, my heart goes out whenever I see an old lush babbling to himself: words do not exist, even if he was in shape to find them, to express the sick, moldy, never-ending misery that the poor bastard is trying to tell you *all about* right now.

But when I say I did something about it, I didn't say I did something intelligent. My chief problem at that moment was that I didn't have time to do anything intelligent. For dreary economic reasons, I found myself having to do a lot of work in a hurry, and my only absolute need was to get to my desk in reasonable shape each morning and snatch a couple of good hours from the fog before it set in to stay for the afternoon and evening.

Obviously this meant doing something about the afternoon as well, so I began to cut back grimly at lunch, and when the craving became too strong in the midafternoon, I ignored the

Cockspur rum bottle, after trying it a few times, because I would
have had to drink it furtively—and I was damned if I was going
to drink furtively—and tried something else that turned out in
the end to be infinitely worse, but that also, if you like small
consolations, worked like a charm for a while and enabled me to
bull, in two senses, my way through my chores as effectively as
I've ever bulled through anything. As long as I live, I shall
always have a special regard tinged with disbelief for the work I
did from the spring of 1986 until the curtain came down in the
fall of 1987. Reading it now, I detect neither the wheezing sound
you usually get from writing rummies nor the broken synapses
of the addict-at-large—although the writer is always the last to
know, I suppose. My short-term remedy had bought me my
two good hours at a price I can barely bring myself to think
about, and in any event still cannot think about clearly.

What I did was simply try an Ativan instead of a drink, and
voilà—instant clarity, instant relief. I didn't crave a drink in the
least, though I continued to have one in the evening for old
times' sake (or three or five). The big thing was, it suddenly
didn't matter to me whether I had one or not. If I was due to
give a speech, or needed to stay sober for any reason whatever,
not drinking became a positive pleasure. And when I did drink
afterward, it was just like old times. I wasn't doing it for maintenance anymore, but fun. Which meant that my addiction was
not to booze as such but to a continuum of sedatives (some
improvement!).

And with that, another golden age came and went, this one
lasting all of about five minutes, but even small blessings belong
on the record, because from now on the very smallest of them
would have some terrible Grimms' fairy-tale condition attached
to it, none more so than this little beauty.

The catch this time was that the Ativans had already ceased to
help me sleep at night, and without that, all their good work of
the afternoon and evening was wasted. The two good hours in
the morning were what this was about, not some golden twilight
later on, so I asked another doctor for another kind of pill to
help me sleep, just for now, until I had time to tackle the total
situation. Even with my awesome ability to hope for the best, I

recognized a temporary solution when I saw one—but I only needed this latest one to hold up for a few more months, and I'd be in the clear and ready to face the music, however grim.

One curiosity that made this folly easier to slide into than it should have been was that relatively small, unfrightening dosages were involved at the time and throughout this whole experience. Later I would hear Paul Bunyanesque accounts from other addicts of whole medicine cabinets consumed at a sitting, not once but again and again, and I could imagine many listeners like me relaxing with permanent relief, knowing that they were nothing like as bad as that themselves. But in fact you don't have to be as bad as that. A crisis can announce itself by nothing more ominous than a need for three Ativans a day instead of two.

Especially if you throw in the new pill on the block, the next one my doctor prescribed to help me sleep. And here enters for the first time a real stage villain. Ativan had been nothing if not anonymous, as faceless and colorless as a gentleman's gentleman laying out your pajamas and disappearing, doing no less and no more than it was hired to do. But Halcion is a regular seducer, a lounge lizard among pills, which promises you not merely a night's sleep but a hell of a good time along the way, in the form of delightfully sunny and light-as-air dreams, the kind that make you wake up smiling, like Scarlett O'Hara after a night with Rhett Butler.

Not, mind you, that I wanted seduction: a light tap with a hammer at the base of the skull would have done just as well. All I needed was *sleep,* not ravishment. So I felt a little of the pleasure familiar to wronged women when I heard much later that this weasely little pill was in legal trouble and might be banned from the country. In exchange for some truly wonderful mornings of work, Halcion would proceed to complicate my retreat from Chemical Heaven beyond measure, as if every good dream had to be repaid with seventy times seven worth of bad ones, as the flights of angels that had once seen me to my rest turned one by one into gargoyles who wanted to party all night, gargoyle-style.

Meanwhile, all was not quite well on the Ativan front either. I wasn't taking notes, so I can't remember when it began, but every now and then I would be drinking away at a cocktail party only to be overtaken by something I keep thinking of as a fog, although it wasn't anything like a fog. In fact, it would be one of my abiding frustrations that I could never describe this sensation, even when it obligingly sat still for hours on end posing for me.

The closest I can come, now that it's gone for good, to defining my so-called fog is in terms of a very light paralysis of the cranial nerves mixed with a total emptiness. And something else, which can't be named because it is not a shared experience. Words are for what other people have been through too, and nobody who has been through this particular experience has ever been able to convey it to anyone who hasn't, perhaps for the simple reason that it has no features to speak of, it is Nothing to the nth power; Nothing heightened to the screaming point.

But as usual, not at first. These early visitations were creepy but not unpleasant, a curiosity more than a threat. I would stop drinking for a while and hold on tight, making conversation, if I must, with enormous effort, as if my teeth were about to fly out of my head (again, not literally: like the fog, it happens to be the only image that survives); and in a short while it would pass and the rest of the evening would be better than ever.

Once again, it didn't occur often; none of my warnings came often until they began to come every day, by which time they weren't warnings anymore.

It all began to come down in September 1987, right after Labor Day, which is the end of the year where I live, and I was in the last lap of my work now, panting and pounding down the track and swinging the whip like a madman. And one bright morning the cocktail-party fog or nonfog rolled, or rather swarmed, in about two and a half hours after breakfast. And this time it wasn't smiling, but became and remained a sense of total, no-exit misery, just as indescribable as ever. It was like hurting all over without feeling anything. It was like being trussed a tiny bit too tight in your skin though the tailor can't find what's wrong. Striving now to locate it more precisely, I sense with a spasm that the arms and shoulders might have felt a little put out and would the word be *oppressed*? and perhaps a squirming in the chest? The memory moves obligingly to whatever part of the body I've just thought of, but mostly to the action parts near the top. Most particularly to the brain, where all the wires were down and where finally, and for the first time, the desolate confusion became so great that work became impossible—or at least it *felt* impossible. (Recently I came across something I *had* to write in this condition and found it surprisingly ingenious, like a chicken dancing with its head cut off. Technique can apparently cover for anything short of rigor mortis.)

Quitting now was simply out of the question. I was so close to my particular finish line that one mighty lunge of hard work would get me there, so I had no choice that I was aware of but, with a sense of certain doom, chased the fog that wasn't a fog away with a second late-morning Ativan, the way you might pay off a blackmailer, knowing he will be back the next day.

In most cases, anyone who diagnoses himself like this probably has a fool for a patient, and soon a very sick one. But for once there didn't seem to be any other doctors around. The one I knew best and respected most told me that the number of pills I was taking didn't sound too serious to him and that I could surely finish what I was doing, throw my pills away, and go to bed for a week or a month with a good book or a library until sleep came back on its own.

Since I had spent many an evening with this brilliant fellow and he knew my body inside and out, I had no narcotic secrets from him and could take this to be a sanction of sorts—but only because I had no choice. I knew it was no real reprieve, because I had felt, as my friend hadn't, the great nonfeeling, the Nothing; but by stringing Ativans judiciously through the day, I was able to keep the visitations short. And so long as I knew they were not going to last, they could do their worst, or nothingest. In fact, as each pill dropped and miraculously wiped the board clean, I began to understand the sheer joy an old addict gets from a fix, not because it makes him feel high anymore but because it makes him feel normal: just not hurting can be intoxicating, and I finished my writing stint downright zestfully, in spite of all I knew; in spite of the hangman waiting out in the corridor, tapping his foot and sending in messages every two hours now.

This is recuperation-as-holding-action, needed more and more often and delivering less and less, until what passes for relief and normality would strike a healthy person as a serious downer. As long as you feel relatively better than you did before, you'll settle. And here was that finish line at last, with the editing and rewriting done at a Charlie Chaplin pace, and I was across it home free. I passed a sleepless night in celebration and braced myself for the worst.

It must have been a weekend, because I remember trying to follow a football game between the New England Patriots and somebody and simply not being able to. The plays were clear enough, I guess, but they didn't connect, they didn't add up to a story. This wasn't a particular game I was watching, it was just football. And I was *uncomfortable,* is the only word for it. Local pain would have been better, more specific; pain draws arrows for you. But my nerves were uncomfortable, and the ones that get together and try to think things through could only register how wretched they felt and how humiliated at not being able to follow this damn game. "I'm generally very brave," as Tweedle Dum says to Alice, "but today I have a headache." I can generally follow football, too, but not today.

So this must be a stroke, no? The evidence suddenly seemed overwhelming. Insofar as the Sheeds had a history of anything, stroke was it: my grandmother on that side had died of multiple strokes at eighty-five, and my father had probably had a small one at about the age I was now, fifty-six. Grandfather Sheed had fallen downstairs to his death, which sounded like a stroke too, although he had probably drunk so much beer by then that it was hard to tell. My mother's family seems to have been more diverse—cancer, heart, the usual bag—I was in no shape to track it down today. They looked, from their pictures, like people who have strokes. But who knows?

More to the point: if what I had now wasn't brain damage, I couldn't imagine what was. In fact, I've heard of brain-damage cases just like this, where the victims perceive the world entirely in fragments. A man throws a ball. A man catches one. How about that? See Spot run. That was me today—except for some small part of the brain that would stay on like a pilot light through everything, judging everything, and ever ready to point out bits of bad news I might have overlooked, but becoming dim and distant when I needed help from it.

But for all the strength of my case, I was never able to sell my brain-damage theory to anyone, that day or ever. My doctor, when I finally reached him, suggested calmly that I call off the little project for today, pop an Ativan, and call *another* doctor in the morning, this time one who specialized in matters of the head.

So—no brain damage, eh? We'll see about that. Although I felt sure my face was a shambles, it obviously didn't come through in my voice, and never would. But just wait until somebody sees me—it'll be straitjacket time for sure.

Yet even at the end of the line, when I checked into an establishment where they examined brains on the slightest provocation, I couldn't persuade them to examine mine. Sick I might be if I said so, but I could never sell them on crazy, which was maddening.

It had always been a notion of mine that sanity is like a clearing in a jungle where the humans agree to meet from time to time and behave in certain fixed ways that even a baboon could master, like Englishmen dressing for dinner in the tropics. But I'd never realized how little you actually had to bring to the meeting. Proceeding virtually on automatic pilot, I was apparently able to produce a good enough replica of a normal human being to fool the average onlooker indefinitely.

You're probably better off not trying to think when you're in this condition because the first thought you stumble on, wherever it comes from, is likely to become an obsession, and for a short feverish while I became convinced that my whole life had been a theatrical performance with never a real moment in it. In vain did the head doctor I went to see the next week try to assure me that I wouldn't have a friend in the world if this was so— how does an actor *know* if he has any friends? how does he know they're not acting too? I had now entered the world of depression, where ideas like this one can sit like boulders at the mouth of a cave blocking the light and utterly immovable, until, just like that, they evaporate. Looking back just a short while later, I couldn't imagine why I'd cared whether I was acting or not—but I did know I should never have read Erving Goffman, who had given me the idea in the first place. God knows what would have happened if I'd been reading the Marquis de Sade or *Mein Kampf*.

The fact that I seldom appeared that sick—sick maybe, but not *that* sick—would complicate my life enormously and lead to a lot of misreadings, even costing me a job one day. But the only immediate lesson I learned was that, as Scott Fitzgerald said of his character Dick Diver, the façade can remain intact after the interior has crumbled—and that a clear eye and a steady voice can stand guard over a seriously disintegrating personality. Half the ordinary people you see in the street could be as crazy as loons and you wouldn't know it from their faces, at least if my own bland reflection in the bathroom mirror that evening was anything to go by.

But enough with the philosophy—right now, it was off to Dr. K. to devise a plan for getting first off Ativans and then off Halcions without too much further damage. And he gave me the only possible advice, which was to cut the pills in two or more pieces and try to come bouncing down one step at a time.

Outside of that home remedy, Dr. K., like all the doctors I would come across, was pretty much flying blind in the region of pills, and we had to learn even the basics together—the first of them being the next step after the one I'd learned back in San Francisco, to wit, that while you may be able to choose which poisons to take, you can't decide which ones to give up: everything has to go. The first night I spent on reduced Ativan rations, I felt as if I'd been plugged into a wall socket, with hideous images springing out at me psychedelically all night long. Faces wouldn't hold still for me. Beautiful women would dissolve into crones, then would become devils, or leering morons.

Clearly, I had to start phasing out of booze too, in some sort of makeshift two-step, a drink today, a pill tomorrow, hippity-hop, just praying that each move wouldn't be too jarring. My daily intake of wine and spirits was so enormous—it even startled me when I recited it for the first time, and Dr. K.'s eyes went wide—that it left plenty of slack, and I was able to cut back quite a lot without minding *too* much.

What I did mind was having to count: it took all the fun out of it. Then again, how much fun was it anyway these days? Outside of the occasional magic night—and I would have these right to the end—when drinking was all the fun it had ever been, getting lit or semilit was pretty much of a chore by now, and the outcome was surprisingly banal. Old drinkers are not looking for adventure but familiarity, the mental equivalent of pipes and slippers, and after I'd quit, it was a comfort to remind myself that I had been there so many times before that I knew every room in the house of booze and wasn't missing anything new.

However, the body has its reasons that the head knows not of, and I discover as I rewind the film that I am reliving scenes in which, if I didn't take a pill, I craved a drink whether I wanted one or not. And I remember one or two afternoons where I sat staring at the clock, as gloomy and apprehensive as a Dublin barfly waiting for the pubs to open.

In less than a week, though, the craving had transferred its holdings entirely to Ativan, hard though it may be to associate such a strong emotion with such a bland love object. Although I still preferred the *idea* of alcohol, it was getting by strictly on reputation by now. The fact was, it wasn't *doing* anything for me anymore. Even a martini barely made a dent in the fog before going over to the other team and becoming part of the fog. Ativans might be dull, but they were still relatively dependable, granting me, even when they were cut in two, a good ninety minutes and shrinking of what passed for my old self. So, alcoholic or not (and honestly, who cared?), I could by the end have much more easily given up alcohol than the other goodies, the ones that worked, the boring, featureless pills. "What use are you?" I remember saying to my last martini. And that was that.

Luckily for me, I had no idea that my floundering excursion into the unknown had barely begun at this point. The only way to survive any kind of depression is to suppose that help is on the way and prosperity just around the corner; and Dr. K.'s invariable formula, "Let's see what happens and call me in two days" (at which point he would simply repeat the formula), kept me pounding hopefully round and round the track through December and January of that endless winter.

But even Dr. K. could only give me encouragement, not information. Although he was the best—and, incidentally, least lazy—of the several psychiatrists I would see in the next fifteen months and he read everything he could find on the subject of pill addiction, even he was a victim of his profession's inflated and pricey version of the American preference for spiritual explanations. Before this nightmare had run its course, I would encounter any number of experts, frocked and unfrocked, fairly bursting to discuss my psychological problems with me, but nary a one who knew anything at all about what was happening to my body. "You're undergoing great chemical changes," they would pronounce over my twitching nerves with all the precision of a fortune cookie, failing only to tell me whether I was going to meet a rich Virgo who would help me to pay his bill.

Meanwhile, my hopes that this process would not be too jarring were shattered again and again, as each step I took shook me to the back teeth. I'll spare both you and myself the details except to say that I recently came across an envelope on which I'd scrawled some notes for my next talk with Dr. K., and even the fading pencil marks look demoralized and jittery, although not as weird as my handwriting would look later. "Fri: Mopy, flat, apprehensive, craving again. 1 Halcion. Sat: Tense, craving but strong enough, and v.g. evening. Sun: Whommf, the worst. Can't stand many more of these. Mon: Woke up beaten, scared." And so on and on, another four days in a life. For some reason, I feel glad beyond words that Saturday evening was v.g. that week.

Could this really have been me? I find it hard to believe this, but for fifteen eternal months apparently it must have been. After that I would walk away so cleanly and completely that the whole episode now seems more remote than a dream. And the envelope with the despairing scrawl on it looks like something found in an ancient tomb. Since William Styron has already written so authentically and well on the sensations of depression (his title, *Darkness Visible,* fits my "fog" perfectly), I would be delighted to leave my own account of it at that. But Styron's book ends just as it gets to the good part, the ultimate walk into daylight, and there's no way to convey the delights of this experience without returning to the darkness and making it visible once again. No two dark nights of the soul are exactly alike, so waking up is full of pleasant surprises.

The one satisfactory principle that I've scavenged from the debris of this mess is that what goes down must almost always come up, and the worst of what follows can be viewed as the downward straining of a catapult that would eventually send me flying as high as I ever got on even the best scotch, and keep me up there longer, in the complacent orbit of the survivor.

Meanwhile, here on earth I had to continue grappling with the appearances problem. Phoning someone to say I had to skip a business lunch, for instance, I could almost hear the skepticism on the other end. What did they want from me—screams? "I don't feel too well." Yeah, sure. Look, what I'm really doing is climbing the wall. We understand. We're not good enough for you anymore (everyone has problems).

If I'd had a Halcion or two the night before, my brain would be flying around my skull by now like a maddened bat, but how to explain this in layman's language? "I hope you're feeling better real soon." The sarcasm hurt all the worse because I've always hated missing lunch and would only be constrained from a suicidal dash for it by my fear of wrecking the car or gibbering when I got there. Even Dr. K. sounded sore when I called off an appointment one day. It seems he had gone to the office just to meet me and felt (no doubt justly) that I should confront my fears and call their bluff. But there *is* such a thing as highway safety.

The only times my condition must have been unmistakably clear to the outside world came when I messed up the sequence of Ativan tidbits and drinks and appeared, I imagine, absolutely pie-eyed. One dinner still haunts me: it was a huge bash at the

New York Public Library, and I had prepared for it by not drinking beforehand but doubling up on the Ativans, which played hob with my timetable but seemed worth it for several reasons, the chief being that I have a vested interest in not making an ass of myself in front of large crowds. Furthermore, tonight I would be meeting a bunch of other writers I wanted to remember the next day—Raymond Carver in particular, whom I admired greatly.

In a sense I got my wish. I remember everything about that evening with a kind of sharp-edged lucidity, as if the people actually had outlines; most clearly of all, I remember Ray Carver, who seemed like the friendliest of men—I looked forward to meeting him properly some time. But not tonight. Tonight was a night to be gotten through like an attack of seasickness on a stormy night in a sealed cabin: just holding on to the railings took all my strength and concentration. The first social drink lit the Ativans like a match dropped into an oilcan, and I might as well have been drinking all day long. Which meant that there was virtually no difference anymore between the effect of booze and pills, except that pills-plus-a-little-booze induced wide-eyed insomnia and unnatural clarity even quicker than booze-plus-a-little-pills did, as if the pills had been ordered to remove all the repose they'd ever given me as quickly as possible.

But if my head was so clear, why was it so woozy? As I sat at the dinner table, I felt as if I was simultaneously fighting insomnia and fighting to stay awake, while my head felt as if it wanted to throw up and be done with everything. Toward the end, a bunch of British Islesy writers, led by the amiable Edna O'Brien, invited me to go roistering with them in Manhattan, and I felt the first of a host of pangs for my lost youth. A hundred such wonderful evenings came back to me in the form of one great big one, like a sprawling mural of jollity. Never in my life had I turned down such an offer, but when I did, they seemed to understand all too quickly and vanished discreetly, like hospital visitors. And just in case I was in any doubt as to what they saw, a photograph arrived in the mail a few days later of myself standing in a group of writers looking quite pixilated, with my bow tie lurching on its side like a sinking ship and the party favor they'd hung on my neck perched roguishly someplace near my ear.

So I'd gotten away with nothing. And that's how it would be from now on, I supposed. The gradual withdrawal from my assorted drugs kept me constantly off balance. And before I had reduced them to a level where they could do no more visible damage, I had run through a double-quick lifetime of the kind of embarrassments I'd been so proud of avoiding, including the ultimate one of blacking out and forgetting where I'd been and what I'd done (nothing interesting, I'm told). Later, when I heard some AA narratives, I was able to say "I did that too." But it was all done in a few months, as if I was cramming for an examination in hitting bottom so I could start rising immediately.

Anyway, Dr. K. and I did get the dosage down, by God, and I was within at least temporary reach of our target of three drinks a day except maybe on Saturdays—but had hit a brick wall with the pills—when an actual medical FACT arrived, like the sound of a gun being fired to end an interminable game. To be sure, the fact did not relate directly to drugs—that would have been too much to hope for—and it entered the house almost by stealth in the form of one of those mildly official-looking bits of third-class mail that tend, nine times out of ten, to get thrown out by mistake or buried in the can-wait pile. Not when you're in my state, however, looking for clues under the sofa cushions. This suddenly looked important, and like an atheist crying out for God's mercy despite himself, I forgot my medical skepticism long enough to rip open the envelope, simply because it had the name of a real doctor on it, and read the contents at a gulp, because they came from what sounded like a real laboratory. The thing every hard drinker and smoker craves, whether he admits it to himself or not, is some good solid medical information to base his decisions on, and that's exactly what I seemed to have right here in my hand, although my relief at receiving it was tempered by a certain stark terror. It's nice to know that God exists, but not so great to learn that He's thinking of sending you to Hell immediately.

What had happened was this. Somewhere in the misty midst of the surreal Christmas holiday season of 1988–89, my miseries had been maddeningly compounded by an unmistakable toothache, which came twanging and screaming through the vapors in the bullying way that physical pain likes to announce itself: "You ain't seen nothin' yet!" And to make things that little bit worse, my dentist couldn't even find where the pain was coming from at first. It didn't show up on conventional X rays, or unconventional ones either, and it took me a second visit, with Dr. T. doing everything but hold me upside down, to turn up the best-hidden hairline fracture in history. And it was only on this second visit, while the search was at its most feverish, that my man chanced upon a pale white patch browsing innocently on the underside of my tongue—common enough among smokers, he said, and only dangerous when and if it turns red, but I might want to have it looked at by a specialist sometime, if I had nothing better to do.

By such accidents are lives saved. Since I had to visit a dental surgeon anyway to have the tooth pulled, it required, thank God, no extra effort on my part, but only a lucky turn in the small talk, for me to act on my dentist's extremely mild advice. "I don't suppose you do biopsies, do you?" I asked, mainly for something to say (we'd exhausted the subjects of the football play-offs and whether my gum was numb yet). "Sure do," he said, or maybe it was "Yup"—it was one of my bad days, and his voice seemed to be coming from a snow-covered tree outside the window—and the deed was done. Thank God again, I didn't even have to come back for the biopsy report, because I probably wouldn't have bothered to.

Both my technical advisers had been at such pains not to worry me about my tongue that when the report finally arrived in its understated envelope, I half expected it to continue in that vein. "Whatever you do, *don't worry*." As if worry was the nation's number one killer.

But that didn't seem to be what it was saying at all. "Patient's tongue is not cancerous *yet*" were the approximate words. "It is *pre*-cancerous. If patient refrains from all tobacco and alcohol, patient's prognosis is good." Huh? The report added something about how laser surgery might possibly help patient too, and I sucked what comfort I could from that, but mainly I was scared to death, and to life, because I had something real to confront at last. "Pre-cancerous" rang in my head like a thousand alarm clocks calling me to action. And thank God there *was* something I could do, if not much.

The smoking clause was easy to comply with in the circumstances: unbelievably painful, but easy, and perversely exhilarating. I was an inveterate cigar smoker, but I was used to going unrequited. Ever since the Cuban cigar embargo at the very start of my smoking career, I'd been scrounging for Havanas like a ragpicker and settling for shabby imitations, two-bit stogies dressed up like royalty. In addition to which all cigar smokers of good and bad brands alike had lately been driven into a corner by public opinion, glaring from every direction like prison searchlights, so that in a sense it was almost a relief to be put all the way out of my misery. If one couldn't light up a great cigar after a good meal in a so-so restaurant, what was the point of anything? In short, it was the perfect habit to give up right now, a heaven-sent sacrificial object to get things started.

So I took one of the two boxes of stogies I'd just been given for Christmas and gave it to, as I recall, the local chief of police, so that *some* good would come of it, and kept the other around for old times' sake and for special occasions. All advice notwithstanding, I'd still rather have one cigar a year than none, and in fact wound up settling for three.*

But of course the really big news was alcohol, around which the lines were now clearly drawn. As of this very moment, I could kill two birds with one stone, or save them with one Heimlich Maneuver, by just giving the stuff up completely. And that suddenly was that. Complications would present themselves later, enormous ones in fact, but for now I was flooded with the excessive clarity of the newly converted, and all I wanted to know was, when do we start? How about right now?

* For the curious: one for my birthday, one for my grandson's birthday, and one wild card, to be smoked in the event of a Nobel Prize or, failing that, an utterly sizzling book review.

I was stalled in Purgatory anyway: every second day, all the witches of London, New York, and Sydney, Australia, held square dances in my head and I had to cancel writing projects or anything else that required a dime's worth of concentration. But if I hadn't had the biopsy, I might easily have hung in there all the same, sweating it out and adjusting to the new conditions. I had known a number of middle-aged men who lived for years in this kind of tense twilight, counting drinks and watching the clock, and always short a night's sleep, and I seemed to be climbing toward this lofty condition when the gun went off, ending one game and starting another.

But not quite immediately. Dr. K. felt that my nerves already had enough on their plate and suggested that we continue to bring the booze down gently in conjunction with the pills—although not stopping at three this time. He added that there were only so many things one should try to give up at a time, and that the quantities involved were not crucial. And God knows I wanted to cushion the fall a bit longer, since even with cushions it was unbelievable.

But I was also getting mortally tired of feeling embarrassed, and I asked if there was anyplace I could just go and get this over with in peace, the way you disappear behind a hedge to throw up. And he said he indeed knew of such a place, where, he believed, they weaned you off your pet habit gradually just as we were doing but where I wouldn't have to wear a bowtie or talk in sentences or keep up any appearances whatever.

All that and Blue Cross too, as I quickly discovered: it was irresistible. And mostly because I was beat to my socks, but just a little because I was curious, I put my name on the waiting list for one of the numerous addiction centers that spangle the landscape these days, offering to do wonders for you in no more than a month.

Thus, idly, did Alice step through her looking glass, or plunge down her rabbit hole, and change everything. I don't know how the Happy Valley waiting list worked in this drug-infested country, but it turned out that I was just their type and they could take me almost immediately. So there was no time for second thoughts. It was like putting your hand up timidly and being accepted on the spot for minesweeping detail. That month would complicate my life beyond description, but it would also afford me a glimpse of the great therapy culture that could be had no other way. "Some people will do anything to get material," said a writing friend. But you don't get the full benefit from a nightmare if you regard it that coolly, and it would be a long time before I would see this one as material for anything except possibly tears.

Unfortunately, by the time it was over, I learned to my exasperated regret that Ray Carver, the patron saint of rummies and the best friend I never had, had died of cancer, after an epic struggle altogether worthy of him. It was, as we used to say, a lousy note, but a good one to end my drinking life on. After a long, happy prime and a short, painful death, *requiescat in pace*. But not yet.

5.

DOWN IN THE VALLEY

"This place you're recommending won't be AA, will it?" said I.

"They're *all* AA," said Dr. K., but added with a small professional smile, "You don't have to listen, you know."

Easy for a psychiatrist to say, I thought, with his years of training. Several I would meet later could actually not-talk and not-listen at the same time, but my work requires a bit more attention, and I knew for sure I would wind up hearing every grim word amplified like an airport advisory to reach every last straggler in the men's room. *"Why are you afraid of AA? What are you running away from?"*

In the new world I was about to enter, the assumption was that it was always the truth you were flinching from like a vampire at high noon, and never from just a cliché or, in this case, a shower of clichés, the bane of my profession. Like many organizations, Alcoholics Anonymous turns its worst face to the world; in fact, its whole organizational apparatus probably *is* its worst face, and its spokespeople are its worst voice. At such meetings as I attended later, I would hear some much more beguiling sounds, including scattered bursts of humor, horse sense, and even skepticism ("Parrots lecturing to sheep" is how

one member, who never missed a meeting, described AA); but
these are precisely the sounds that are shut off sharply when
organizations address the outside world.

So far all I'd picked up was the sound of the parrots, squawk-
ing peevishly at anyone who'd listen, particularly in the sports
pages, which is where I tend to hang out. Just, for instance, let
some recovering athlete make the mistake of saying, "I really
owe a lot to AA," and the parrots would be all over him in the
next week's mail, insisting that members of AA should maintain
their anonymity at all costs—presumably on the grounds that if
they slip, people will blame the movement and question its infallibility.

Since in my own average lifetime, I had known several people
who had backslid most conspicuously from AA, infallibility
must be a tough sell anyway, and I couldn't imagine why they
made such a big deal of it. Weren't they building their membership up for a big letdown? Meanwhile, I guess we were meant
to suppose that the letter writers were not AA members themselves, but merely interested observers who happened to know
the organization's bylaws by heart.

Whatever they were, they certainly never missed a trick but
would be out again in force—the same ones by the sound of
it—the moment some other athlete was daft enough to blurt that
he thought he was really "getting on top of my drinking problem." This called for a truly thunderous reprimand, and the
poor beggar would be treated to the scolding of his life for his
overconfidence and grandiosity. "An alcoholic is *never* on top
of his drinking; he is always just one drink away from disaster,"
etc., etc. Terrible and swift is the Lord, and slow and humorless
are his followers. If this was what meetings were like, I thought,
give me an early burial under a downtown bar at the height of
the happy hour with someone trying to sing "Kelly, the Boy
from Killane" overhead.

The overwhelming impression given by these truth squads
was that to give up drinking you had to submit to a root-and-
branch brainwashing, after which you crossed some great divide
that separated you from the rest of humanity for eternity. Nothing in my experience told me otherwise. Most of the few AA

customers I had known were nervous-looking citizens, usually
somebody's uncle, who scurried away from festivities of all
kinds and put on windbreakers and wouldn't tell you where
they were going, although on other nights you might see them
gloomily filing into church basements to talk about booze booze
booze until a normal man would expire either of thirst or boredom.

The image was so ghastly and widespread that a number of
my acquaintances, who were physiologically more than ready to
dry out and give up, were damned if they were going to submit
to it, and they never got to find out if there *was* another side to
it. Ironically, the best of this association really is anonymous,
but the worst of it you can't miss. And the only members I was
aware of besides the lugubrious misfits mentioned above were
the triumphalists, all pink and shiny and gregarious, people who
talked in bumper stickers and had only one mood; people without light or shade or even tones of voice; undifferentiated energy
masquerading as people. "Remember—one day at a time!" these
ghouls would exclaim heartily, as if for the first time in history;
and then, masters of paradox, they would add, "Tomorrow is
another day!"

Was there any way of just giving up alcohol without becoming a "type" at all—either a wistful loser (or "dry alcoholic," as
they're called in the club) or a sleek winner who has given up
too much of himself and turned into a Fuller Brush salesman?

More to the point—even if I escaped one of these cartoon
fates, would I still be able to write worth a damn? People who
depend even a little on inspiration for their livelihood tend to be
as superstitious as ballplayers about where it comes from. And
since alcohol can do some truly wondrous things for your imagination, at least when you're young, it's tempting to suppose
that the whole thing comes from there. Upton Sinclair, the no-
torious nag, once made out a list of all the American writers who
had been destroyed by drink, and absolutely everyone was on it;
to the point where a child of twelve, or forty, could see that if
you *weren't* on it, and *didn't* drink yourself to death, you hadn't
a ghost of a chance of making it as a writer.

There never was such a subversive list, especially if you tried to match it, as I did now, with a list of writers who had given up booze and tried to keep going without it. Damon Runyon managed okay, but he'd stopped drinking almost too early in life to count; Raymond Chandler wrote all his good stuff while dry, although Dashiell Hammett couldn't write a word that way; and among contemporaries, Elmore Leonard stood out, and I was sure there were others. But even if you threw in John O'Hara and his windy late novels, it wasn't much of a list compared with Sinclair's, and the only encouragement I could get out of it was that the born-agains seemed as a group to be, if not deep or major, at least agile and capable of the word games and improbable associations that might be attributed to alcohol.

But canceling this completely was the fact that they *weren't* major or anything like it, and never mind that there have only been about three major Americans or that my sample was too small to prove anything. A bad proposition can always cancel out a good one when you're depressed, and it didn't occur to me until the fog cleared that all the best American books seemed to have been written by people in their twenties anyway (thirties, latest), after which it didn't matter *what* they did with themselves.

But there are no good thoughts to be had in the state of permanent semiwithdrawal I had settled into. The whole point of tranquilizers is to depress your nervous system, and mine had done such a number on me that anything that entered my head seemed quite unbearably sad; and just in case it didn't seem quite sad enough, the part of my brain that stayed lucid through everything continued to make sure that no worst case or hideous possibility ever escaped my attention. It was as if the family optimism which I'd inherited from both parents and which for years had turned bad news into good almost automatically, had gone into reverse and was turning flowers into weeds and beautiful faces into skeletons as fast as it could go. I would have sold my soul for one cheerful image.

The one thing I was not looking for was a browbeating, but this, from all the evidence, is the first thing they issue in an AA institution—a nonjudgmental browbeating, to be sure, but I doubt if my nerves could have told the difference.

In fact, I had already experienced a small taste of the medicine that I assumed was in store for me. I had gone to see a local doctor who specialized in addiction and who was said to be a "straight shooter" who "leveled with you." A straight shooter he certainly was, straight between the eyes, and level with me he did too, in the manner of Jerry leveling with Tom in the old cartoons by running a steamroller over his bones.

"Specialist in addiction" was putting it a bit strongly, though. As far as I could tell, he knew nothing about pills whatever and didn't want to know. "In all my experience, I've never *heard* of anyone taking Ativans in the daytime," he said, like a Victorian faced with the ultimate depravity. My little stratagem for finishing my work placed me, it seemed, almost beyond the human pale. To his way of thinking, Ativan and Halcion and Librium and, saints deliver us, Percodan were all just buzz words for booze, concerning which he didn't seem to know much either, except that addiction to it was a disease that would undoubtedly kill me in, I can't remember whether he gave me two years or two months, if I didn't immediately enter the nearest AA branch office or rehab center, which he even began to dial for me as we spoke.

Little Red Riding-Hood could not have been more shocked. "You're not a doctor at all, you're a . . . a . . . an AA recruiter." Here I had come looking for some simple physical explanation of what had hit me, and the guy had not only dodged the question slyly (something I would get used to) but, while doing so, had practically sent for the guys with the nets and the white coats.

There are, as it happens, any number of fates worse than death waiting out there, and this guy was one of them. As I reeled out of his office, I decided that a month spent in such company as his would surely drive me crazier than any combination of chemicals yet devised, and such was his skill at recruiting that it would take me another wretched four weeks and a cancer scare even to consider going anywhere at all to attend to my condition, and then only with Dr. K.'s repeated assurance that Happy Valley wasn't like that at all—that he had an old friend there who really was a doctor and not just another straight shooter, and who would steer me through the rest of this mess with a minimum of empty threats and idle blather about dying.

K. was right—or half right—about his friend, anyway, and thanks to him, Happy Valley would not prove *quite* as weird or beside the point as it might have, i.e., I learned one or two actual facts from him that had at least a remote bearing on my condition. Before checking in, I had to clear it with my employers, and they couldn't have been friendlier. My immediate boss even consulted an expert *he* knew, who passed on one more unscientific suggestion to add to my growing collection, namely that "I'd better have a good support group."

What the hell do I need *that* for? I remember thinking. Don't I have enough troubles without having to worry about other people, and whether they're "there for me" today? Suppose they don't answer the phone, suppose they don't feel like it? And that's when it all came back to me, the memory of my last big illness and the satisfaction I'd gotten from surviving it. If I hadn't wanted a support group then, why on earth would I want one now? Wasn't it the problem for addicts that they'd *already* been leaning too hard, on both things and people?

So far I hadn't encountered the "I'm okay, you're okay—but you'd better lie down for a year or two anyway" school of therapy, so I assumed the idea now was to get back on one's own feet with as little fuss and public attention as possible. Being quite accustomed to falling down in the literal sense of the word, I knew that nothing gets you back up there faster than pride, of which I still had maybe an ounce, and embarrassment, in which I was suddenly richer than the Sultanate of Brunei, or whatever. How the hell had I let this happen? What crazy mixture of laziness and optimism had brought me so low, and how could I sneak back up unnoticed?

Meanwhile, all I asked of the outside world, I decided shakily, was all I had ever asked of it, which was alternately to be left alone by it and immoderately entertained, as I saw fit—that and to be given some more information (a theme that would continue to swell to a roar as I went along) concerning what exactly was wrong with me. The spiritual side of things, I could take care of myself.

"Grandiosity" would be the word I'd later hear applied to this attitude, but in truth I felt about as grandiose as a kitten. The above spiel sounds like brave talk, now that I can put it into words, but it was more like a dying gasp at the time. ("Go 'way," mumbles the cadaver to the pallbearers, aka support group, "go carry somebody else.")

All I wanted from Happy Valley was a little peace and quiet while I gently let the poison out of my system, and maybe also some tips on how to hurry it up. Beyond that, I was neither thinking straight nor snorting defiance as I checked into Happy Valley. My wildest hope was that somewhere on the premises might conceivably lurk a brilliant mechanic who could give me a jiggle and start things purring again just like that. That, on a less successful scale, was pretty much how it had worked with polio. I'd learned nothing from the doctors, but I'd met several good physiotherapists who seemed to have learned the machinery of polio from hanging around the shop, and I'd learned a bit more from other veterans; and the counselors at Happy Valley were alleged to be a bit of both—therapists and veterans. At any rate, the catalogue listed them all as graduates *cum laude* of the gutter, so I hoped that somewhere in the interstices of the party line one of them would actually let slip something useful.

But whether they did or not, I knew that the only way to find out was to go along with them as far as I could. As Rilke said of criticism, you must open yourself to the work of art completely before you begin to judge it. And I knew I would get nothing out of Happy Valley if I entered the room arguing. Blue Cross or somebody was paying good money for this, and they wouldn't get their pennyworth if I just recited my own opinions over and over, and stuck out my tongue.

So when a guy said on my first full day in the Valley, "Do you accept that alcoholism is a disease?" I know I had every intention of answering "Anything you say, sir." But I guess I didn't, or, if I did, I didn't say it right—because for the rest of the month, the authorities kept bearing down on me about this in the furtive style of the proselytizer ("Have you given any thought to," etc., etc.); and later, at my passing-out interview, the chap of the first day said, "I believe that he's finally come to accept alcoholism as a disease."

I had? If I'd known it was so important to them, I'd have rent my garments agreeing with them the first time it came up, just to get it out of the way. It really was all the same to me. Although alcoholism was like no other disease I'd ever heard of, I assumed they had some definition I didn't know about, which I'm sure would have been okay with me. In a lifetime of drinking, I'd met maybe half a dozen people who might well have been diseased: they didn't enjoy drinking and gulped the stuff like medicine, yet would kill their mothers or themselves to get it. If that wasn't a disease, it wasn't like anything else either. But did I really have *that*?

My own view, which I did my damnedest to keep to myself, was that the disease proposition had probably begun in most cases as a necessary cover to give drunks a little breathing room while they wrestled with a temptation more powerful than anything nondrinkers can imagine, sex being the only thing that comes close. But to be overmatched against a particular temptation is not necessarily to be diseased—is it?

Please let me argue, just this once. In retrospect, the only temptation that bothered me the whole time I was at Happy Valley was that one, the craving to thresh things out and maybe bang a few heads, and I'm afraid it showed, because I wound up being considered a cynic despite my most solemn efforts and despite the fog that rolled in every second day, blanketing my cerebellum in what felt like thick fur. Like any addict of anything, I knew that my addiction to arguing was bad for me, and in my heart I didn't even want to do it, but I could barely keep my reflexes on hold as one fat pitch after another came floating my way.

This was the first of the several misunderstandings that would bedevil my stay in the Valley, and since it must have landed on the very first page of my dossier, it might reasonably be called the mother of them all. People who don't enjoy arguing, or aren't used to it, always take it too personally, and whatever resistance I may have shown, if only in my expression, to disease dogma was immediately read as proof that I felt personally threatened by it. Once again, if I had known this, I could truthfully have said, "What's another disease to me, gentlemen? Call it whatever you like." But what I, or my expression, probably *did* say was something dry and irritating like "A disease isn't a matter of opinion, is it?"

Bad move. What I had taken to be an abstract discussion of a question that didn't concern me one way or other was actually the entire syllabus and the only question they cared about, and I had just unwittingly spun myself a web in which I would be stuck until the day I left. I had, it seemed, virtually talked my way into official denial of a disease that had given me thirty-five great years and at worst two lousy ones—a disease that, if I had to do it all over and human nature had remained what it is, I would probably have stood on line to catch again. (Second thoughts about this would be along shortly.)

To be fair to the institute, it had at least two other bits of evidence to suggest I was indeed in "denial"—not that I ever *denied* I was in denial, mind you. On arrival, I had told Dr. Y., the so-called "good" doctor, that as far as I was concerned at this particular moment, I was addicted to pills and nothing but pills. The idea that Ativan addiction *automatically* meant alcoholism was new to me. I was still digesting it slowly, so what I was saying was, please don't worry my head about it today. Give me, as they were saying that year, my space. "I'd like a drink right now, but I would kill for a pill" was my not particularly striking way of phrasing my difficulty—but I *did* lie about this, because I wouldn't have killed for either of them. What I was trying to do was sum up everything I'd learned so far, which was that pills worked, they brought relief, and booze didn't, and Dr. Y. seemed to understand this. "You've just been doing maintenance drinking anyway," he said.

That's it! (Nice phrase, too.) But even he didn't quite mean it, because a couple of days later he asked me why I had so much trouble admitting my drinking problem, as if we'd never discussed it before. "Because if I admit it, I'll have to quit—and who wants to do that?" I thought to myself but didn't say, because of course I did plan to quit, *whatever* they told me, it was the chief reason I was here, and I just wanted to get on with it without bogging down in all this airy-fairy talk.

But airy-fairy talk turned out to be of the essence, the only approach they knew to this thing, and there was no way I could reason or sweet-talk my way around it, even with the good Dr. Y. And the first rule of this approach was that the patient's estimate of his own condition is objectively worthless, except as possible evidence against him.

My statement vis-à-vis pills and booze was a perfect example of this: the Kafka character believes that his own summary of the case may actually help the judges to understand it a little better. Silly fellow. In fact, of course, there was only one thing I *could* have been doing in *any* of my statements, because it was all anyone did around here, which was to deny my drinking problem. And the whole object of their therapy, blocking out every other issue, was to get me to admit that I had this problem which was really a disease and which could only be kept at bay—never, God forbid, cured—by going to AA meetings for the rest of my God-fearing life.

"Doesn't anyone want to talk about pills around here?" I wanted to shout. "Don't they affect the equation even a little?" Not if Happy Valley had anything to say about it, it seemed. Dr. Y. was probably the least doctrinaire person within miles, but even he could throw me only a small bone to quiet my yapping about pills. "An Ativan is the equivalent of a martini," he said, which seemed like a promising line of inquiry. It seems that alcohol and the benzodiazepine drugs have a family resemblance and similar aims in life, so that a lot of collusion had been going on behind my back. But he didn't pursue the chemical implications any further, presumably for fear it might lead us away from the straight and narrow, the Tao, the twelve steps to paradise. Even though Dr. Y. was a real doctor in a nest of swamis, even he had to bend his knee to the great American superstition that all problems are basically spiritual.

So that was the best I could do. Although I would meet a lifetime supply of alcoholics in the next few weeks and not one of them would have the same symptoms as I or even seem to know what I was talking about, I was stamped and labeled as having the exact same thing *they* had, and I couldn't get a straight word out of anybody—except Dr. Y. on every second Tuesday—concerning the specific physical sensations I'd been receiving: where they came from or how long they might last. If this was really a disease I had, it was a mighty incorporeal one, with virtually no physical aspects at all. Or maybe the counselors just hadn't been told about them.

What made Dr. Y. an oasis despite himself was a faint suggestion, no more than a hint behind the ear, of irony. We might as well do it the AA way, he said, "because it's the only game in town." And I felt he was playing it in that spirit himself. He had his part to read and I had mine, but every now and then he would step outside his lines and say something in human-speak (I won't say what for fear of identifying him), the kind of thing one friend might actually say to another over a bar or kitchen table. And later, at our encounter group, he would seem to distance himself slightly from the set speeches of the counselor, only stepping in occasionally to break the clinches if one of us had the temerity to answer back.

"You may not agree with AA the first time you hear it," he said on that first day, "but just put it aside for now, and maybe it'll look better next time." This seemed to me to be giving his doctrine a hell of a big advantage; any crackpot notion could win if you gave it tenure like that and let it hang around till it looked good.

But I wasn't here to argue, *please* try to remember that, Sheed. If I'd always felt as good as I felt that first afternoon I wouldn't have been here in the first place. I'd driven myself up (or down depending on where we are) this very morning, and was still reasonably full of highway vinegar as I fenced with Dr. Y. Only later as I sat alone in my room, facing my first night of detention and absorbing what the Irish might call "a sense of my situation," did I return to my more familiar state of depressed anxiety.

Maybe it was the dinner menu that did it. My wife is a marvelous cook, and, unlike most heavy drinkers, I treasured every bite of her output. But suddenly I was back in boarding school, with all its associations, on the first night of the winter term.

And to hammer me even more firmly into the past, the single glass of wine which Dr. K.'s old regimen would have dictated for this evening was apparently to be replaced by a glass of mankind's number one enemy, water.

Evelyn Waugh himself could not have been more indignant. Surely the whole point of growing up was not to have to drink water with one's meals? It seems funny enough now, but I guess it can't have been at the time, because I remember protesting hotly and then doggedly that I was supposed to come down *slowly*, not all at once, and that someone had better fetch me a glass of wine right now.

"We don't have any alcohol on the premises," said the lady sternly, and I can picture the word *denial* forming in a comic strip bubble above my memory of her head and multiplying into a dozen bubbles in the next frame, as the word flew around the compound. "Patient Ninety-three is in denial."

But I believe that what was happening was far weirder and more primitive than denial. I almost wished they'd bring me a glistening Beefeater martini, my usual tipple of choice, so I could make my point by refusing it, the way I'd been refusing the things for weeks now; or a glass of Teacher's scotch and water, my backup selection, the image of which positively bored me today. (Cheap vodka, the staple of alcoholics, didn't even enter the equation: if that was all that was left on earth, I would have quit years ago.) It was just the one glass of wine that I wanted, for ritualistic reasons and because I thought I'd been promised it.

So little did I crave even wine for its own sake that at my hurried lunch on my way here this morning, I'd actually left half a glass of the stuff on the table because I was running late and I'd be having another tonight anyway. I guess the fear of going cold turkey also rattled me some that first evening, because I'd only seen it in movies, where it was as blood-curdling as the special-effects people could make it. On the other hand, I'd already descended so far from my once-giddy intake that surely I must be close to firm ground by now, in which case the phantom glass of wine would have been neither here nor there.

But I would continue to have trouble with wine long after I'd ceased expecting it at meals because the conviction had lodged deep in my soul that wine was civilization, wine was France and Italy and beautiful women; beer was not. Beer was bar stools in Jersey and windbreakers and getting drunk with the guys, and *those* I could give up, although not lightly—they had their charm too. But wine was not like regular drinking, and it would take me longer than this to accept that I would have to give it up along with the other stuff. Wine went with great dinners in three-star restaurants overlooking the sea, dammit, and not with getting cross-eyed at parties. Wine didn't even taste that good on its own, yet a great meal without it was simply unthinkable, and so at this moment was a lousy one in a strange place surrounded by snoops. I required its cheerful presence, if only to look at.

However, all I got for my ranting was a month of suspicion that might or might not have been avoided. Unfortunately, I was, and would remain, much too fuzzy to take notes, but they did give me an Ativan or something to keep from going dreaded cold turkey alone in my room, and I can't say for sure how much I slept that first night, but somewhere between waking and sleeping the gargoyles came back for a final roll call—not exactly gargoyles but normal faces that dissolved into hideous ones along with a sense of utter abandonment and desolation.

For the most part, the nights and days at Happy Valley run together in memory, so that by now there is just one endless night followed by one action-packed day. But that first night was different, because it marked the end of the old regime, and I was still recognizably my old self for the last time as I seemed to watch my past life march off slowly into the distance. I knew even before they'd started on their brainwashing that I'd never have another drink, and I also knew that it wasn't this or that drink that I was going to miss but the whole carefree way of life, the "What're ya having?" "amusing little St.-Emilion" way of life, which had never looked more resplendent and achingly desirable than it did as it marched over the horizon.

Depressed already both by pills and the absence of pills, I felt like all the wives and mothers in history standing on docks and train platforms waving and sobbing, except that their grief was presumably real and mine totally artificial: the fact is, my nerves were so scrambled and skewed that I could probably have screamed with sadness over anything you mentioned—frozen vegetables, the 1906 pennant races, anything at all. Alcohol was only the worst among equals.

Somewhere around dawn, I finally found relief in the realization that it was too late for a drink in real-life time; and with that thought came a general cooling of the engine. The old life I was looking at had actually marched off a couple of years ago, had it not? And its real name was not booze but youth, which is a very different thing. Breaking it down further into frames, what I missed was particular scenes that booze had helped me to celebrate, not the booze itself. And the idea that these scenes could not be enjoyed without chemical assistance was an insult to all concerned. If you can't get anything at all out of a sunset or an old friend without the help of a drug, never mind which one, you're not really enjoying either of them—and incidentally, you're not the jolly specimen drunks usually take themselves for but more like a corpse kept alive by injections.

Embroidering on this—and insomnia gives you lots of time for embroidery—I remember deciding that what we had here was common or garden idolatry. Even so fine a thing as a Beefeater martini should probably not be placed at the center of the universe (a great burgundy, I wasn't so sure about: you can't expect a miracle the first time you go down on your knees). Mankind's original sin was obviously not sex—God presumably put those parts there for a reason—but it might conceivably have been taking sex too seriously. Whether the subject matter is sex or alcohol or even, why not, apples, the minute you say "This is *it*—and to hell with the rest of it," out of the garden you go.

Taking full advantage of the morning coolness, I tried to imagine some of the old scenes without glasses or bottles and found them quite startlingly pleasant, for which discovery, much thanks, because the Valley people were about to pronounce a withering curse on my past life and would spend a month abjuring me to kick over every trace of it. But I knew in the back of my mind that what I wanted was to have my past life back, only more so; to live it again, only better. And this would be my talisman through the vale of amnesia.

The Happy Valley world picture had to be put on hold yet another day as we came smack up against the irreducibly physical the next morning. Outside of the curious exchange over the disease question mentioned earlier, my indoctrination was suspended while they peered for the first and last time at the body I had for some reason brought along with me. Dance around it though the authorities might, the big reason most people go on killing themselves in these various ways is that stopping is simply too painful. So the staff has to pause in its preaching every now and then to check on one's vital signs (no sense preaching if the patient has passed away) and one's trivial signs as well, giving me in the process the checkup of a lifetime, which I passed for the most part with insolent ease.

It was exhilarating in a feverish kind of way, at least compared with the nights surrounding it. If I listened closely, I could practically hear my blood pressure bubbling like a teakettle, and at any moment I expected my head to start whistling as well. My blood pressure had actually begun to rise ominously sometime before I got to the Valley, and now for several days it soared into the wild danger zones, before coming gently to rest at perfect. But that, along with a slight trembling in the fingers that left almost immediately, was about the sum of my dreaded withdrawal. Compared with what they put the wretched Ray Milland through in *The Lost Weekend*, my farewell to alcohol was a stroll in the park on a warm day, and I realized with chagrin that I could have taken it months ago and saved myself a lot of grief.

Or so I thought for the rest of that dozy day. Everyone knows it's better to tear the adhesive tape off with one pull than to drag it off hair by hair, and if giving up pills the next night was going to be anything like as easy as going off booze, my troubles would be over just like that.

And so they were—exactly twelve incredible months from that day. Not that the next night was so bad in itself: in fact, it would look pretty good in retrospect, one of the better ones here. It was just totally sleepless, like the night in San Francisco. And as they never tired of telling me here, "Nobody ever died of lack of sleep." I did my best to believe this astounding proposition—although how could they be so sure?—and simultaneously resigned myself to the prospect of fainting ostentatiously in public sometime next week and teaching them a good lesson.

On Day Three I was feverish again and almost too tired to move, so they gave me their standard test to see how much phenobarbital it would take to give me a *little* sleep the next night and calm my system enough to start straightening me out in earnest. I told them I felt much too sick to be indoctrinated today, so they grumpily pared my program down to a single AA session in the evening, which incidentally convinced me for the moment that I'd rather die in the arms of a pink elephant than ever attend another one.

The standard test which Dr. Y. had given me earlier that same day had consisted quite simply of handing me a real knockout pill and watching to see what happened, and I hadn't kept him waiting long. In fact, I'd just started telling him how amazingly fast pills work on me, if they're going to work at all, when it hit and I felt like Humphrey Bogart chatting with the Fat Man as the room spun and the face in front of me began to swim, and the next thing I knew, I was lying on my bed listening to some cleaning ladies talking bawdy in the next room, a soothing Shakespearean sound that brought great, if brief, peace—but could this be possible? I looked at my watch, and it said that less than an hour had passed since my appointment with Dr. Y. had begun.

And this pill had been their H-bomb, their best shot. So a normal dose of a normal sedative obviously didn't have a chance. But Dr. Y. was blinded by the speed of my test and gave me a normal dose anyway, and it made no more impression than buckshot in the hide of a charging rhinoceros. So I passed another utterly sleepless night, marked only by the cat-and-mouse game I played for the first time of many times with the nurse who peeped in on me every hour on the hour. Since I tend to look equally corpselike awake or asleep, I had to make it my business to look lively every time the door moved or be recorded as having slept for an hour, which for some reason seemed quite intolerable.

These spectral interludes continued off and on the whole time I was at the Valley, forming a tableau of their own, alternately giggly and desperate depending on the chemical balance, which seemed to be completely out of my hands. The nurses played several old-fashioned, womanly roles wonderfully well during these interludes, from earth mother to entertainer to pal, before disappearing like vampires before daylight. What these visitations had in common was that they were all quite real and they all seemed like dreams.

On Day Four, they put me through all my paces dead or alive, starting with group therapy and winding through various sessions of this and that, which seemed designed primarily to keep you moving from one end of the grounds to the other in order to keep you from thinking too much. It reminded me of my old English school, which raced us around and around to take our minds off sex.

The most useful lesson I learned from any of these strange make-work drills was my discovery that I could follow every word I heard just as well on no sleep as on eight hours, and even answer back occasionally in my head, though this I continued trying to cut off before it got into gear—write a hundred times on the blackboard "I didn't come here to find out how clever I was." To be sure, the fog kept moving in and out as before, taking with it a good half of what I'd heard and jumbling the rest forever; and this did seem to have some faint connection with how well I'd slept the night before. But the central office that takes in words and fills in the answer forms seemed to need no sleep at all and probably never had. At maybe my third encounter session on Day Five, I would be chided in the gentle, cushioned way in which harsh words are delivered at such meetings, for my apparent obsession with sleep, and my first thought was "But of course—that's what I'm here for." And my second thought was "There's more to life than just booze, booze, booze, you know"—there's also snooze, snooze, snooze, ha ha.

But for once they were onto something. The truth was that I'd always felt quite absurdly helpless without sleep, and I had been much too quick to advance it as an excuse. In fact, a memory comes back to me, wearing a bright red face, of my once trying to have an examination postponed on that ground—a horrible example of the things some invalids think they can get away with. The memory also obliged me to admit that I'd done just fine at the exam, just as I would get by at Happy Valley on no sleep at all so long as I stopped telling myself "You're sleepy, you're sleepy."

Since these insights did not visibly relate to booze, the class blessedly moved on to the next victim, leaving me alone with my prize, my insight. "So what?" said the voice in my head abruptly. This part of me seemed to need less sleep than anybody but was already up and about, pointing out any black clouds I might have missed and snuffing out small rays of hope with a swipe of his claymore (I believe he came from the Scottish side of the family). Some days he seemed so refreshed by his insomnia that he told me not only why there was no hope for *me* but why there was none for anyone else in the room either.

Since the rest of my brain wasn't functioning at all, I guess I should have been relieved to find old Uncle Fergus, my inner pessimist, keeping the store open. But it's hard to warm up to Fergus. My alter ego is, or was, in fact a hopeless depressive whom I'd known off and on since childhood; and for the last few crazy years I realized that I'd actually been feeding this creature, this dark side of my brain, its favorite kind of food, downers and more downers, which might as well have been strychnine. So a thought from him was worse than no thought at all. The best brain in the world cannot think its way out of depression, because all its ideas are poisoned at the source.

Counting my blessings was at least getting to be quick work around here, which was a blessing. Since I couldn't think of anything to say out loud for those first few days that connected with anything anyone else was saying, I lived pretty much inside my own head, where I learned, for instance, the answer to a mystery which had baffled me for thirty-five jolly years: at last I knew why drunks tend to cry at some point in the evening. They are simply paying their sin taxes as they go, and the price of living on depressants, with sobs now and pains in the head tomorrow.

Since I, contrariwise, had never cried a drop while drinking, except for tears of joy and glee, and had seldom had hangovers, my back taxes must reach to the moon by now. But Happy Valley seemed as much in the dark as anyone as to exactly how much I owed or when, if ever, I'd be through paying. In vain did I ransack the minuscule library, which seemed, like a ship's library, to be stocked with books that people were trying to get rid of, and the heads of the various authorities. Nobody could tell me the news I needed to hear: that depression ends, maybe sooner than you think, and that if you can just hang in there, avoiding downer-uppers and upper-downers, whether you're addicted to them or not, life will eventually make it up to you.

Although American bookstores perennially burst with optimism, people who have had polio are immunized against most of it, and I couldn't find anything on the shelves that was remotely encouraging and at the same time believable about my condition, which, like polio, is a hard fact entirely beyond the reach of self-help and autosuggestion, the twin crutches upon which our optimism totters.

So I decided, most reluctantly, that maybe someday I'd better write something myself.

6.

NOTES ON A BRAINWASHING

Since patients were forever coming and going at Happy Valley, there was no such thing as a course of instruction. You might hear the thing you needed to know on the first day or the twelfth or possibly on your way out the door. The stuff just went round and round, like that neon band of news that used to circle the *New York Times* building from morning to night. They called it a "program" and advised you to get with it, but getting with it turned out to be like entering a London fog at Chelsea and leaving it at Westminster, or vice versa, who can tell? So any attempt I make now to describe me going through it has to be purest impressionism, a study in fog on fog.

Indeed, as I write this, a memory comes back of once trying to get home in a real pea-souper in old Fog City itself. Incredibly, the buses are still moving, so slowly that a square hit from one would barely nudge you, but their lights do tell you that there must be a street over there, which means that this is a sidewalk; and when the wall you're gripping runs out, you're close to a corner, but which one? Is this a Kensington wall, or a Chelsea?

Same thing now. It feels today like a Sunday-type of afternoon, so categorized by its sheer emptiness and sense of foreboding: anyone who's ever attended a weekly boarding school will recognize a Sunday afternoon a mile away. Actually, I have no idea what day it is, except that I am about to meet my counselor the next morning for the first time, and I decide to move things along by jotting down a few notes about myself to kick us off with. But in the desolation and nervous dysfunction of the moment, these turn into the most scathing psychological portrait anyone has ever drawn of anybody—a study of warts on warts this time, in my new, severe manner.

To my everlasting relief, the counselor shows not the slightest interest in my indictment—he is not a shrink, and doesn't want to pose as one—and I plunge with him back into substance abuse and denial with a high heart, as if I've made a good and terrible confession to a priest who doesn't speak English. When I return to my room, I tear the notes into small pieces, consigning them and my memory of them to oblivion. I shan't write anything else the whole time I'm here—not *just* because I'm too confused to but because, like a fat child asked to do push-ups, I don't feel like it, for the first time in years. There is no joy in scribbling any more, and no point. Depression is marked off from the other diseases of mankind by a somber baseline of indifference. This is like the one operation you *don't* want to talk about or show anybody, the Purple Heart you throw in the garbage. I knew that I had a great subject here, a hundred great subjects, and that I would never see any of them again. To hell with it. For once in my life, I didn't even feel like showing off.

With exceptions. After his normal dose of phenobarbital had failed to impress me on my fourth night, Dr. Y. gave up and slipped me a real mickey in the form of a King Kong fix of phenobarbital, with a view to weaning me back to regular sleep with gradually diminishing doses. I slept like an angel and woke up singing. My God, this was a beautiful place. The morning air hit me like a Christmas morning hitting Mr. Scrooge, and I quite startled our den mother or matron or whatever by singing along with her at breakfast, and unobtrusively straightening out her lyrics (I trust it was unobtrusive). By lunchtime I instinctively wanted to have a celebration lunch to welcome such a day into the calendar, and I pictured the headwaiter at our favorite Chinese restaurant slippering up to say, "Ah, Mr. She, your favite martini?"

Here, I realized, was my nemesis; not depression or inadequacy or all the stuff they would hurl at my head for the next few weeks, but the same gargantuan, half-insane urge to celebrate life as much and as often as possible that had gotten me here in the first place. And as if to drive this simple truth home, I dreamed that night that I was buying drinks for everyone in the bar, including a double for myself, to celebrate the fact that I'd given up drinking. And someone nudged my elbow and said, "That's not quite the way we do it."

No, indeed. By the next day I was back in the swamp, getting my ears pinned back about the insidiousness of booze, which was such that if we accidentally swallowed a trace of alcohol in some cough medicine, the speaker assured us, we'd be doomed forever. So I wouldn't even be allowed to celebrate with cough medicine.

The moments of exhilaration and clowning around were so rare that I remember every one of them like heavenly visitations sent to keep us from going *quite* crazy, and to inform us that life can be beautiful and hang in there. But they were invariably followed by days that said quite the opposite in thunder, and I would sink so far in the other direction that around the end of Week One, Dr. Y. decided to put me on Prozac, the wonder drug of the season; and a week after that, a Wednesday, I had *another* good day. And I fell on this one too with glad cries, like an Englishman spotting an egg in 1943.

Otherwise, the bad days were the story, and I'll only say as temperately as possible that anyone suffering from anxiety-depression should stay as far as a large continent permits from programs designed for substance abusers; talking may be a perfectly good cure for some things, but to my sick ears it sounded like voices just outside your window while you're trying to sleep off a fever. What they were saying was so dull and *unmusical*.

Perhaps the best example of the riot of cross-purposes I'd stumbled into came toward the end, when my counselor trotted out, as if for the first time, a colorful phrase he had actually used at every one of our meetings, and I winced as I saw it coming.

"Yes—the truth hurts, doesn't it?" he purred. "It's not the truth," I muttered, "it's the repetition," which on bad days could reverberate in my head like a trash compactor in an echo chamber. "Well, you'd better get used to repetition in AA," he said. "Because that's what it's all about."

The counselor, Lord knows, was doing his best. But he was like a doctor who has taken a degree in only one disease and therefore treats all his patients for, let's say, measles, because what else is there? Since I was in my last week by then, I was thoroughly familiar with the "single disease" theory and just anxious to get home and sit in gorgeous silence for a while.

I can't let myself off so lightly now, however, but must return to that first week, where it is now definitely Sunday, a real one this time, and I've been impressed into something called a rap session, so named presumably because the instructor had taken turns rapping us on the knuckles and slapping us up alongside the head. To wit.

"You—yes, *you!*" It was obviously too late to hide in back of the sofa. "When did you have your first drink?"

I honestly had no idea, but I could tell that that was no kind of answer for the sergeant here.

"I guess I remember sitting in the college bar and thinking I'll never get to talk to these guys if I don't have a drink with them," and in the anxiety of the moment I guess I really believed this story, although as I remember it now, my first drink had probably been a bottle of Schaeffer beer my mother had allowed me to try three years earlier at a farewell party before we returned to England in 1946; and if that was forgettable, how about the pint of something called, I think, "Old O'Dougherty's" that a friend of mine and I had smuggled into a school dance and gotten sick as dogs on?

The thing was, I had to say something, and the college bar version at least gave us some good stuff to talk about: feelings of inadequacy and other soul-searching staples that seemed to fit the spirit of the program. Maybe it would give Rover here something to chew on and would take his mind off my trouser leg. But the rapper was a regular dyed-in-the-wool measles specialist, or subspecialist, because he quickly broke in to "Cut the crap," as he would say in his straight-shooting way, and to pipe, "But it really doesn't matter, does it?" "What, who?" I shot back, and he said, "What *matters* is that you had that first drink. Right?"

I cannot vouch for the other particulars of this dialogue, or browbeating, but I believe the man then said, "Suppose you found yourself on an island where the custom was for everybody to drink all day and night—would you go along with that?" To which I honestly answered, "No—I've been with people like that, and I couldn't keep up with them."

I wasn't trying to be a smart-ass, I was just trying to survive and get this guy off my back. But he wouldn't quit until I'd taken all my measles medicine, and although he talked and even looked like a storm trooper, I'm sure he thought he was helping us the best he knew how with this good, brisk, straight-from-the-shoulder talk. As I say, it's a hell of a way to treat depression, but it did deepen my acquaintance with a single-disease dogma the army way, by stuffing it up my nose, where it can still be found.

Dealing as I was from about a one-card deck, I was in no shape to decide whether it was even remotely possible that all the raggle-tag citizens I began to bump into around here had exactly the same thing wrong with them. But even in that shape, I could see the irresistible convenience of the proposition. With a small nation of addicts yammering at the moon and hammering on the doors, each one of them convinced he is a special case, who has time for details? These embattled institutions couldn't possibly hope to hand out customized treatment to all these bums. America's drunks alone would overwhelm every doctor and therapist in the land just by breathing on them. And in recent years, the drunks had been joined by an equally unruly horde of heroin, cocaine, and everything-in-the-medicine-chest addicts, all in need of a therapy fix right *now*, while they're still in the mood. ("And don't blame me if I go out and kill someone tomorrow, if you turn me down for treatment, man.")

What to do, what to do? The only possible way to treat such a continental mass of supplicants was the *same* way. But where it had at least seemed plausible to tell alcoholics that they all had the same disease, could it really be possible, let alone provable, that the beautiful dreamers of heroin and the ecstatic insomniacs of cocaine *also* all had the same disease?

Enter, in the nick of time, the new miracle drug, "the addictive personality," which makes the whole world of highs and lows kin. Never mind the physical aspects of addiction, which can drag down anyone (to wit, hospital patients hooked on morphine) regardless of personality; and particularly never mind the legion of cigarette addicts who couldn't *possibly* all have the same personality, unless you expand the word to meaningless infinity.

These exceptions would have cut no ice at all with the rap sergeant, whose attitude was simply "Look, we're dispensing this stuff here and it seems to be working"—and in one sense, it certainly was: in my four weeks in the Valley, and later, during the year I spent intermittently checking out AA meetings, I ran into case after case where the speakers seemed to be talking themselves by main force into the symptoms of "addictive personality" and conforming to type a little bit more each day— until their suggestibility and pliability and inner softness seemed like the real symptoms, while the ones they'd started out with were just decoys. These people would agree to anything, it seemed, in order to come in from the cold and warm themselves at the fire; and since those who didn't were deemed incurable and constitutionally incapable of facing the truth—yes, the stuff they were dispensing worked. How could it not?

But in another sense, I wasn't quite so sure it was working, because I'd already met at least three people who'd been here *before*. What did this mean? Did you have to keep *doing* this stuff? Think about it later. As I reeled from the rap session that first Sunday, I simply felt vaguely, and I can't tell you how vaguely, like a recruit who's been stuffed into the same-size uniform as all the other recruits, because it's the only size they have. "One disease fits all." Well, why not? I hadn't come here to argue, and maybe the uniform fit better than I thought.

The other thing I'd learned from the rapmeister was that the world of sobriety was even more disagreeable and unlike the civilized world than I'd feared. Around here it was perfectly in order for the grown-ups to treat us like backward infants and jump all over our answers and, if we did manage to say something smart, insist on the last word anyway.

"In my judgment," begins the patient, or straight man, and before he can get any further, the authority figure pounces on him like Robin Hood jumping out of a tree onto the fat sheriff's back. "*Your* judgment—you mean the judgment that got you up to a kilo a day [or whatever]? The same wonderful judgment that left you staring at your face in toilet water every night? I thought you'd handed your judgment over to Mr. Smirnov [or Herr Heroin or King Cocaine] on permanent loan. So is *that* the judgment you're appealing to now?"

If I had answered back, I would have said, "That's right—and it's the same judgment that brought me here, Jack. Silly me, huh?" This was a particularly tough argument to keep out of: obviously we hadn't used our judgment before, and it was high time we started doing so. But what purpose was served by ridiculing this battered old faculty? Surely we had to patch it up and send it back into battle anyhow—so what was the point of tearing it down like this?

Which shows how much I knew about brainwashing. Soon after that, maybe the next day, I got another big fat clue. Every morning began with a group therapy session, which differed from a rap session only in that we were allowed to talk a little longer before the gavel came banging down on our heads. Anyway, the subject this day was something called "low self-esteem," a phrase which, incredibly enough, hadn't yet reached my ivory tower in this spring of 1988.

Did it have anything to do with the virtue of humility that little papists like me had been taught to cultivate? Only kidding. I wasn't that blessedly detached from the culture around me, the air we all breathe. In our breathtakingly ignorant society, no lesson has been more thoroughly and universally learned than the absolute necessity of loving oneself, before one can hope to love anyone else; the message hit the motion picture screen as early as the mid-forties and has been hitting it and the Box methodically ever since. The only thing that took me off stride was this namby-pamby way of putting it. My own self-satisfaction had always been such a robust, full-bodied affair that it was hard to imagine squeezing it into such a prissy formula.

"Self-esteem" was, moreover, a phrase that put me fatally in mind of a Jane Austen clergyman patting his stomach. "Mr. Collins was a man of considerable self-esteem, to the vast amusement of his friends and the mild astonishment of such parishioners as gave thought to the matter"—and normally, this would have had me off and running into, maybe, a Dickens variation. "No one in the city had ever questioned Mr. Pickwick's self-esteem, although his title to it was sometimes a matter of the most intense debate," and so on.

But that is the difference between sick and well: nothing strikes you as funny, and nothing the outside world can do to you seems worse than the way you feel already. I had by now swallowed a gallon of infelicitous verbiage around here, and my palate was quite numb. If self-esteem was the way they wanted to put it, fine with me. It didn't amuse me, but it didn't bother me either. It was gray on gray.

This being said, it did seem that accusing us of low self-esteem at this point was pretty much like shooting fish in a barrel. Anybody who felt good about himself at this particular time and place must be self-deluded indeed, not to say nuts. Outside of the sheer embarrassment of being here in the first place, we were almost by definition physical and nervous wrecks, incapable of feeling good about anything. As I mulled the question in my mind, preparatory to placing my head in the stocks for the group's inspection, I realized that my own self-esteem was usually as good as my last review, subtracted from or added to the vast reserve one needs to get into the writing game in the first place, and adjusted to the last decimal by how I felt about that morning's work.

In other words, as with many artists from the best to the bogus, my work was myself by this time, and it stood in for all the blows and all the praise, the raspberries and the roses that normal people receive in person. The typical artist, in my experience, barely even takes in compliments that don't relate to his work, unless they come from beautiful women, and he certainly isn't interested in compliments or insults to his *character*. Tell him he's drawn a great line or written a perfect bar of music and you can follow it with every term of abuse known to man: he won't even hear you. "Perfect. The fellow said my sonata was '*perfect*.' "

But suddenly I was stripped of my alter ego, my stand-in. I hadn't worked that morning, and I hadn't wanted to. And just like that, I wasn't a writer anymore—but I wasn't anything else either. So okay, I have low self-esteem—tell me what to do about it, and let's get started on it.

Round and round the circle we went, each of us lower in self-esteem than the one before, like tourists competing in the limbo, the dance that ends in a crawl. But the antidote never arrived, or, if it did, I missed it. Instead the message seemed to be that feeling bad about ourselves was a step in the right direction and that if we ever started to feel better, it probably meant we were succumbing to "grandiosity," a catchall word worthy of the Jesuits. There was no escaping from grandiosity even if you decided to make a break for daylight: it waited at every exit as Pride waits for the young Catholic.

In my determination to play ball, I decided that perhaps what they meant by low self-esteem was what I'd always thought of as a lack of confidence. In which case, we were in business (and besides it was my turn and I had to say *some*thing). Once my own spiel was dutifully delivered to the group, I fell to daydreaming about the subject. My peculiar upbringing, which had shuttled me back and forth over oceans and class barriers, had left me as alert as a jungle fighter to all kinds of signals real and imaginary. As soon as a new guy entered the pub, I'd ask myself, How do you talk to *this* one? English or American? Sports or weather, or Whither the Novel? The mysterious moods of drunks are of no help in this respect. Nine o'clock's nice guy is ten o'clock's psychotic killer. So you could never put your gun away. Then, again, England, with its quagmire of unwritten rules, presented one kind of problem (I can still hear the mumble-titters along the table because some damn-fool Yank has lit a cigarette before the

Queen has been toasted. Too priceless) and America, with its impenetrable politeness, presented another. You could make every kind of chump of yourself in America and never know it. Indeed, I'd been watching Englishmen do this very thing all my life, and had borne the embarrassment *they* should have felt, on my own back, like a martyr in a farce.

So maybe that's why I drank (as if one needed a reason)? In my heart I knew this was all nonsense as soon as I thought it. If my myth about wanting to talk to the guys at the bar was based on anything at all, I had the story the wrong way round: I would have *stopped* drinking to talk to them. Booze blunts your social instincts and makes you horribly vulnerable, a transcultural chump all ready for roasting, and I had always avoided drinking among strangers if I could help it, or even among friends who wouldn't match me drink for drink, like two nations agreeing to disarm at the same pace. All in all, embarrassment had been a great force for sobriety in my life, if not the *only* one, and had kept me from making God knows how many silly phone calls to famous politicians and friends I hadn't seen for years, besides saving me, at least since college days, from the irremediable sin of talking back to policemen.

Stop daydreaming, you in the back! The worst thing you could do in group therapy was not to speak at all, and I'd already seen one laconic character, a rustic old New Englander, pummeled mercilessly for not opening up and letting us share him. So whenever the talk turned to self-esteem, as incidentally it tended to do (Steinem is right) if women spoke first and proposed the agenda, I offered them this again, a displaced Englishman's infinite fear of embarrassment, because it was the best I could do. Who knows—maybe it was true, it sounded bad enough to be true.

Meanwhile, the real bad news kept on coming hot and heavy. The Valley had only four weeks to cut us down to size, which in my case would reduce me from about three inches tall to barely visible. A diet of humility designed for knocking the stuffing out of a monster of arrogance can make short work of a borderline depressive, and most of the time I neither agreed nor disagreed but just lay there and let the bulldozer do its deadly work. If I didn't have low self-esteem when I got here, I'd sure as heck have it by the time I left.

A month of this pounding seemed, as you might suppose, to stretch to infinity like the winter term at a boarding school. But for a complete brainwash it was probably barely enough. So in the manner of a cop leaving the lights shining in your eyes even while he's not actually torturing you, my counselor presented me with a lugubrious pile of books (plus a bill for them, which rankled) to absorb between sessions. Fortunately, he didn't follow me into my room, so I didn't have to make things worse by reading them—just having them around and dipping occasionally was dreary enough. For instance: "When I came into AA, was I a desperate person? Did I have a soul-sickness? Was I so sick of myself and my way of living that I couldn't stand looking at myself in mirrors?" No, I decided, playing along as best I could. I was sick of feeling lousy, period. And when I looked in the mirror, I saw nothing worse than a damn fool having a very bad day. But the book was insistent. "What makes AA work? The first thing is to have a revulsion against myself and my way of living." And so on.

The above thoughts were recommended respectively for January 1 and 2 (I didn't get to January 3), presumably every year come rain or come shine, even as a priest must remind himself even on holidays that "dust thou art and unto dust thou shalt return." In fact, the little black book they were drawn from could almost pass for a priest's breviary in its stark black sobriety. But it is *not* a religious book, they were suspiciously quick to tell you, because AA is *not a religion.*

The speed with which religion was invariably disowned, in almost audible italics, led me to suppose that someone must be into deep denial about this—a denial that reached a crescendo in a series of talks we had to go to after group therapy, roguishly entitled "God and All That." It seemed that there was no hope for any of us if we didn't submit our sick souls forthwith to a Higher Power. Bill Wilson, the founder of AA, had strongly recommended this procedure, and a recommendation of Bill's instantly became a commandment etched in stone to his followers, almost the way a founder's words are sacralized in a real religion.*

This imperative did much to explain the extreme variation on Christian humility that had been mainlined into my veins ever since I got here. Even the rationale for it was the same. In order to submit fully to God, one must shed every vestige of one's old, false self to find one's true self in Him. It is a leap of faith, even if you already believe, thrilling and scary as a tunnel of love to the zillionth power, but the light at the end was said to be worth it, *if* you make it. If you don't, of course, you're stuck, with nothing to fall back on. With all belief in yourself gone, you now *have* to believe in a Higher Power, or be damned.

So what kind of Higher Power were they offering here, what sort of light to justify the leap in the dark? At this point we seemed to hit some kind of snag. The desperate jauntiness of that title "God and All That" had already given me a clue, and as soon as the sermon began I had the whole picture. The speaker was like some kind of minimalist Christian minister who, having insisted on a particular doctrine, hastily proceeds to empty it of all content until Voltaire himself could agree to it, but not a single soul anywhere could die for it.

This was a serious gap. Even my own Catholic Church, which offers a God entire and undiluted and well worth dying for if one can only believe in Him enough, doesn't expect many people actually to do so. The flesh is weak, and little Catholics are not generally expected to give up their old selves completely or take leaps in the dark, but only to do the best they can. Yet Happy Valley was demanding a level of self-abnegation of *all* of us, including some fresh-faced teenagers recently blindsided by cocaine, worthy of Trappist monks and Hindu holy men, in the name and service of—what?

Where the Unitarian minister gives you a stripped-down God, the counselor today went him one layer further. The Higher Power didn't have to be God at all, but whatever you'd

---

* It wouldn't be fair to my lugubrious pile of books not to mention that I found Wilson's own story fascinating and clearly the record of a significant man, well worth saving from at least some of his followers.

like it to be, the Higher Power of your preference. Although the speaker's preference was obviously AA itself as the ultimate in Higher Powers, he didn't even insist on that. The straight talk and hardheadedness they so prided themselves on evidently ceased abruptly just as we approached the heart of the matter. Everything about AA, as taught here, positively *ached* to be a religion, but religion is a well-known turnoff, so they leave the altar empty.

A lively discussion ensued as we rummaged among various alternate gods, trying to find one you could possibly lean on, and I pitched in with my own William Jamesian, or was it Bergsonian, interpretation of the phrase. One's Higher Power was the force that makes flowers grow through cement, or lions survive in high mountains, or humans (to use James's own example) lift several times their own weight to rescue loved ones from wreckage. It was the *élan vital*, the life force, and I knew it well from polio days.

The discussion was so all-inconclusive that I wondered why they kept circling back to the question and didn't just move on to something else. As it was, our various Higher Powers seemed to cancel out and weaken each other. My reading of it didn't seem to interest anyone else much, but theirs didn't interest me either. In fact, I never sensed much connection between any of the various inner lights on display at such sessions.

For myself, I was soon off and daydreaming again, and remembering the last time I had made a sustained pitch to my official Higher Power, which was when I asked God, by name, to help me out with polio. For as much as three years I had prayed nonstop for a cure, until at age seventeen I had come to my senses in the icy waters of Lourdes, and had realized I was not going to get one—and that I didn't need one. I was used to polio, which meant as far as I was concerned that I *was* cured, and my prayers had been answered. But a habit dies hard, and for some years after that I had continued to utter reflexive mental prayers for every emergency—"Dear God, help me with this and that"—until one day I saw how childish it was, and what an invitation to stay childish, and I gave it up just like that, although not necessarily the faith that inspired it. The problem of why God allows suffering that so vexed Ivan Karamazov seemed from my experience to prey on people who have to watch pain more than people who directly suffer it, and to this day I haven't met a single polio veteran who had any trouble with the problem of God and pain. But generalizations about this subject are by their nature a hopeless mixture of the subjective and the imaginary, and I can only report that such pain as I've encountered myself has made religion seem more reasonable, not less.

But not this time. If I was ever going to return to my rather whiny intercessions, it certainly wasn't going to be now. I had gotten myself into this mess, and it was up to me to dig myself out as best I could. I would have felt, once again, *embarrassed* to drag God into this. And besides, I had just an inkling, not yet a full-blown insight, that harping on spirituality was not the route for me, that this was as much a sensual experience as a spiritual one. I'd heard somewhere that abstinence from booze and tobacco enhances your taste buds, your sense of smell, and even your eyesight (the jury is out on hearing, though I now believe music sounds better too). And that's what I concentrated on now. Once upon a time, I had discovered the incredible pleasures of eyesight when I put on glasses for the first time and found myself staring transfixed into the window of a hardware store: I had no idea that power drills could be so lovely. So I enjoyed imagining that sobering up could be like buying the equivalent of glasses for each of my senses. And every now and then, I would get these emanations, even down at the bottom of my well, of strength returning on a scale I hadn't experienced in years. Although the light might be snuffed out ruthlessly a minute later, I could remember where it was and what it looked like. When I got out of here, I reasoned, there would be a huge self-indulgence gap to fill every day—drunks devote an incredible number of man-hours to their own pleasure—and at least some of the pleasure came from anticipation, which was something I could start on right away during those flickering moments.

My standard pipe dream, probably common to prisoners everywhere, usually took the form of picturing my old life pretty

much as before, but tackled from a fresh angle—instead of slur-
ring my way past the hostess and the cops on the way home, I
would dazzle them with epigrams. And I would sniff the night
air as never before, and thrill to the scrambled eggs I planned to
make when I got home.

But if there was one thing Happy Valley frowned on more
than anything, it was your old life, which to them was a tracery
of pitfalls and potholes. Obviously, we must start all over—the
great American temptation; we must be born again and yet
again, as often as it takes. But here we hit another snag, because
along with the problematic God they were offering us at journey's end, came a threadbare, unfurnished heaven to move into
with Him, Her, It, Them. One session was devoted to the
subject of weekends and how to get through them (there was no
question of looking forward to them); and the sheer thought of
finding something useful to do in the house or out in the yard on
a lank Sunday afternoon made me almost ungovernably
thirsty—for the first time, I realized, since I'd been here. If
anything could make me reach for a drink over the warnings of
my precancerous tongue, it would be a weekend spent on the
Happy Valley plan.

And then there were the daily trips to the Happy Valley
workshop, where we were encouraged to lose ourselves in mod-
eling clay or woodwork. For fear of looking unoccupied, I
reached for some crayons and dashed off a couple of the kind of
cartoons I used to draw when I was stuck in bed at the age of
fourteen, and the supervisor greeted them with the gushing enthusiasm of a parent at a show-and-tell. Such promise! I really
should think of taking this up seriously.

Trouble was, the cartoons took eight minutes tops, so I'd
have to do an awful lot of them to fill the day, and they weren't
going to get any better. My art had frozen in place at fifteen, and
wasn't about to start moving now: Grandpa Moses I wasn't. As
for woodwork—again I felt the tickle in my throat. These people knew more ways to make you thirsty than Budweiser and
Miller put together. But I knew that these things, woodwork
and yard work and make-work, wouldn't really drive me to
drink, they'd drive me to despair, and someone would find me

hanging by a promising homemade noose from a freshly whit-
tled rafter on a Sunday afternoon in August that I was just trying
to get through in order to get to that day of days, Monday!

But Happy Valley's own heart didn't seem to be in salvation
by woodwork either, because most of the time the workshop
was occupied or closed, and the inmates just stayed in the television room, where they sat in long rows staring at the cartoons.
I'd never seen grown-ups looking at TV cartoons before, and I
wondered what went on in their heads. Were they thinking or
what? And if addiction was a disease of the total personality,
and if we had just four weeks to do something about it, was this
really the best way to spend the time? Shouldn't we be talking to
each other or reading something?

Before I left, I would make several good friends who did like
to talk, and independently we built our own world in the midst
of the larger one, but the institute itself didn't seem to know
what to do with us between browbeatings, except play records
over and over again of a hearty, good-sense clergyman, telling it
like it is: it was vain to protest that perhaps three hearings was
enough for one of Father Goodbody's jokes, or that the shiny
pink face I (perhaps unfairly) pictured the jokes issuing from
was exactly what I most feared about sobriety. The records were
smilingly compulsory ("Laughter is the best medicine, and we're
going to give you your dose right now!"), and I just sat there
considering—was I, too, destined to turn pink and shiny?
Would I too make hearty jokes? Never mind. If I didn't thrill to
Father Goodbody, I was in deep denial.

That was on weekend nights, when the local AA chapters
were not in session. The policy during the week was, as noted,
to keep us occupied almost every minute, so we wouldn't go
getting ideas. But come Saturday, the place seemed to change its
mind and leave us completely to our wretched devices, height-
ening the normal gloom of a Sunday to a screaming crescendo of
angst, and thus preparing us for life on the outside, I suppose.

By Saturday night one wanted company so badly that I actually found myself looking forward to our weekly pummeling
from the rap sergeant the next day and to the group therapy
session that started the real week, frustrating though this invari-

ably was. Group therapy, one would imagine, would be the one chance for us to connect with each other; the word we used over and over again was "sharing," which suggests a certain vestigial give-and-take. But no sooner had one speaker tried to address what the last one had said than the counselor would jump in like a boxing referee on steroids, breaking up clinches before they could even form.

"You're supposed to address the group," he would bark, "not just Fred." I suppose he figured that any advice we gave each other was bound to be bad and he would only have to undo it later—so why not jump in with the good stuff right away? "The way you *should* feel . . ." he would actually say, which is how you know you're in the middle of a brainwashing. The next step would obviously be a correct set of dreams for each night of the week and a uniform personal history.

I guess it all came under the heading "ironing out our differences," because it turned out that not only did we all have the same disease but we all needed exactly the same medicine for it despite the crazy-quilt nature of our group. Alongside the taciturn old-timer, who was a Valium head, sat, for instance, a jolly matriarch from Providence who had, like many of us, stayed at the party a wee bit too long and had no trouble talking whatever. Well, twenty lashes and five Hail Marys for the two of them, says the judge, peering dimly over his spectacles.

Across the way sat the teenagers, including one who, to the untrained eye, needed a good spanking before you could even *start* talking to him, and a fresh-faced lad of a kind you'd be delighted if your daughter brought home some night. The kids—who came and went in the usual rotator band—were for their part, divided into cocaine addicts, who'd thought they could beat the game, as kids have thought since time began, and everything addicts, who'd started on their mother's medicine cabinets and moved on to glue sniffing and anything else that could be sniffed, swallowed, or injected.

Back on the other side of the net, the veterans tended to be mostly drunks who were congenitally suspicious of anything called drugs and quite immune to other forms of feeling high. Thus, variously equipped, the bunch of us sat talking blindly past each other, "sharing" but making no contact, with the sound of the referee's whistle squealing constantly in our ears.

My heart went out particularly to the kids, who were being pounded day and night with industrial-strength therapy when a few kind or sharp words might have done just as well. A couple of times, I actually broke through the lines to try to impart a little common sense—nothing brilliant, which was quite beyond me, just the stale fruit of experience. Even if we did all have the same disease, it surely made a difference at what age we'd gotten it. Along with all the flotsam of pop psychology that had drifted into this place had come an across-the-board egalitarianism that I couldn't quite swallow even in my 97% absorbent phase. Addiction might make the whole world kin, but it doesn't make it the same age, and even a worthless life accretes experience that can't be had any faster, some of which is worth passing on.

To wit, to a boy suffering from obscene tantrums, I suggested a couple of insults with G ratings that could probably madden his tormentors just as much as his puny supply of swearwords. He was particularly taken with one recommendation for use on enemy taxi drivers: "My, you're ugly—I mean hideous," and is probably on his way to becoming a theater critic, if he hasn't been killed yet.

It was exhilarating to try sneaking such pearls past the supervisor, and I remember two other small successes. To a girl who said she planned to declare her complete independence from her family when she got home, I said, speaking for parents everywhere, "You mean you're going to pay your own bills?" No, it certainly didn't mean that. "Well, then, it won't be real independence will it? It'll just be words and dreams, like before."

I *said* my advice wasn't brilliant. It's just that you can never be too sure about the obvious—*somebody* might have missed it, as this young lady, along with half the new republics in Russia, had missed the boring connection between independence and money.

My third client hadn't missed a thing, but had actually gotten the gist faster than any of us. "Well, supposing I go home and try my best, but just can't make it the first time and I have to come back here—that wouldn't be so bad, would it?"

No doubt the official answer to this was simple enough—
something about not "projecting" into the future and taking
things "one day at a time" (never forgetting, on the other hand,
that "tomorrow is another day"). But the boy had been listening to the music, not the words, and the tune they were playing
over and over was "The Prodigal Son." Never has an organization had such a soft spot for fallen sinners—and why not? The
disease, as they describe it, is so overwhelming, and its victims
so weak and helpless in the face of it, that defeat is almost to be
expected. Every fall from grace is a testament to the fierceness of
the enemy and incidentally to the absolute necessity of their
own role as therapists. The fact that our hyperactive counselor
did not answer right away spoke volumes.

Since I considered defeat completely out of the question, I
couldn't afford to be in two minds about this myself, and I
stepped up smartly into the vacuum to say, "When you came
here this time, Jack, you probably had a brass band to see you
off, and people murmuring 'What a mature fellow, what a wise
choice.' Don't expect any of that next time."

In each of these cases, the kid looked around as if a lightbulb
had just turned on above his or her head. *Hey, that's right*. As
I say, you never know about the obvious.

I only wished, though, that I felt half as snappy as the above
interjections make me sound. The truth is that (1) these were
almost the only words I can recall saying voluntarily and (2)
having decided not to argue, I'd almost forgotten how to, and if
they said we were all absolutely powerless against booze, fine
with me, boss. Indeed, I'd gone along so thoroughly that when
I finally got out, I half expected the first bottle of Beefeater gin
that I saw behind a restaurant bar to walk over to my table and
pour itself down my throat.

And it didn't have to be gin, they warned over and over. A
wayward spoonful of that old devil cough medicine or even
mouthwash would be enough to start any of us off, and blood-
curdling tales circulated of people who'd picked up the wrong
glass at cocktail parties and been turned into ravening monsters
by a sip of someone else's vodka and tonic.

Even when you're not arguing, certain propositions stick in

your throat. And I wondered whether this tom-tom insistence on our helplessness might not have something a tiny bit self-fulfilling about it. Simply as psychological strategy, which everything was around here, the "fatal dose of cough medicine" doctrine seemed like a two-edged sword. On the plus side, it put the fear of God into us, which seems to be a necessary precondition of abstinence. All my life, I've heard people say that they really ought to quit drinking (and by the time they say it, they're already lit); and the next time one sees them, they're at it again, drinking themselves miserable, sipping and swearing to quit in almost the same breath.

The absolutism preached by places like Happy Valley certainly has this to be said for it: it breaks these deadlocks and induces an exhilarating sense of danger. The enemy is everywhere, even in your medicine cabinet. The stakes have been raised, and every moment is an adventure.

On the minus side, one person's bracing whiff of fear is another one's stark terror, and at one of our compulsory AA meetings I would witness a lady consumed with panic because a favorite eating place was about to install a bar. Where to go, how to hide? Life on the run suits some people better than others, and forbidden fruit exerts different appeals to different temperaments: one man's wonderful challenge and chance to defy the gods is made of the same material as another man's sweat-drenching nightmare. The forbidden fruit is going to get you eventually, thinks the second one. So why not get it over with? I remember as a child standing on the platform of our rinky-dink village train station and reaching reflexively for the railing in back of me as the express train roared toward us—only to find my mother gripping it tight too. Flinging oneself in front of trains, or from high windows, has absolutely no appeal *except* inevitability, yet for just that moment, my mother and I and, I believe, countless others could have been addicts of flinging ourselves at trains.

If reasonably normal people (my mother wasn't an addict of anything but detective stories) could be tempted by such altogether uncomfortable fates, imagine the mental state of a tosspot who is told over and over that one drink will return him to hell.

The appeal to surrender, to lie down and give up, or sit back and enjoy, plays right into his court. After one sip, he won't be accountable, old buddy. He has a disease that certifies him as helpless, you see. And we'll understand his fall, unto seventy times seven. It is no disgrace to lose to such an overwhelming enemy.

But the authorities also assured us at regular intervals that their methods worked, and again I took their word for it, only registering small blips of dissent on my own good days or right after I'd heard yet another veteran reminisce about his days at Betty Ford's place or Hazelden. Was *that* how it worked—repeated immersions? Never mind. In such a total atmosphere as this, and with your spirits as low as chemistry can make them, you believe what you're told, by God, and you accept any rescue that presents itself.

And yet and yet. I recall wondering, even in that state, if they weren't asking people to give up a little too much of themselves, if they weren't cutting away too much live tissue to get at the tumor.

My counselor framed the matter succinctly for me when he said, "You have to believe that your sobriety is the most important single thing in the world."

No, it isn't, I thought, there are a hundred more important things. A thousand.

On my occasional frisky moments I even wondered whether they weren't making unnecessarily heavy weather out of this whole thing. Drinking is bad for you, so don't do it. How's that for a program?

Only kidding, guys, I know it's much more complicated, or we wouldn't be here, right? These playful spasms were soon over, and angst was always just around the corner. So shut up and listen. The Happy Valley way of doing things *worked,* worked, worked; it worked because we believed it, and we believed it because it worked: all I had to do was buy into this equation at either end and all would be well.

I must have settled the matter in their favor a dozen times—and yet, the continued assaults on our own resourcefulness and ability to help ourselves continued to bother me, like an itch in the center of my head, every time I heard it. At one particular meeting a kid piped up to say that he'd been practicing his willpower lately and felt pretty good about it, and you would have supposed that he had blasphemed the Twelve Steps themselves. Speaker after speaker worked the lad over, until the AA meeting began to resemble a Communist show trial. "Trying to lick this thing with willpower is like trying to stop diarrhea with willpower" was the showstopper. And I thought, before I had time to correct my thinking, "So what? You can't stop diarrhea by going to meetings either." Metaphors have to do a better job than *that*, baby.

But the kid seemed quite crushed, which I suppose proved that his accusers were right. If he lost his moxie this easily, it certainly wouldn't have stood up long to the pressure of friends urging him to have just a little nip in honor of that good man Saint Patrick.

What spooked me was that they didn't even know this guy before passing definitive judgment on his willpower. Lots of people presumably go to meetings because they're having some trouble with their drinking, even *they* don't know how serious, and they hope to learn something here. But there are no degrees in the mind of a hard-liner. If you're here at all, you *must* be helpless, now and for the rest of your days, unless you put yourself immediately in the hands of the Higher Power of your choice. To the true believer, there is no such thing as a little bit alcoholic or a small drinking problem, and the believer's mission, as laid down in the twelfth step, is to help you to see this too. Otherwise he can't do a thing for you. And if this absolutism turns you off, as it has several people I know and who knows how many others, too bad for you: your heart is hardened in denial, and you're not ready to give up drinking yet. Bill Wilson's first step has been promoted from a useful suggestion to the narrow and only gate through which initiates must enter, even if they have to shrink themselves like Alice in Wonderland to do so.

At an intramural AA meeting, manned mostly by my fellow shavetails, I sensed that we were watching each other like ferrets to see who would say the magic words "I'm an alcoholic" next.

Nobody was telling us to say them, we had to arrive there on our own or our confession was of no use; but it had become clear that if we *didn't* arrive there, we were not being honest with ourselves, but were locked in denial, and would have to stay shivering outside while the others warmed themselves by the fire.

So one by one, we came over—myself, I must admit, with fingers crossed and only because I felt silly saying "Hi, I'm Bill, and I may or may not be an alcoholic, but I'd like to get a word in edgewise." The few stout souls who did use this formula seemed like second-class citizens, and all of them came out with their hands up eventually. Whatever one's motive, there was the same giddy relief in the air afterward, as if another soul had found Jesus and Happy Valley had done its job once more. And I'd guess that the new converts were quite pleased, too, at having caused such glee, and were soon caught up in it themselves.

It was an instructive brushup on all the old playground lessons. "Hey, Sheed doesn't think we ought to pray to win football games. Isn't that right?" The score is 7–7 at halftime, and we need all the help we can get. So you wind up *leading* the damn prayer. Since I planned, for my tongue's sake, to give up drinking forthwith whether I was an alcoholic or not, the more good reasons I could find to support my resolution the better. So sure, "I'm an alcoholic." Why not?

The next problem was that I didn't consider a lifetime spent at AA meetings a sufficient inducement to quit drinking. Although AA was, I suppose, an incontrovertible improvement on DTs, my problem now was depression, and all I could see before me between here and the grave were hundreds of men in windbreakers and women in faded jeans dragging plastic chairs across the floors of church basements, in order to say yet again, "Hi, I'm Fred, I'm Mabel, and guess what? I'm an alcoholic."

To the depressed, all things are depressing. And months hence, when the tide had turned, I would find AA meetings so entertaining and packed with genuine, un-TV-like drama that I hated to give them up. But to my abraded nerves, the clothes and chairs and voices jarred all the time I was at Happy Valley like acid rock played into an infected ear, and I could barely take in what they were saying. So a diet of that was clearly not what I needed right now.

Unfortunately, what I *did* need, namely my usual Marx Brothers fallback view of the situation, was quite beyond my scope. There is no point in telling a depressive to come out laughing, or fighting either. Next to exhorting him to relax, no advice could be more grating or beside the point. Fighting back was all I knew, but it would have to wait. *Fight?* I could hardly drag myself out of bed.

Au contrary, as Miss Adelaide would say. At another kind of meeting, one of the spunkier inmates had summoned the gumption to say, "Some people have the idea that AA can become kind of a crutch itself after a while. So what do you say to that?" "I would tell them"—and I can't remember the first part of what the speaker said, except that it was the usual ingenious piffle, but the last part had me *almost* up and roaring. "What's wrong with crutches anyway?" he said with all the purring complacency of someone who never gets answered back.

Reflexively, I gripped my canes. And if my own gumption had been anywhere to be found today, I would have bellowed, *"I'll* tell you what's wrong with crutches." Once upon a time, I'd wriggled my way down from crutches to two canes to *one* cane, and sometimes none, as I swung the bat at softball games, and even the feet at dances; and now, in my fifties, I was glumly retracing my steps and had recently gone back to two canes, and no softball, and could make a case that my melancholia had begun with that: my most persistent worry even at Happy Valley was, it now surprises me to remember, that my right foot would drop and I would need a second brace, a second AA, to use today's metaphor. If they'd handed me crutches as well, I would have burned them or drowned them and gone to bed forever.

Since I already had one incurable disease, I decided then and there that I'd just as soon not have another one. So it came as a prodigious relief when help arrived from the least likely of quarters (there were no likely quarters around here), namely our Sunday rapmeister himself, who paused long enough in his weekly hectoring and badgering to give his own definition of what an alcoholic is or is not. "If you can give up drinking whenever you have to," said this wonderful man, this prince among bullies, "then you're not an alcoholic."

Eureka! I searched my soul with dawning delight. To be fair, I didn't strictly speaking know if I *could* give up booze, because I'd never tried before. But the rewards for doing so had never seemed so sweet. It seemed that if I could just persuade my mangy old willpower to go along and grunt "No" from time to time, these people could never lay another glove on me, or rap at me, or straighten me out in any way, shape, or form. Better still, I would never have to give one more thought to my self-esteem for as long as I lived.

Right now, the question of whether I could do it would have to be put on hold while I waited for my nervous system to be repaired, if it *could* be: like one of New York City's bridges, it might have passed the point of no return. I had no firm reason to suppose I would *ever* feel better, and through the foggy wretched time that lay ahead, the Happy Valley brand of scare talk would continue to weigh heavily on me like a convoy of tractors crossing the Williamsburg, and the smear campaign against willpower and self-reliance would send shudders through my whole rickety structure.

On the plus side, though, their warnings gave me more reasons to abstain from booze than I would ever need. The truth was that I would have had to be absolutely insane to try drinking in my current condition. Besides my cancer deterrent (which they absolutely refused to take seriously) and my oft-stated desire to get back to work (they'd heard *that* one before), I had a motive they *had* noticed, which was an obsession with sleep. And surely they knew, as I knew, that if I had a drink now, the insomnia would be instantaneous and ferocious, the waking nightmare to end waking nightmares, and this would come on *the very first night*, before I'd even hit my stride as a recidivist. So what was the point of all this jawboning? Why did I have to be told over and over not to do something so totally crazy and unrewarding?

The quick answer is that some of us really were that insane, so all of us had to take our medicine—if we were so sure we didn't need it, we shouldn't be here. And this was reasonable, I supposed. I *shouldn't* be here, but I didn't know where else to go.

People in search of a medium-strength brainwashing are just out of luck these days because the Happy Valleys of this world are geared to desperate customers only, not pantywaists who've gone over the edge; so if one of the latter staggers in by mistake, he shouldn't be surprised to find himself flung on the operating table being prepped for major surgery. There is never a minute to waste, because the prototypical drunk who strays into these places, or is tricked into coming, is probably only passing through sobriety on a whim, his own or someone else's, and as soon as he's rebuilt his strength, he'll be off and flying again like new, unless they can break his will, his wings, in the short time he's in their power.

Enter next a pale-faced wreck (well, they all look like that when they get here) who's been taking depressive drugs until he can hardly raise his head—well, never mind about the details. He drinks too, right? So he's a drunk, and all drunks have the same disease, and whap, into the black hole he goes, where they hit him with everything they've got. If I could just have made it into the depressive ward, presumably I would have been safe.

Up to a point. One day, I had lunch with someone from that ward, and the sadness was quite overwhelming, such that it could not have been made worse even by the slapping around he'd have got in my section. Depression needs no help from outside; once it turns up the screws, it doesn't matter where you are. My case against Happy Valley was not so much that it makes one even more depressed, since in most cases that would be impossible, but that there were so many things they didn't talk about, or warn me about, in between their bursts of ominous prattle. Of the many gaseous words I heard there, only a handful were of any use at all. One purely factual lecture sticks in my mind, concerning the subject of drinking and sleep, the gist of which was that I'd worn out the cushion that made alcohol a sedative and would henceforth find it a stimulant. And there was another one about allergies to formaldehyde, which, to my fevered brain, made clear why outdoor swimming pools made my feet itch.

All this and cancer too. Believe me, doctor, I'm sold—you don't have to hit me again. I'm not going to drink anymore, okay? I hadn't been going to when I got here, and I certainly wasn't going to now, even if I had to hire a gorilla to lock me in my room. But my resolve obviously didn't show, because it did not spare me the Child Psychology I treatment from my counselor at our penultimate session. "I can just see you a month from now," he said, hardening his voice like a marine sergeant in the movies, "back at the bar, sippin' away." ("I'd rather die, sir!" I guess I was supposed to say.)

I asked to be excused from my last meeting with this dangerously overheated man, because I couldn't face going another round with his pet phrases, so I suppose his impression of me as a hopeless weakling was confirmed forever. But his hellfire preaching had already sunk in sufficiently to convince me that abstaining from booze was quite beyond unassisted human power. So in the same muddle of despair and curiosity and nothing-to-lose that had brought me here, I asked if I might try some Antabuse before leaving, the stuff that makes you violently ill on contact with booze.

For the curious—the Antabuse made me violently ill even without contact with booze. But my request for it impressed the authorities mightily. "We didn't think you were serious," they explained, completing the cycle of misunderstanding. Mother of Battles, what did I have to do to convince them I was serious? Here I thought I was being Job on his dunghill, and they thought I was trying to be Groucho. Thus perish all clowns.

On my way out the door, they tried to set me up with one more rap session, this one to include my wife. But knowing the nature of their rap sessions—and the nature of my wife, bless her—I managed to veto it. Later on, I might have enjoyed the riot of crossed purposes and clashing cultures or, alternatively, the strained efforts on both sides to understand each other, repeatedly frustrated by the language barrier—but not until my head felt a little better. Not until I saw the point of jokes again.

Now that I was heading back into the real world, I had to decide how to handle whatever this thing was on my own. And as with polio, the first step seemed to be to keep the cast as small as possible. I might be sick, but my wife certainly wasn't, and there was no way I was going to drag her into this, or ask her to adapt her life to mine. Outside of the impertinence of the request, I believe it would actually have increased the pressure. If booze *was* going to be a problem, I didn't want to add a thirsty, reproachful wife, or friends who didn't call anymore, to my caseload. It's a lot easier to write a book by yourself than to bring a play to Broadway with actors and technicians oinking and bleating along the way. Yourself you can ride herd on; yourself, beat down and discouraged as you may be, is the least of your worries.

The other thing is that if you want to ease your way back into the human race, you have to accept it pretty much as it comes. Addiction is, among other things, a social disease, and you haven't really licked it until you can face the world just as it is, with a smile or a growl as you prefer. And this meant emphatically *not* asking it to change, or to pay me any mind whatever.

Brave talk, and at the moment not much more than that. But, as I hope the next two chapters will demonstrate, this was the right medicine for me—although, as they may also indicate, I would barely know I was taking it half the time. While I was still at Happy Valley downing my phenobarbital every night, I was subject to bursts of lucidity, and could form these Napoleonic plans; later, I would find myself just hanging on. Yet, at my most incoherent, I would still know that it was my fight and no one else's, although advice was welcome from any quarter, and I would overdose on shrinks for a while.

The question is, Would this medicine have done anyone else any good, or was it specific to me? The answer depends squarely on whether one has an incurable disease or merely (to use a phrase the therapists had almost drummed out of the language) a bad habit. For my own purposes, I had me a beautifully simple test of whether I had a disease or not. If I took a drink or a pill right now, after the hazing those two rascals had just put me through, I had a disease, all right. And if I ever gave anyone cause to send me back to this place, or to start me on another course of temperance studies anyplace at all, I was not only diseased but crazy. The invitation to my wife was the snapping point, and the thought of being talked about and planned for, like a sick kid in the next room, was enough to have me up on what was left of my hind legs and howling. Disease? I'll show you disease!

But it turned out to be an academic question, because not only would I find booze precisely as easy, though even more painful, to give up than cigars, but I was about to enter a zone where it would all seem like a bunch of sounds anyway: disease, Higher Power, self-esteem—the rain streaking across the windows and the wind banging on the roof made more sense, and explained themselves better. And since we have plenty of both out our way, Happy Valley rapidly lost whatever reality it had and became one more strange dream in a period of strange dreams—you know, the one where you're sitting in kindergarten with your bony knees sticking out from the desk and a dunce cap on your head because you have flunked Life itself and been sent back to start over. Talk about being born again—some of the other students in the dream are babies, others seem to be at death's door. But you're never too old to learn your ABCs.

Well, it was no skin off my nose, they could do what they liked now, because at long last I was swinging down the driveway in my own car, giddy with freedom and with the thing I came here to cure, insomnia, which was staging a last hurrah but *felt* as if it was leaving—I can't explain it better than that. Therapeutically speaking, Happy Valley might have been using a howitzer to kill a flea, but the flea *was* dead, I knew it, and ever since I have slept like a baby, if any pill-taking insomniac out there wants to know.

Now all I had to do was get over the howitzer, and thirty-five years of fun, and I'd be in the clear.

7

LOWER THAN LOW, HIGHER THAN HIGH

My dwindling doses of phenobarbital had been timed perfectly to run out the night before I left Happy Valley, and a strange night it was. Once again, I didn't sleep a blink, but this time the nurses didn't bother to look in every hour. From now on, my insomnia was my own affair. I had actually proved on previous nights that the situation had progressed just enough for us both to close the book on it. With a flyspeck of pheno I could catch a fly's worth of sleep, and this placed me pretty much in the mainstream of American insomnia. Thus Happy Valley had, with certain fairy-tale reservations that I'll get to, done what I asked it to and alleviated the worst of my sleeplessness. If I didn't sleep that last night, it was not from the chemical bomb damage so much as from feverish excitement, of a curiously neutral kind, not happy or unhappy, just excitement, as if some weight had been lifted off my nerve ends and they were capering and doing aerobic exercises in the moonlight.

The next morning, my wife came to fetch me, and I still felt giddy enough to insist on driving the last seventy-five of the two hundred–odd miles home, sleep or no sleep. On the final lap, we stopped at a supermarket to pick up some stuff for supper, and I thought I had died and gone to heaven: the color and variety of the merchandise glistened like Christmas toys after the austerity of Happy Valley, where they had confiscated my Irish Breakfast tea bags, presumably on the grounds that my wife might have secreted a razor among them with which I might try to kill myself, and I could have wheeled my cart up and down the aisle forever. And when we got home, I thrilled just as much to the sight of my very own telephone on which I could call absolutely anybody I wanted, from the mayor of Tokyo on down. At Happy Valley, we had fought like rats over a single pay phone, and I had been obliged to reel off a friend's credit card number each time and pray to God that my party was in, because there was no way he or she could get back to me, since the poor old whore of a phone was always in use.

So I sprayed the landscape with calls like a teenager until the novelty had worn off, and ate supper jubilantly, and went to bed hopefully, only to find some truly grotesque waking dreams waiting there to inform me that the party was over and we were returning to Hell immediately.

Once upon a time, some friends and I took a trip to Tangier and environs in a Volkswagen bus, and were dazzled by the skill of the local grease monkeys at fixing one's car just well enough for it to be driven out of range before breaking down again. But the Moroccan mechanics could have taken lessons in fine tuning from Happy Valley. I had roared out of the shop that very morning purring on all cylinders, but here I lay in a steaming heap in the therapeutic equivalent of the middle of the desert, a million miles from nowhere.

Withdrawal from phenobarbital, I would now proceed to learn, was about as bad as withdrawal ever gets, and infinitely worse than anything I'd experienced so far. But once again, it proved impossible to get any hard information. The assorted shrinks and medicine men I talked to on the outside had frankly never heard of the problem, and neither, to my surprise, had any of the folk at the local AA meetings, except for someone who had heard it was bad, and "could last a year, could last three."

The voice at the AA listing in Manhattan was the most ignorant of all, and also vaguely derisive: if I hadn't known better, I would have sworn the man was as drunk as a billy goat, as Jean

Stafford used to say; but of course AA is the closest thing you can get to a saloon outside of the real thing, and some members never lose the style. "Phenobarbital?" he rasped, his red nose no doubt gleaming into the phone (I see no need to be charitable about this guy). "Phenobarbital? You on *that* stuff?" And then in a lofty tone, "Thank God, I never had that problem myself! Nossir—not phenobarbital." And so on. (This might be a good place to pass on my theory that every organization should put its brightest employee, its superstar, on the phone, while hiding the imbeciles in top management where they won't be noticed. I guarantee business will pick up.)

It says enough about the people at Happy Valley, I think, to add that I didn't even bother to ask *them* about my situation. The sum total of their medical advice on drug-related depression had been to put me on Prozac right away, which, as I would learn, is the nearest thing to washing your hands of the whole affair. The best that could be said about Prozac in my case was that it tends to turn massive depression into acute anxiety, which is at least livelier; and that it keeps you awake, or very lightly asleep, to enjoy it. Indeed, if you *do* sleep, your nightmares are likely to be so jazzy and frantic that I found myself in the bizarre position of fighting to stay awake, a strange turn of events indeed. But that's how I spent my first night home.

But I still hadn't discovered the *worst* thing that can happen on Prozac, outside of homicidal rage, which is that it can cause urine retention, a totally maddening condition in which you would sell your soul to urinate and can't. A slight physical affliction is not necessarily a bad thing when you're depressed because it takes your mind off your troubles. But urine retention takes your mind off nothing. Quite to the contrary, it walls you in with your troubles and makes you feel you can't get rid of anything.

This is certainly not meant to be a book of vengeance or an indictment of a particular institution, but a commentary on a way of doing and looking at things that seems to be going around these days. The official Happy Valley reaction to the first signs of my new problem was typical. The outside doctor whom the faith healers there depended on, if one of their diseased patients ever actually got sick, came round to check out my prostate, which he pronounced about right for my age: a little trouble peeing was, it seemed, among Santa's collection of goodies for the elderly, which I was now just old enough to apply for.

And that was it, as far as Happy Valley was concerned; they'd done their bit. When the problem got worse, they simply sent for the same doctor and he said the same thing, probably adding something about seeing a specialist when I was safely out of the garage.

This I did when the problem got unbearable, which was immediately, but I'll spare you the urological details, which are both messy and uninstructive, except to say that (a) there is no more poignant problem in life than trying to decide between slaking your thirst with a sip of something and sparing your bladder the extra ounce of torture and (b) a catheter is fun for a while, but leaves you—me, anyway—feeling as wet and slobbery as an infant.

Since this scourge would wind in and out of my phenobarbital withdrawal like background music, punctuating my darkest moments with pangs of operative angst, I'll run it through quickly up front. The high point of the experience was a thrilling, strangely carefree midnight run by ambulance to the local hospital on a catheter emergency (our ambulance crews are a riot, if you're in the mood), and the low point, if I must pick one, was probably the moment the specialist said he'd exhausted his pharmacopoeia of muscle relaxants and bladder enhancers and could see no alternative to operating on my prostate—a procedure I'd heard horrible things about. In fact, I'd have called this the last straw, if I didn't know by now that there was always another straw waiting.

Fortunately, I decided to get a second opinion from the only urologist in the local phone book, and this country doctor had the smarts to ask me what pills I was taking, and the whole simple truth came out. Prozac, if your eyes can handle the fine print, "may cause urine retention." He added that all antidepressants have this particular side effect, except for those of the Desyrel family—a fact you'd suppose they'd know at a place like Happy Valley that doles out these medications like party favors. But such is the platonic line they draw between soul healers and body repairmen that the doctor who signed my first Happy Valley prescription for Prozac had never even met me, but was doing it on the say-so of my guru, who "thought I seemed depressed." (I have since learned that at least one previous tenant at Happy Valley had suffered the exact same Prozac aftereffect I had, but had left no trace on the collective memory.)

So you can see why I didn't bother them with my phenobarbital adventures—I wouldn't even have known whom to talk to. When my counselor called up a few weeks later to ask how I was doing, I did tell him about my medical adventures, and all he had to say was, "Are you going to plenty of meetings?" So much for the *minutiae* of medicine. Although he too had told me that I would be undergoing formidable "chemical changes," these, whatever they might be, paled next to the necessity of recognizing my disease, and deciding on a suitable higher power, and *going to meetings*.

Thus it came to pass that *every*thing surprised me that year; I was prepared for nothing. The phenobarbital withdrawal actually lasted one month, but because I didn't know that in advance, it seemed like eternity, which might be defined psychologically as *any* period of time to which you can't see the ending. Like some *Twilight Zone* character who thinks he's on the surface of the moon and goes insane with despair just outside of Reno, Nevada, I was actually within spitting distance of the happiest six or seven weeks of my life and didn't know it.

The knowledge would have helped more than words can express, particularly on the nights when I contemplated suicide—or not exactly *contemplated*, that isn't the way it works, but felt I had no choice. I have heard people accuse suicides of selfishness, but it's not like that at all. Your own interests don't enter into it, and neither do anyone else's. You have to do it, that's all, and the outside world has no more say in the matter than the wallpaper or a painting on the ceiling, both of which are the outside world too.

I thought often of Chesterton's saying that "suicide is an insult to every leaf on every tree," which had answered all questions of this kind for me during the glooms of adolescence, but which rang no bells now. "So what?" was all I could say. Leaves have their problems, I have mine. My heart goes out to suicides who leave children behind, and beyond measure to the children themselves—it was nothing personal, one wants to tell them, the killer had no choice. But if you haven't been there yourself, you can never know this.

What I remember mostly is a dull certainty that I would do it the very next time the temptation reached a crescendo; the compulsion would hit like the tallest tidal wave in history and carry my battered remains out to sea, and I'd get some rest at last. And every time, I, by the grace of God, survived one of these power surges, the understanding was always that the next one would be *worse* and quite irresistible.

Yet of the several such waves that I endured while craning my eyes for the next one, I now recall only two with any clarity. And I remember them because of how I responded to them, not because of how they felt—in themselves they were all foam and noise and are all gone now. The first time I "had" to kill myself, I simply phoned up my old friend Dr. K., who had given me his private number for emergencies like this—and will certainly go straight to Heaven for doing so. Although the time must have been three or four or infinity in the morning when I dialed, the man responded as if this was just the call he'd been waiting for. "This makes me feel like a doctor again," he said, in the single pleasantest line I've ever heard, and together we sweated out the urge to self-slaughter until it was replaced with blessed sleepiness.

As we chatted along, I learned, almost in passing, the whole secret for dealing with depression *and* temptation—though like most such secrets it would prove much easier said than done. Close inspection suggested that the giant wave was something of an illusion. What I was actually being hit by was a rapid series of incredibly bad moments, unbearable but brief, with a small but perceptible breathing space in between. And what I did with this space was the key. If I panicked, the panic would join the moments together, the way the mind's eye joins frames of film into a movie; if I tried to escape, I would be hit again on the way out, and again and again, seemingly faster and faster after that. And if I tried to look on the bright side, I would really have my face mashed in it.

The trick I finally tumbled to that night and the next could alternately be described as passive resistance or steering into the skid. Having reposed my soul as best I could, I said, in effect, "Hit me again—show me what you've got" and found some small pleasure in keeping my eyes open and trying to analyze what followed. An old *Life* magazine photograph comes to my mind—God knows who took it—of a photographer who has just strapped himself to a palm tree during the great hurricane of 1938 to get a better view. Both the man and the tree appear to be stretched to breaking point by the storm, but the camera clicks back triumphantly, taking pictures of pure wind, and having the last word. That was me, now.

The strategy didn't, believe me, help much—but every little bit is welcome, because the second thing you learn is that there's a span to these things, they don't last forever unless you cooperate with them and prolong them by panicking. So you learn a hundred ways to stall (counting your breaths like a Zen master is a good one), not because any of them will make the problem go away, but just to take a few minutes off its running time, and not have to bother Dr. K. in the middle of the night again.

With the second attack of suicidal dementia, I took the law into my own hands. My wife had gone out for a few hours and I had the place to myself. "So," I said, or thought, to my demon, "here's your chance—put up or shut up; kill me or leave me alone." It sounds melodramatic now, but the drugged life *is* melodramatic—the scenery and sounds are all out of Edgar Allan Poe—and these words seemed like calm good sense in the circumstances. So I set to work, with the slyly deliberate slowness of a city road crew, figuring out ways one might kill oneself, *if* one decided to (the stalling mechanism was already in full gear).

Pills were out, because we didn't have enough in the house—and if we did, there was no guarantee they would work. Bud MacFarlane, the Irangate bungler, had woken up with a nasty headache after a thousand or so, while other hopefuls, if that's

the right word, had reportedly been transformed into brain-
dead vegetables just before they reached the other side. Knives
had always fascinated me, but a story my sister had told me
came back from across the years about a girl at her school who'd
slashed her wrists, and had then run around the building screaming for help. Although I believed my resolve was firmer than
that, I also knew that it was an easy job to botch. Only a skilled
surgeon could be quite sure of hitting the spot, and even then,
someone might walk in and I'd have to *explain*. And then, as I
lay on my back with tubes dripping out of me, explain again—or
worse, not have to explain because the story had gone the rounds
already. Knives could open up avenues of embarrassment dead-
lier than veins.

Continuing on through the arsenal—thank God we didn't
have a gun in the house. There is no stalling with a gun, you
either do it or you don't, and the number of impulse suicides
performed this way by people playing chicken with themselves
must be legion.

We didn't have a high window either, and the idea of flinging
myself repeatedly from a ground-floor window entertained me
for only a split second—jokes might have been expected to help
once upon a time, but when I tried them, they tasted unbelievably *harsh*. I not only couldn't see what was funny about them,
but wasn't dead sure what the word *funny* meant.

Still, I knew what the word meant to other people, and I
knew that the sight of me trying to hang myself would be objectively speaking, very funny indeed, as I tried vainly to tie
knots in unobliging ropes and to kick chairs away that wouldn't
budge. The last thing you want when you're trying to kill yourself is to be laughed at, it must clash horribly with whatever
you're trying to say; but all I could picture now was a wall of
grinning faces looking on as Buster Keaton tries and tries again,
and all I could think was that I wasn't very good at this kind of
thing.

You never know what's going to come in handy, and I thank
God now for giving me neither mechanical skills nor mechanical
imagination, because I was damned if I could think of any other
way to "off" myself short of going to the city and looking for a

tall building with windows that actually opened, and trying to hang on to my death wish as the elevator stalled inevitably between floors.

Otherwise the cupboard was bare. I had to do it, but I couldn't do it. And with that matter hastily decided, the impulse receded just enough and there were no more waves, only sulky little ripples, and finally, stillness.

Looking back, it would be easy to say that the nonsuicidal among us will always find stumbling blocks and reasons for postponement. But it certainly didn't feel like that. It's beyond my powers now to imagine, let alone describe, how much intenser these thoughts were at the time than they look now as I place them calmly in a row on paper. It was as if certain screws had been tightened to breaking point that month, causing the core self to seek relief at any cost. "I can't take any more of this!" is the cry of the suicide, even if he doesn't know what "this" is.

But perhaps the best way to convey the difference between then and now would be to say that I couldn't have written the words down at all back then, because I couldn't write anything down. During one of my up moments in the Valley, I had agreed to an easy magazine assignment on the assumption that I'd surely be well enough to handle it by the time I got out, but every time I stabbed at the assignment with my pencil, my handwriting came out so scratchy and primitive that it could have been done by my foot.

The last killer assaults of the retreating phenobarbital had by now been augmented by the side effects of various antidepressants, starting with Prozac itself and then, when that failed to do anything more than make me jumpy, all the others in the book. But I never found out whether the pills might have helped, because I never got past the side effects, of which my nervous system contained an encyclopedia: if one patient in a thousand experienced dizziness, that one was me; ditto for backaches, nausea, drowsiness, and insomnia. As a species of cherry on top of this sickly mess, we finally placed something called L-tryptophan, which triggers nightmares that advertisers might have called a breakthrough in the form: nightmares that would have made Dracula howl in his coffin.

But I could never really know what caused what. There were mornings when, from no apparent provocation, I would just lie in bed with my right arm shaking convulsively, and everything else trembling slightly in sympathy; or I would look into the mirror and start to cry like a baby—and realize how silly that looked, and turn away sobbing, out of range of my own eyes. It is in this kind of condition that people sometimes have to make life-and-death decisions. Judge them kindly—but don't make suicide any easier for them.

So my dream of drying out quietly, of "throwing up behind a hedge" and returning to society my old debonair self, had back-fired quite badly. At Happy Valley, I had at least been able to keep up appearances by the loose standards of such places; but I was beyond that now. "You looked awful," witnesses have confirmed about that period, and the worst of it is that I wasn't even trying *not* to look awful. My motto from polio days, "If you can't feel good, you can at least look good," seemed both pointless and unachievable. And even the thought that someday I would regret this and wish I'd handled it better cut no ice.

Nothing anyone did or said could have made me *feel* better, but feeling bad would have been infinitely more tolerable if someone had told me how close the rescue team was. But since my advisers so far hadn't even warned me that the attack was coming, they could hardly tell me when it would leave. ("Beware the pink cloud" was all they had said.) For all I knew, I had a condition no one had ever heard of before, let alone found a cure for. And the best I could find by way of a diagnostician in my regular neighborhood was, yes, another shrink with another magic pill. The last thing in the world I needed was another pill.

Reviewing the alternatives: it would be, as noted, a royal waste of time to urge defiance on such a wreck as I was that month. Nothing is more dismal than a pep talk when you're depressed, nothing rubs your helplessness in more cruelly. In fact, even passive resistance is too much to ask of you in this state, too demanding and businesslike.

The upside, I finally figured out, to being depressed is simply that you have no obligation to do or feel anything at all, but just to hang on. To Hell with feeling good, to Hell with fighting back. Time is on your side, believe this, and indulge yourself in helplessness—and, if possible, food. Although, at the very bottom of the pit, food loses all taste and interest for you (so to Hell with that too), I found on intermediate days much childish comfort in ice cream, which begins to look pretty good as the booze empties out. I was thin as a stick by then, and could gorge my heart out—making up for any excess by fasting on the few good days that came along, days so good that I didn't need the consolations of pleasure. Of these, I distinctly remember a good Tuesday (although I usually considered Tuesday the February of the week) and a good Thursday sometime later. The up times were spaced wide apart, just enough to keep one going but no more, and they usually ended with a sense of foreboding worthy of the brothers Grimm. "We're leaving now," say the good spirits, "and don't hold your breath till we get back." But it was nice to be reminded that such things as good days existed and that when they came, no amount of booze, tobacco, or even ice cream could make them any better.

But these were just beacons in the fog, every bit as frustrating as they were encouraging: the light could be coming from miles away, for all I knew. Reality right now was the down days, when I would sit frozen in an armchair by the window, praying only to end my time on earth a *happy* vegetable, a vegetable that at least felt no pain. If I could gather sufficient strength, I would then dial the number of my new phone pal, a veteran counselor who was also a human and who, rare among his breed, recognized that there was more to life than alcohol. In fact, he sent me a paper he'd published somewhere proposing that there might be such a thing as "sedation addiction," as opposed to common or garden alcohol addiction, which was the closest anyone had come to what actually ailed me. But so far it was not much more than a phrase, and when we addressed my case, we had to fall back on the limited language of booze.

"If it took you thirty-five years to acquire a habit, it's only fair you should spend a year getting over it," he said—giving me at last a time frame, however unscientific.

"Some people say that depression is just anger turned inward," he said another time, but this rang no bells at first. Another friend would later say that I had seemed full of anger during this period, and I had to take his word for it. All I could remember myself was a screaming discomfort alternating with abject misery and a longing to get over both of them, which I suppose may have added a peevish cast to my countenance.

But anger? I simply wasn't aware of any. And having danced a few pointless numbers with Denial, I was leery of emotions I wasn't aware of. The great discovery popularized by Freud, but dating back to Sophocles and beyond, that a great deal of mental activity is subconscious had, in my lifetime, given a blank check to every manner of quack, and the word they were writing on the check this year was *anger*. Next year, who knows? In the fifties my gang and I had weathered the menace of *latent homosexuality*—the less you were aware of which, the more likely you were to have—so I knew what a seductive waste of good, middle-class time these phantoms could be.

Nevertheless, I tried, for the sake of form, to get mad at something outside myself, and if I succeeded, I wasn't aware of that either, and I still felt just wretched. The joke on me is that I now believe my friend was quite right—you *can* rage your way out of depression; but only when you're ready to.

Two things that did bring slight relief both came from furthest left field and were entirely specific to myself. One was the devising of an absolutely perfect mnemonic, one that cross-checked forward and back, for a friend's phone number. "Look, Ma, I'm thinking!" This activity had, by some magical means, automatically cleared a track for itself, temporarily pushing aside all manner of gook and sludge from my brain; so if thinking is your thing, *any* kind of thinking (car tinkering sounds ideal), now is the time to do it—if you can, of course. On the very worst days, it's impossible, the sludge is immovable and threatening too ("Touch me, and you'll be sorry!"), so you resume your dead man's crawl right away and just hang on. It's all you have to do, because *time is on your side, goddammit.*

The second escape I found was in music. Public television,

God bless it, was running a special on Duke Ellington, and salvation arrived as the Duke began stroking the notes of "Solitude," tenderly but fastidiously, as if releasing his miraculous, healing song from the piano by some high-priestly ritual. My own spirit climbed with each harmonic shift until I knew, with the certainty of a tonic chord, that I was close to the end of my own imprisonment.

But every man has his own remedy and his own songs. Mr. Styron found classical music liberating, and I could see how painting might do it as well, or looking out the window. When you're getting over depressants, your senses begin to open one by one some time before your mind has caught up, and I found myself riveted by swatches of scenery, or even by extra-clear pictures on television. These things would, I sensed, make my heart really soar if only it could, if only it wasn't held down by invisible steel threads.

Up, up, and away. The Ellington dream came almost at the moment of waking, but before my eyes open all the way onto daylight, there are still a couple of spaces to fill. What about booze all this time, for instance?

Happy Valley had so impressed the notion on my fuzzy mind that alcohol was at the center of the universe that I emerged facing in that direction, expecting all my troubles to come from the array of bottles that seemed to line the outside world. When you're depressed, everything depresses you, and not being allowed to drink, i.e., to feel good on demand, naturally comes right at the top of that kind of list.

The first morning I got back, an old friend came round to say hello, and asked innocently if he could have a glass of wine. And I thought, this man is *free*, he can do what he likes. Although the last thing in the world I wanted just then, or had ever wanted, was a glass of wine in the middle of the morning, I now felt unbearably restricted at not being allowed to have one, as if I'd been flung down a well bound hand and foot. I could *never again* walk into someone's house and ask for a glass of sherry or prize malt scotch, for all that they're both overrated, or reach for a gin and tonic to cut the heat of a summer day.

Suddenly vistas opened in every direction of having to toast brides with orange juice, and of celebrating winning games with Coca-Cola, and of watching friends everywhere drift away from me into Nirvana while I sat tethered to my soda pop. They had told us at Happy Valley not to "project," not to think beyond the moment we were in; but the human mind is made precisely to do those things; living half in the future and half in the past is how we know we're not cows. And besides, Happy Valley didn't really mean it. The very evening after I was told not to project, a speaker at one of our AA meetings told us about some chap in his eighties who decided after fifty years or so that it might be okay to have a drink, and "he was gone just like that."

My friend with his glass of wine proved to be a harbinger, like the first spirit to visit Scrooge. That very same day, or the next one, we celebrated my homecoming the only nonalcoholic way we could think of in our narrow repertoire by going to the movies, where we saw *Moonstruck*—a film which, as probably no one else has ever noticed, is basically about drinking wine. Every few minutes, the characters on screen seemed to stop in their tracks to schmooze over a bottle of chianti, incidentally *celebrating their freedom to do so,* while I writhed in my invisible chains.

It was the same with novels—drink, drink, drink on every page—and I'm sure it would have seemed the same with TV as well, if I'd been any kind of a beer fancier. In fact, the whole damn world seemed to be made of booze and I was surprised I hadn't noticed it before. So I decided to ignore the mother-hen warnings of Happy Valley and stick my head right into the lion's mouth and *go* to cocktail parties, and to such of my old haunts as didn't fill me with nameless melancholy.

It was a case of backing one's own self-knowledge, which they'd derided so mercilessly in the Valley, against their own general-issue, one-size-fits-all catechism. "The best defense is a good offense" had won me no cigars with my counselor, but I knew it was the only way to go. Either I could cower in my bunker and wait for the booze to get me, or I could march right up to it chanting "In your face," or "Our team is better than your team."

If I chose the first, or Maginot Line, approach, I would be clos-
ing off a great deal of the world and making my life much nar-
rower—but I would not be making myself any safer. In fact, the
enemy would seem that much closer, encircling me from all the
houses and bars I'd ceded to him. And in the misery and lone-
liness of my safe space, I would be that much more vulnerable.

The rule I decided on to keep all the doors in town open—and
I pass it on for what it's worth—was simply never to have a
drink on the spur of the moment. If I wanted to get back on the
stuff later, fine. But I would have to make the decision in some
cool moment when the temptation was not the loudest voice in
the room. And, just to complicate the litigation, I further de-
creed that the case must be heard before a full court, with all the
witnesses allowed to drone on to their heart's content. The truth,
that it was simply not in my best interest to drink, would surely
out eventually.

But, first things first. The rule for my social debut was simply
to keep muttering "Out of the question, out of the question"
until I got home again, or forgot what I was muttering about.

"What are you drinking? . . . I see you're not drinking . . .
God, I hope you haven't given it up permanently." The outside
world was its usual helpful self, clucking around me like chick-
ens in a burning barn. "Oh my God, you poor thing. Did the
doctor say how long you'd have to give it up for? Don't you
find life dreadfully dull without it?" If I'd been in any doubt
that giving up liquor was both impossibly difficult and utterly,
devastatingly unrewarding, these people were here to set me
straight. I could see how some drunks might prefer just to keep
on drinking than to face this gauntlet, this Greek chorus of woe.

Yet I could also see a possible source of amusement in their
worried faces, to be enjoyed when I felt a little better. The level
of anxiety in some of them was so intense that it dawned on me
that these people might be in much worse trouble than I was.
And even some of the less concerned ones reminded me of the
boys at school right after I got polio. "Could I be next? How
would I take it if I was?" If W. C. Fields here can quit drinking,
anybody can.

For some time after that, I felt on and off like a test case, a health object, as I had when I took my first faltering steps in 1945. Can a guy who has manifestly enjoyed his booze as much as I had just walk away from it? There was a definite need to know in my neighborhood. Some people manifestly didn't care, and bless them. Perhaps later I could pose as a good example for the drunks, but right now I needed some hard proof for myself that sobriety beat working on a chain gang in Georgia, that there was some joy in it, that it wouldn't always be the living death that I was passing through now.

Phenobarbital had so skewed everything that I had taken it for granted that I *must* be tempted, and it was only when the first cocktail party ended that I realized that I hadn't even come close to temptation or needed to use my mantra once. "Out of the question" was a fact, not an opinion. My recent memories of booze were so alternately painful and boring that even with the witchlike warnings of Happy Valley chiming in my ears and assuring me that I couldn't help myself, I wouldn't have accepted a drink at gunpoint.

Which gave me some breathing room, at least for now ("Beware the pink cloud," trilled the witches, who were not going to let me off the alcohol hook till there was no hope left for them), but no great joy. It meant I could go anywhere I liked—bars, wine tastings, Irish wakes—but it didn't mean I wouldn't feel dismal when I got there. The only difference between a good evening out and a bad one was that sometimes I seem to have been, out of sheer ancestral memory, the life of the party, while at others, I was the return of the Mummy's Curse. But it was all the same to me. My body had its moods, but the man within was down to two, lousy and plain miserable.

The only thing worse than going out was staying home in the prison of one's thoughts. In fact, the only time I came within sight of anything resembling temptation was on the way out the door one evening when I thought if I *wasn't* going out I'd certainly have to have a drink. Yet going out even to the most bibulous households resolved the question completely. I certainly wasn't planning to have a drink *here*, and make a fool of myself.

But since I wasn't going to have any fun "here" either, and I couldn't spend all day watching movies in which people didn't drink, I decided to hit some AA meetings instead. There at least, I would be safe from the clank of glass and the glug of liquor pouring, and from the need to explain anything to anybody every few minutes.

But not, of course, from incessant palaver about booze. This would become a problem later—how on earth were people to get their minds off drinking if they talked about it all the time? But right now I didn't care what they talked about. I just wanted to be among fellow souls who had been in the sewer themselves and knew what it was like down there. You couldn't even *invent* a misery at an AA meeting that couldn't be topped by some-one—though the remedies they proposed for insomnia were as goofy as any I heard on the outside: "tincture of orris root" would have seemed scientific by contrast.

My interest at the moment had nothing to do with AA's effectiveness and everything to do with fellowship. On a level of pure impression, I noted that AA clients divided, as one might expect, between those who went to meetings to help each other, and those who went there simply to moan and rattle their chains. Those shadowy uncles of yours who leave the party to go to meetings aren't much fun when they get there either, and my quest for happy teetotalers was only medium successful. But when I found one, he or she was likely to be very happy indeed: and I formed the rickety hypothesis that people who drank to improve reality would probably be happy people in the afterlife as well, but people who drank to escape it would often be almost as wretched as ever. Sobriety can only do so much for you, and it doesn't finally guarantee happiness any more than drinking does, only less pain.

Among the helpful members, there was a further division be-tween the ones who played it by the book, and could only com-municate in the lingua AA with its steps and its sponsors (your shadowy uncle would be one of these), and the ones who dared to cut loose and talk like friends. I quickly fell in with one of the latter, an old sailor whose horizon couldn't help being large, however hard he tried to narrow it for group purposes. Jack, as one must call him, was the first to talk about the fabled pink cloud without simultaneously reading me a list of warnings about its dangers. Maybe he surmised that the shrunken cadaver he was talking to (I'd lost a good twenty pounds) didn't really need any more bad news right now. Instead he launched, as one old sybarite to another, into a glowing description of the endorphin rush that awaited me at the end of my travails. "I've been up there ever since," he said, "and I expect you will be too."

It would be too much to say that my heart leapt at the prospect, because leaping was beyond its capacity, but at least it didn't sink, which made this a good day. And I would suck what nourishment I could from Jack's words as I jogged cautiously toward the finish line, which proved to be much closer than I had dared to hope. On April 14, almost two months to the day since I'd started on my phenobarbital run, I hit what can only be described as a wall of emptiness. A blank. A sheet of glass you could put your hand through. I sat at the kitchen table staring out the real glass door in back and trying intermittently to jot down my thoughts, but there were no thoughts worthy of the name. The word *existential* kept occurring to me, but I had no idea what I meant by it. I also remember writing some stuff about high pressure areas, troughs, low fronts—my mind was like a weather map that had gotten stuck. The air had stopped moving and nobody knew how to start it again, and the clouds just sat there like bumps on a log. Nineteen eighty-eight was a year when the actual weather got stuck a lot, right over my head, as if the whole universe had been taking pills. So it was child's play to transfer the scene to the inside of my head.

But I couldn't say for sure *what* I wrote, because after carefully tearing the page from my notebook to read on a better day, I found when that day came that I couldn't bear to have it around any longer. Before balling it up and throwing it into the fireplace, I took a last quick look, and found it totally without interest, as empty as the mood it was trying to describe. But I *still* couldn't bear to have it around.

If my notes that day contained anything more concrete than weather reports, it would probably have been a reference to a speech I had to give in Connecticut on the eighteenth and how impossible that would be. The reason I remember the dates so well is that it isn't normal to feel as good on April 15 as I felt the next day. It's my fixed belief that I was watching Ron Darling pitch for the Mets against the Expos when it hit—but my equally fixed belief that I was racing to meet a magazine deadline. Both would have been possible in the rush I remember feeling as the phenobarbital finally left my system, cursing like Peter Pain in the old Ben-Gay ads and squealing like the Gadarene swine on their way to the sea. Hot damn! I felt good. The clouds had finally moved along and been replaced by this gigantic pink number out of Disney, in which I rolled and wallowed like a child.

Thus began a seven-week spree that would prove to be as close to heaven as I expect to get and almost worth the pain of getting there. It was also unlike any other kind of spree I'd ever been on, in that, among other things, I would wake up every single morning of it, not holding my head, but thirsting for more of whatever it was; and more after that, until my lungs almost burst with joy. The years peeled off me like old skin, and they peeled off everyone else too, so that when I left the house that day, the old men and women on Main Street looked for a moment like the GIs and young brides they had once been, scanning the postwar real estate ads in the store windows and almost laughing with relief; and all around them the countryside seemed to be greeting its first spring ever with everything in its arsenal, robins, daffodils, the works. If I'd committed suicide— what was it, two weeks ago?—I would have missed this sensational apparition altogether.

And even the buildings in New York, when I drove there a couple of days later, had shed their grime for me and glistened like diamonds as they must once have glistened for Edith Wharton and Scott Fitzgerald. I fell in particular thrall to the Twenty-fourth Street block between Madison and Park avenues (Willa Cather country) and drove out of my way just to be on it again. Talk about the street where you live, today I even loved the street where the *street* lived. This noble block, I decided, represented the Empire City at its absolute imperial best: generous, sure of itself, endearingly pompous. It was ancient Rome without the orgies, I babbled on gleefully, a Rome you could trust.

But back in the country once more, there was a white pad-
dock fence *à la mode de* Kentucky that ran that block a close
second, and without leaving home there was my very own
kitchen (what age am I now, about five?) and all the remarkable
things in it. I found myself taking a particular shine to the coffee
machine and the whole routine of priming it each day—so much
so that I would fall asleep at night chortling at the prospect; and
then, with Mr. Coffee, or whatever his name was, gurgling
cheerfully in the background, I'd turn on the television set,
which I had never known for sure *had* shows in the morning,
and marvel over the ravishing beauty of the commercials and the
irresistible charm of the hostesses, any one of whom could have
launched a thousand of my ships any time she said the word. In
fact, I found myself falling in love, like a P. G. Wodehouse
character, with all the women on television—safety in numbers,
indeed—and with womanliness itself.

At the first several AA meetings they'd marched us into at
Happy Valley I'd noted that the speaker seemed invariably to
have divorced his wife early on in recovery, almost as if it were
part of the program. And I'd assumed each time that he'd done
so solely because the old lady reminded him too much of booze,
either because she'd been for it or against it (spouses can't win).
But now I saw that an ungovernable surge of libido might have
something to do with it too. Happy Valley had actually encouraged us to be selfish in our blind pursuit of sobriety, so *that* was
taken care of. If a new girlfriend helps to get your mind off alcohol, go for it—once you're sure it's safe for *you* to and you
won't start *you* drinking again. Infidelity in the cause of sobriety
was no crime. Conscience was for healthy people, not for weak-
lings like us.

I'm sure if Happy Valley was a real place, it would protest
hotly that it didn't mean it that way, but in the moral vacuum our
counselors had set up around the message there were no two ways
about it. So long as we didn't drink and WENT TO MEET-
INGS, they didn't care what we did with ourselves—which was
all the encouragement our self-indulgent characters required.

Or would have in my case, if my Higher Power hadn't had
more than one string to His bow. My problem was that, outside

of my precancerous tongue, which I now believe a genuine diseased alcoholic would have sailed right past (the evidence connecting cancer and booze is slender and quite ignorable), I could think of no better motive for abstinence than the universal fact that drunks are a pest, and a disgrace to their families. If that was really the way I was heading, my first grandchild, who was on his way to being born that very summer, would grow up to remember me someday as Grandfather the Drunk, "the death of the party," and avoiding this at all costs was, let's just say, the form my selfishness took.

And the same went for leaving the wife who put up with you when drunk and deserves something a lot better now than being abandoned.* Drying out may be a heroic feat, but it doesn't automatically entitle you to a trophy wife.

Nevertheless, you're likely to want one like crazy, and it surprises me that in its selective high-mindedness, AA makes so little use of this most potent of sales pitches. Although sex can apparently be used to sell everything under the sun from automobiles to insecticides, it is seldom if ever used to sell sobriety, where for once it actually applies. People often get high for the sake of sex, but they should be warned in advance that, whatever drug they use, diminishing returns will set in ridiculously soon. There isn't a habitual drunk or junkie in the world who can match the performance of an average sober citizen who started with the same equipment, and many cannot compete at all after a while. Which, since sex is pretty good to begin with, makes the brief enhancements of drugs a losing proposition indeed, a sucker bet. There are probably good arguments against a TV campaign featuring recovered addicts making out like bandits, but if it just showed active addicts striking out miserably with the sex of their choice, it might do wonders.

At least among the younger set. Some older addicts get beaten down so low that their libido seems well and truly beyond repair anyway— so what's the use of quitting? they ask hopefully. But

* If she's a degenerate drunk herself, bets are off: you can't help her much if you're in the gutter with her, so kindness and selfishness may both dictate separation, if only to allow your partner in booze to hit bottom and start rebounding, if she's going to. And there endeth the sum of my advice.

they're letting themselves off the hook too lightly. There's a lot more to a libido than getting laid. For instance, at the very last AA meeting I ever attended, six long years ago, one of the speakers decided to digress a moment onto the general subject of spring: for the first time in months, it seemed, he'd been able to get in a good day's work on his garden and the sonofabitch was really beginning to shape up, you know? By chance, the next speaker had had the exact same experience and the next and the one after, until this whole roomful of barflies seemed to hum with excited talk of hollyhocks and nasturtiums, and whatever it is that gardeners talk about. And meanwhile the sun streamed in and a breeze that smelled of every flower in the catalogue, and booze suddenly seemed a million miles away.

If this wasn't sex, it was the next best thing, a dazzling display of libido, considering the age of the speakers. And with this canticle of canticles still ringing in my ears, I bade a final good-bye to the Program (several times I had stopped at the door like an eavesdropper, but I'd finally run out of excuses. You can't go to AA meetings *just* to be entertained.); it would never get any better than this for my graduation day. By now I *knew* these people and their backgrounds in morbid detail and knew also that several of them had come within a whisker of being the rural equivalent of Bowery bums, quite beyond human reach. Yet here they all were, unprompted and unrehearsed, reciting one by one their sheer joy at being alive, as if the Paraclete had just flown in the window. I hadn't been in a bar that felt that good in twenty years.

And that to my mind was libido, the stuff that makes certain teenagers write poetry as compulsively as they fall in love, and was causing me right now to make eyes at my coffeepot and marvel at the consistency with which a steam kettle pauses before whistling. The joys of domesticity seemed to suit my temperament peculiarly well, considering that I hadn't even suspected their existence a year ago. And if they ever palled, a million years or so hence, there was always the smell of the hardware store downtown, surely the most reassuring smell in the world, and the infinite fascinations of the five-and-dime; and beyond the village, trees and plants everywhere that I'd like to learn the names of someday—and, in short, the concept "dull" had been suspended indefinitely. Things were interesting just for existing, and if they didn't exist, that was interesting too. My temperate parents once told me that they didn't know the meaning of the word *boring,* and I told them they'd been missing a treat; but obviously, I had too.

It was, as the song says, "almost like being in love," and you don't have to be a Freudian to call it a sexy feeling: it was, in fact, the same sense of *latent,* potential sex I remembered from my Catholic boyhood, as one came to the end of an abstinent Lent and boom! it was Easter and suddenly there were so many buds popping out of nowhere that you half expected to wake up some morning with a bed of crocuses growing in your armpit. This is the kind of "sexy" that makes some priests and holy people so preternaturally happy but is so close to sex itself that it can explode all over the place if one is a little less than holy. Sometime around then, I read the collected letters of that fitful Christian John Cheever, and found him on one page writing a quite sublime account of the joys of grocery shopping as he rides his pink cloud through it, while in others he is testifying to an almighty surge of sexual activity limited only by the absence of a third sex. (It was my impression from a slight acquaintance that what Cheever really wanted was to make love to everything in the world individually and collectively in an unparalleled display of pan-randyness. Never was such an itch combined with so much genuine love.)

Anyhow, I knew just how he felt, and how everybody else felt too: I knew that the waitress's feet hurt and that the salesman on the phone was probably bored with his job but anxious about losing it, and that the garbageman had never thought it would come to this. But these were not tragedies—after depression there *are* no tragedies, just situations, stories, only a few of which are irremediably heartbreaking. In my endorphin maelstrom, I felt empathy with all the victims that were just then starting to flood the market, but along with that, much more curiosity than pity in most cases: let's see how he/she handles this one.

In this mood, I glanced through some of the advice columns in the papers, and was astonished to find that half of them seemed to recommend immediate therapy or counseling, of which I'd just had such a bellyful, to what sounded like perfectly normal people. What on earth did these folk need with therapy? Didn't they see how *interesting* their problems were? Granted that human life is incredibly complicated and difficult, anyone possessing one fifth of the strength I felt now simply from not being depressed (it wasn't new strength, just old strength realized) should be able to take on most of it without recourse to the doctor. So tell your readers to go dancing, overeat at least once, or buy a book about Napoleon (*not* a about self-help, or self-anything. Tell them to forget themselves for five minutes. The air outside is wonderful). But don't advise therapy.

Yet not only did the counselors advise therapy—they even suggested a sickness to justify it. "You may be depressed and not even know it," they murmured, thus casually opening up a vast new market for themselves and their colleagues. "Are they kidding?" I almost screamed with rage in my happiness. "Not *know* it? Are you *crazy*?" One of the few virtues of depression is its uncompromising honesty: it leaves you in no doubt whatsoever about what it is, and what it is *never* to be confused with is mere sadness, melancholy, or regular household angst, any of which can be put to use for you right away in songs, poetry, and the sheer joy of moaning low and driving everyone else crazy.

By introducing a note of panic into what Freud called normal human unhappiness, the newspaper swamis could well be tampering with people's circulation and inhibiting their growth. Anyone who's had dealings with the clinically depressed knows that they are not just a little sadder than the rest of us: a new element is involved, a sterility, a small death.* Depression produces nothing, no songs, no poetry, no life, and is good for nothing until it leaves. After which, as I was learning, a million flowers may just bloom.

Meanwhile, outside the house, my worst fears seemed to be

* This is the view from recovery, and is perhaps a little too stark. Obviously if clinical depression is caused by, let's say, a serotonin imbalance, then lesser imbalances might cause lesser depressions. But one devoutly hopes that the relevant science someday becomes exact enough to obviate the gloomy self-diagnoses denounced above.

coming true. If not exactly pink and shiny yet, I had become unmistakably gregarious, smiling unwittingly at strangers (at least, I guess I was smiling because a lot of them smiled back, and an abnormal number went so far as to say "Hi") and exchanging meaningless small talk with anyone who would listen. I only realized the depth of my decline when I noticed that bores were hanging up on *me* now, and avoiding my eye in the street. But who cared? I was so sunk in sin that I couldn't even see anything wrong with acting like a one-man fraternal organization, a Babbitt for our times, a Bubba of the North.

It wasn't all hearts and flowers, however. I remember driving one day into a gas station in the Bronx, demanding attention for something or other—I have no idea what. What I do recall is everything melting before me as in a dream, with every last service station roustabout, down to the most sullen, hopping to, and practically curtseying, as he scurried to meet my whims. The habitual slow motion of these places had turned to ragtime, and I reveled in an exuberance of anger that I wouldn't have suspected was in my nature, along with a fussiness that wasn't there before either. If I lived long enough, maybe I could sit in a director's chair someday demanding millions of retakes, or march into stockholders' meetings and turn great companies upside down with my impassioned nit-picking.

And when it wasn't exaggerated anger or extravagant serenity, it was laughter, the wilder and sillier the better. I understood perfectly the flights of manic humor that seemed to sweep through certain Jewish friends from time to time—the so-and-so's didn't drink! Anyone can be funny, anyone can be clever, if he's going to stoop to being *sober*. Conversation seemed almost unfair in this condition: I could think of two or three possible comebacks to anything that was said, and call my agent about which one to use, in less time than it took Errol Flynn to switch swords from hand to hand. To think that I'd been afraid that sobriety would sap my powers as a writer. Good grief, sobriety was fairly flooding the switchboard with similes, word associations, and *mots justes,* all tumbling over each other to get into the sundry pieces I seemed to agree to write every time the phone rang.

Maybe it takes sleeping pills as well as booze to produce this condition, and believe me, it isn't worth it, but I was for the moment legally drunk on lucidity and self-satisfaction. And drunk is the only word for it. I remember shaving one day and thinking what a totally splendid fellow I was, to be sure—or not so much thinking it as experiencing the thoughts passing through me. Anyone who has ever observed a wimp in a saloon gradually deciding that he is possibly the greatest man who ever lived will recognize the phenomenon. If the wimp has one ancestor whose name is remembered for anything, you'll hear about it in triplicate (though why people expect so much from their ancestors when they've already *met* their relatives is beyond me); ditto if he's spent one night to remember in Paris or lurked on the fringe of one famous battle.

This is the part of the drunken dream in which only good things happen, the guy pursuing you breaks a leg and you can speak perfect Chinese, but never fear, the bad part will be along shortly—for the drunk, but not for me. Although I had the considerable advantage of knowing that the self-satisfaction was all balderdash, the flip side of recent miseries, the grandeur hung on anyway for days like a punch-drunk sycophant quite impervious to reason. "But you *are* a prince among men, you *do* know that, don't you?" Let him be. It's a pleasing sort of nonsense, and you've certainly got some pleasure coming.

So how about that speech on April 18? Incredibly, only three days had passed since that worst of days in the kitchen, and here I was, on my way to Connecticut to give my speech, and I wish I had lined up a year's worth of them in that incredible month, because as we flew up, I found myself, for the first (and last) time ever, absolutely on fire to get up on a platform and start swinging. So where was my famous stage fright, the conviction that words would fail me and I'd wind up opening and shutting my mouth soundlessly like a goldfish? Where was that, pray tell? And what about the fear of nameless embarrassment, unforeseen disaster, and permanent disgrace? Nowhere to be seen. In fact, I wasn't even worried about the sudden onset of coprolalia, the burst of obscure Latin obscenities and the emergency exorcism.

Let me at them, was all I could say to my lifelong phobias. The student body, as I waded regally through it, looked like the most intelligent collection of kids ever assembled, and I only wished that there were more of them, thousands, millions more. Because today was the day I got even with my stage fright, and began my fabulous new career as a lecturer—between landmark movies, that is, and company takeovers. I guess there are some people who feel this way all the time, and I'm glad to have been let in on their secret. Total chemical mastery.

Although I'd brought a prepared speech, I jettisoned half of it as I went along, and made fun of the other half. What was the point of having wings if not to wing it? Behind the ad libs were more ad libs, and in front of me was an audience of old, dear friends who had picked up the spirit and seemed to be laughing in anticipation of jokes I hadn't even thought of yet. When it came time for questions, I felt as if I was fielding the things behind my back and returning the answers between my legs. Why hadn't anyone told me this was so easy?

One question did stump me, though, for just a second. A woman asked me why a fine-looking fellow like myself had allowed such a dreadful picture to be used on my last book jacket, and I was tongue-tied with memories as the last horrible months seemed to regurgitate themselves like garbage coming up through the drain. So I simply asked myself how Dorian Gray would have handled this and decided he would have said, as I did now, "I must have been having a bad day."

The truth is, though, that when that jacket photo was taken, it had seemed quite flattering and absolutely the best that could be done with me. Now it survived as graphic evidence of how far I'd come, the perfect "before" picture to go with the "after" picture of scrawniness and bounce that appeared in the local paper the next day. I had lost a ton of gray flab from the distillery that once was my system, and had not yet converted it to pink flab with applications of ice cream, the great equalizer.

But it wasn't just the picture—that whole day could have been corked up and used as evidence. The pink cloud, which I'd been warned to be on guard against—not *quite* without reason, as we'll see—is also the best proof there is that sobering up is worth it. The next time Happy Valley sees the likes of me coming, it should be advised that this, the argument from happiness, is the big one, the clincher, as far as us hedonists are concerned. You can only get so much mileage out of wringing your hands over the past; in my own case, the good memories so outnumber the bad that the hands soon cease to wring anyhow and start to applaud. I had a *great* time drinking.

But this was great too, and it was positively the best I could do from now on. The other party was over, this one was just beginning. And this one was better, so far, because it never seemed to end.

After the speech I felt a little deflated—the first hint of a problem that would later mushroom into a major nuisance. To wit, as I walked past the bar abutting my hotel lobby, I realized with a plangent pang that I would never go into one of those again and casually order a scotch or a break-the-bank martini. Drinking had always been preeminently the way you made good times better, the way you kept them going. But what did I do with good times now—just sit and stare at them? Tell myself how really good they were?

It passed, pushed out by the next surge of happiness—surges that could get so strong at times that I recall one morning a few days later lying in bed feeling so happy that my head began to hurt and I realized I wasn't enjoying this anymore, but couldn't find the switch that turned it down. Whether most people have such susceptible generators to cope with, I don't know. Although everyone who's been on depressants has a pink cloud somewhere in his system all ready to roll if he ever dries out, these clouds seem to come in all sizes, and I can't guarantee everyone a jumbo, large-family-size one like mine. But then, the bigger they come, the harder you fall off them.

Looking back, I judge the ecstasy or high fever to have lasted not much more than ten days or so, to be followed by a more manageable serenity; but that may be because my orgy was interrupted somewhat artificially, and in a way that may actually have said more about my drinking and pilling adventures than all the omniscient generalities of Happy Valley rolled into one.

In brief: that April we received an unusual number of interesting invitations in Manhattan, all of which I pounced on greedily. And when I got there, I found, as I had barely dared to hope, that the joys of lucidity more than made up for the pleasure of having a glass in my hand, especially by the third party in the same evening, by which time I could easily win all the arguments and remember all the lyrics as well. I also found to my huge relief and mixed dismay that my character hadn't improved at all: I still wanted the most of everything that was going.

Between festivities, I noticed something else—that I was leaving some blood behind in the toilet every time I used it—quite a lot of blood, in fact. But we'd be returning to the country in a few days, where I could check into the hospital and find out what was what, *without missing anything*. Meanwhile, I took some antidiarrhea medicine, with the vague thought that it might stop up *every*thing for a while, and continued to revel.

Well, it wasn't as if I felt the least bit sick. In fact, I felt quite wonderful as my wife and I headed into our last giddy round. The final event was a PEN club blowout, and a record of my spectral presence at it remains in the form of some snapshots taken by the late Jerzy Kosinski, himself soon destined to enter the shadows—or perhaps he was already in them—but very chatty and incandescent that night. My own appearance in Jerzy's pictures is quite skeletal in a cheerful and, as it's easy to see now, acutely anemic kind of way. Later in the evening, I would almost faint in the men's room and have to sit there gathering strength before tottering back to my table—but I still felt marvelous, and had another sip of wine, which I'd found to my relief I could do without complications (wine tasted awfully chemical though, dangerous but not particularly charming, and it was no hardship to stop at one).*

What's more, I felt marvelous all night, and the next morning too. In fact, I insisted on doing the driving back to the country and probably even sang as I drove, that being the form my happiness takes, if the company can stand it. All of which sug-

---

* If this sounds too blithe to be true, that's how it is with pink clouds, and why they warn one against them: real alcoholics think they can walk on water, too. But since Happy Valley had been wrong about everything else in my case, and since I've never tried giving up booze before, I had to find out how much space I had to move in. No doubt my counselor still expects me to come to grief on my ninetieth birthday.

gests that when your endorphins are pumped to the max, they can perform without any backup at all, because after waiting an unusually long time for lunch in our usual watering hole, I finally fainted for sure, and came to in a hospital bed with tubes sticking out of everywhere and a strong suspicion that I might be legally dead.

The good news was that I had at least licked my blood pressure problems, because I didn't *have* any blood pressure now, or pulse either, to speak of. The bad news was that I had bled halfway to death.

In my favorite apocryphal story about anybody, Sigmund Freud overhears a bunch of his colleagues vainly trying to analyze some hard case or other, and finally breaks in to say, "Gentlemen, you forget—this boy has a rotten character." That was me all over. If the hospital had asked me, on one of its innumerable forms, what would you like on your tombstone?, I had the answer ready for them: "Here lies one party too many." Somewhere among my ancestors, whom I picture as alternately the noblest and shabbiest of specimens, jostled together higgledy-piggledy like the slums and skyscrapers of New York, lurked a regular Elsa Maxwell, someone who liked parties and their potential for surprise so much that he or she didn't even need a drink to enjoy them.

Anyway, here I lay, at least half dead, the *reductio ad absurdum* of party animals, and still uncannily pleased with life, like one of those superwatches that tells perfect time at the bottom of lakes. At one point, to my surprise, I wept, but I hastened to assure onlookers that I did so out of sheer physical weakness. It seemed important that this should be made clear. Depression had not returned. Far from it. They said, "Poor you" and "Some people have all the bad luck," but they were quite wrong. This could not have come at a better time. It even gave me a chance to race through the part of "perfect patient" again, to my own amusement. (I doubt anyone else noticed.)

Intestinal complications are surely the messiest of health scenarios, and no doubt the most unrewarding to read about too, even for sickness buffs. So I'll slide past the details, except to note that for the next three days, I experienced the maximum, first of discomfort, then pain (I can never again see a bicycle tire being pumped without flinching), and then acute discomfort once again, until I'd had enough of each to know that the worst that can happen to you physically does not come up to the knees of mental suffering. And yet, and yet—if offered a choice of one more day of either, I'm still not sure which I'd choose.

At any rate, physical pain leaves you with your wits about you, and I remember my sporadic pleasure at watching spring continue to assemble outside the window, and my intermittent glee as my young doctor insisted that he *never* caused pain ("What kind of doctor do you take me for?") but only "slight discomfort"—for which he prescribed massive doses of Demerol, which, in turn, Happy Valley had conditioned me to reject, to my blinding "discomfort." This doctor never did find out where the blood was coming from, because the flow stopped just like that before he could trace it to its source. So he called it "diverticulosis," as if he knew all about it, and forbade me to eat strawberries and corn on the cob for the rest of my life. No more wine, no more strawberries. Why was this man laughing?

One last thing that sticks in my mind from my fling with hospital life was my bizarre pleasure, in that setting, at watching a fashion show on television. The models in their bright dresses seemed not only the antithesis of the emergency room, but also of AA with its shabby windbreakers and faded blue jeans, and beyond that of what I realized to be the ultimate low point in human history: England in 1946.

Other people may return to Manderley in their dreams, but for me the trysting place is more likely to be a Carmelite church in Knightsbridge, where all the women seem to be dressed in the same mustard coat with their perms concealed in the same faded bandanna, and underneath both—one knows with a horrible certainty—the frock they've been wearing since 1939 and washing since then, too, to a limp, universal off gray. To complete the ensemble, lisle stockings sag despairingly into sensible shoes, which are worn down either on the right side or the left, the fun being to guess which. Meanwhile, for music, everyone, everywhere is either coughing or trying strenuously not to—sniffing, gurgling, and muttering "Oh dear, oh dear" before, as a posi-

tively last resort, fishing the ancient handkerchief out of the
shapeless handbag to blow the whole mess into and clear the
decks for another round.

So imagine the pleasure of finding oneself awake and magically transported to a runway seat in Milan or someplace to
watch beautiful models sashaying past in bright autumn prints,
flipping a hip and twirling round so that their skirts flare out,
prior to sashaying back where they came from. As I lay there
with tubes carrying unknown substances in and out of me, I felt
as if color had just returned to the world, after the longest
winter in history—although I suppose it had really only returned to my Ativan-coated eyeballs.

After the fashion show came a televised visit to some great
castle or other, and that was gorgeous too, in this case not so
much for color as for sharpness and nobility of line, as if my
eyeballs had been missing out on edges too. You can only judge
how far down you've been from the height of the bounce afterwards, and I must have been down all the way to China because
I was now up on a level I hadn't been near since a time twenty-
five years before when my family and I had driven from An-
dalusia and a winter of unrelieved black on white, on up through
various intermediate hues, as Spain tried grimly to lighten up,
and finally into the bright watercolor splashes of southern
France.

My elation back then as we swept into that bower of light,
and my glee right now over Signor Muchobello's fall collection
a generation later, had it in common that they had both been
most thoroughly prepared for, as Lent prepares one for Easter,
and yet both came as complete surprises, which is the difference
between real pleasure and the kind you can order anytime you
like from the waiter.

Lifelong drinkers can have a baffling time of it adjusting their
minds and tempos to the caprices of natural happiness, which
commonly misses appointments and shows up the next day,
skips weddings and looks in on funerals, where I once got the
giggles over the choice of music and had to squeeze my jaws
shut in order to appear solemn. Happiness is the ultimate practical joker. A bunch of friends get together to have fun, and

nothing happens. One of them goes home, looks at the cat, and bursts out laughing.

Despite its reputation for anarchy, alcohol actually keeps your emotions severely in line, so you can have them precisely when you want them ("You don't expect me to tell that joke *sober*, do you?"). When I was fifteen, I remember gazing at the lakes of Killarney and thinking, okay, so this is beautiful—why don't I feel anything? And what can I do to *make* myself feel something? A few years later, I would know: a glass of wine, or even the prospect of a glass of wine, can do wonders for scenery, while a nip of Wild Turkey bourbon can send it over the moon. Wild Turkey is so good it should hang in a gallery.

"Good ale does more than Milton can / to justify God's ways to man" as A. E. Housman said. But what do you do when your ale is taken away? Obviously I'd been worrying about this much too much. The lesson I should have learned in Killarney that day, and what every kid should memorize before he takes his first drink or drug, was that while a sober person can't feel good on demand the way a drunk can, the pleasure, when it does come, rings truer and has much more *to* it than drunken happiness. At *seventeen*, for instance, I was poleaxed by the Roman Forum, and I can't imagine even Wild Turkey adding anything to the shivering excitement except a coat of sentimentality and vague well-being. "Isn't this great? Boy, this is really *great*." Thus speaks the drunk at Niagara, the Taj Mahal, *Rocky V*, or his high school reunion. It's all great, just great, in ever-diminishing intensities, so that by the end of the trail, his highest high cannot compete with normal happiness, let alone with the explosions of joy you get when all the endorphins kick in at once. Imagine that you have been gradually dimming all the lights in the house, for the charm of it, until you can barely see, and then turning them back on in force, and you've got it.

But the glare has its harsh side as well, which you notice after a while, when you want to turn it off and get some rest, and this is why the Happy Valleys of this world are not entirely wrong to warn against the pink cloud. The pleasure game is all about contrasts, and where any addict may be overjoyed just to feel normal again for a few minutes, a pink clouder is outraged *merely* to feel normal. Is this it? Does the ride really end here, in the same poky neighborhood you escaped from in the first place?

Shortly after I got out of the hospital, I noticed that life seemed to be getting just a little bit flatter in the same way you notice the days getting gradually shorter in winter. I still felt good, yes, on the whole—but good for what, precisely? Where do you go with this thing? I felt *latent* with happiness, as if I needed something else to clinch it: I itched, the way an amputee must itch, for my old habits. Or some new ones. Or *something*.

At this point, I suppose, the incorrigible addict starts tying his sheets together with a view to escaping all over again—and maybe enjoying another ride back on the pink cloud. But fortunately for him, AA is full of people who've tried this already, who have been through the whole cycle twice, sobering up completely and becoming drunks all over again, and the second recovery is absolute murder. So if horrible examples can do anything for him at all, he'll be wise to decide at this point that it's better to wait for the slight boredom to pass, and for the pink cloud to reassert itself.

But what do you do when the boredom, *angst,* terror keep getting *worse*? Right now, everything seemed to be running faster and faster in that direction, until by the end of seven weeks or so, I began to experience something much worse than flatness—in fact, I would have given anything to feel flat again. But before the very worst came, I began to feel *moldy,* a condition that probably deserves a few words, though I'm not sure what they might be. ("What does 'moldy' mean?" asked my wife. I don't *know,* but it's what I felt.) At first I blamed it on the alien corpuscles I'd received in the hospital, which now outnumbered my original supply and presumably outvoted it. But the donors must have been strange people indeed to lead me through such a number as the band began to play next.

So was I about to lose my pink cloud forever? It certainly felt that way. The descent felt *decisive,* the way gravity feels decisive. This must be the make-or-break point for addicts, and thank God I wasn't that tempted by either booze or pills because I knew just how they felt otherwise. At this point, I believe a mirage must appear to them, an alternative pink cloud, which Dostoevski (who seems to have been *every*where first, like Kilroy in World War II), as usual describes best, although he wasn't actually talking about drugs at the time. In *The Brothers Karamazov* Alyosha has a vision of the world's peasants dragging themselves painfully around the diameter of the globe in the inevitable chains just to catch a split-second glimpse of the Beatific Vision, the Face of God; after which, they consider the exchange so well worthwhile that they start on another round.

No wonder AA pleads with its children not to "project." Optimism and memory combined can be so seductive that, even when you're onto their game, they can *still* lead you astray, if there's nothing else doing. What's so bathetic about the Beatific Vision of drugs is that, as the addicts reach for their chains again, they know it's a hoax and that every round trip brings a little less God and a little more pain, *ad infinitum.* But even the dim memory of God and of living in hope is better than this unearthly flatness, this sense of having crashed from your cloud and been abandoned forever—because, as I was now discovering, they don't lower a ladder for you to let you down gently from your pink cloud, but push you off rudely at the last moment and leave you there for the crows.

For a while, I remember, I had buoyantly told people who asked how I felt that it was like California weather—just one damned perfect day after another. But then, it wasn't quite perfect anymore, and I would, without warning, experience a peculiar sense of having a funny taste in my head, at first mildly but later overwhelmingly, along with its psychological analog—a sense of not quite belonging here, of being an isolated cluster of nerve ends left in a parking lot on the dark side of the moon, and quite at my wit's end about how to get through the next few hours, which were typically afternoon ones, between the drinks I hadn't had at lunch and the several more I wouldn't have before dinner. (After dinner I was usually home free.)

It would pass, and euphoria would return, shaky and slightly diminished. But meanwhile, the scene shifters were at work in the background, starting in late May and early June, setting the stage for the next act. And from what I could sense of it, we were going to try another tragedy, a long one this time, like the uncut version of *Long Day's Journey into Night*.

But what I wanted more than anything in the world by now was still the same thing, namely, to be told precisely what was going on and what, for God's sake, to expect next. In fact, what was going on was that I was almost exactly halfway through the course, my hazing, which meant I had only to hold my breath for another six months and my troubles were over. Yet, without this knowledge, I might have dropped out at any time. And missed the best party of my life.

8.

Down Again, Up for Good

Once again, the agent and herald of change was my tongue, a weird little object if you think about it for any length of time, but then aren't they all? During the recent intestinal unpleasantness, when I nearly bled to death, I'd been offered two startlingly different views of my less conspicuous organs: a Jules Verne *Journey to the Center of the Earth* series of quickies through the colonoscope, as we careened through the blackness of my own lower intestine with lights flashing, and a more detached, Jacques Cousteau type of survey, courtesy of barium meals and enemas, of the whole jivey ensemble, featuring the stolid peristalsis working away quietly alongside various unidentified pistons to keep the show on the road even as I sat there; while never to be ignored, the foppish appendix waved about menacingly to the lower left (my right), eternally in search of a role. Who knows, if Walt Disney had ever made a movie of this scene, kidneys and adenoids might seem almost as lovable as dolphins and baby elephants, and maybe, if they couldn't get Peter O'Toole, I could get to do the voice-over for an appendix someday.

Although the tongue didn't quite make it into either picture, my view of it was altered forever by what I'd seen of its colleagues. The tongue would henceforth no longer seem merely the megaphone and public relations office of my soul, but a piece of immensely vulnerable machinery, right out there on the firing line. If one thought the appendix lived dangerously, consider this baby, perched at the very crossroads of my universe and exposed to everything that came my way (thank God I wasn't worried about my eyeballs as well: the risks those guys run are in the Indiana Jones class).

Thoughts like these can actually seem quite charming on a sunny day, but terrifying when the weather turns. The first time I went to the cancer hospital, I was intrigued that the doctor spent most of his time peering down my throat, where, he explained, most of the tongue lurked in a nether world, far removed from the sunshine of one's mouth. "I'm looking at your voice box," he said casually, introducing an element that I'd never connected with my case—wasn't the voice box miles away from here?—"and everything seems to be shipshape." Swell, okay, nice to meet you, Doc, can I go now and let's hope I don't have a parking ticket, were my somewhat inadequate responses to this ominous development. (So what else is new, besides the end of the world?) It would take a while for the news to meet and merge with the malaise of afternoon. The only thing that bothered me so far was a sore spot at the side of my tongue that the doctor said over the phone probably came from biting it and was nothing to worry about. Since the sore also seemed to come from my occasional sips of wine, I gave those up (they weren't that great) and proceeded not to worry. But worry is ultimately a matter of disposition, and it was just a question of time before the encroaching moldiness and the strange taste in my head lit upon this promising material on their rounds and detonated it.

As usual, the warning I got was minimal and alarmed me without preparing me. Picture a perfect Saturday lunch on a friend's sunny deck, followed by a cocktail party which was okay too, but something was going wrong here, very wrong— and then a night spent in a misery of suspense, as if my bed had been wheeled into a waiting room on some unspecified charge—a Franz Kafka waiting room, where the whole purpose was waiting, that's all they did there. (If the people in the room ever saw the doctor and found out what was wrong, they might stop worrying, and we can't take the chance.)

The next day, we had friends out from the city for lunch, and I remember a curious alternation of excitement, as a twist in the conversation revealed a possible new direction for a piece I was writing, and terror, as the meeting of panic and cancer got closer and closer, and the friends left, and it got closer still, until sometime toward morning it hit, and all the goblins that I thought had left my system for good with the last of my drugs came pouring back like clowns *returning* to a circus car. And I imagined the doctor I was going to see tomorrow taking an electric saw to my tongue, and slicing off first the part that talks, and next the part that eats, and finally, his eyes blazing by now, hacking the whole thing down to a nubbin, prior to releasing me back into life, where I suddenly find myself, in my waking dream, gesticulating wildly for help, but what help could there possibly be? Some people in the crowd smile and some stare straight ahead, but what difference does it make now? What can anyone do for a man without a tongue? And how would he go about asking for it?

And then, what will *tomorrow* be like for a man without a tongue? I gibbered with fear, and I was beneath fear, groveling fathoms below its surface and even below the place where tears start. God knows what kind of appearance I made the next day when I saw the real doctor and heard, between my own toneless whimpers, that I had indeed been biting my tongue, and that I really *needn't* have worried. The man gave me some ointment to ameliorate the problem and assured me that I still didn't have cancer, any more than I'd had it six months ago when I first read the biopsy and started on my adventures. I had, in short, abased myself over nothing.

In one sense, this episode was the end of a sequence as well as the beginning of one. Whatever else lay in store for me, I would never again experience *this*—the kind of abject terror in which you feel yourself simply no match for the elementary forces of life and would, on the whole, rather be dead, except that you're scared of that too. Some people are equipped for things like sickness and dying and some people are not, and you'd like to be excused immediately, though—please, Mister—not killed. (Sent to the nursery, maybe.)

I imagine many men have felt like this on the battlefield, and considered themselves cowards ever after, yet there is nothing as fixed as "cowardice" about it. Although I was certainly the last word in cowards that day, I had previously faced far worse without even a whisper of this kind of fear, and would face it again. Later in the book, I'll give an example of my usual cruising speed of cowardice—but words cannot express the difference between "post-tranquilizer-addiction" fear and other kinds, which is one of life and death. The bravest of souls voids himself on the way to the electric chair, when all hope is gone. But tranquilizers can suck the physical hope out of you too, and leave you just as empty as a condemned man. To describe the indescribable a little more precisely: the pills have ceased to work as shock absorbers, and your old ones are too rusty from disuse to help, and everything lands flush on your exposed nerves. Your emotional immune system is shot.

But it comes back better than ever, don't ask me how. One of the dividends you pick up later, if you hang on, is a sense of rude healthfulness and invulnerability. What can anyone do to you now? The worst has happened. The rest of your life is strictly on the house, a dividend. But first you have to wait while the longest freight train in history rattles slowly past.

Outside of a horrendous July Fourth weekend, that my interior chemistry apparently mistook for Halloween, and I sat up shaking and trying to read till dawn, I'm fuzzy about the dates. All I know is that I'd already seen and been reassured by the cancer doctor, but I *still* seemed to be descending, and would continue to for several more months. At the beginning of this second bout of depression, or "Son of Nightmare," I might get as many as two good days a week on which the pink-cloud phenomenon would play itself out in miniature; then one such day; and by midautumn next to none. At first, when a good one came, I thought "Okay, this is it, it's all over now. I'm cured." But later, I would learn not to get my hopes up so high but to see each reprieve as an isolated beacon in the fog, precious evidence that my nervous system might still be made to work again, if I lived long enough to see it.

Seeking *some* scientific grounds for hope as well, I asked around for a CAT scan of my head, only to be told that the machine couldn't record the finer points, the small print, of mental breakdown, and I also asked about biofeedback and anything anyone could think of, finally settling for some kind of test where they fasten things to your skull and record something or other—but naturally my appointment fell due on one of my best days and I could barely remember why I'd come here. A doctor a day keeps the symptoms away, and I *knew* they wouldn't find anything wrong this time—*tomorrow* was when I should have come, as Yogi might say.

Meanwhile, I hadn't heard quite the last of my cancer fears, which still simmered just below the boil. Once I got thrown for a loop because someone complimented me on losing weight. "I have *not*!" I shouted. (Cancer suspects live in terror of sudden weight losses.) More seriously, I got it into my head for God knows what reason that Doctor X. at the hospital had not been leveling with me about my condition but was sitting on worse news than he could bring himself to tell. X. seemed like a kindly sort of guy, and he might have taken one look at the pitiable wreck I imagined myself to be that day and decided "We can't tell this man the truth—now or ever. It would probably kill him," or whatever doctors say to themselves. But what could I do about it now? Call up X. and say, "Tell me the real truth, so long as it doesn't hurt too much. And try to make it *really* convincing this time"? What's the answer to a guy who won't accept good news and can't handle bad?

To find out, I called up my favorite other doctor, and he said, "Don't worry, he'll tell you when it's bad, all right," which I accepted, to my surprise, just like that. And then my friend most shrewdly added, "It sounds to me as if something else is bothering you, not this." And with that, the cancer bubble faded forever, leaving me with nothing to fear but reality itself, and with a nervous system that sometimes hurt so much I could cry, and did—not once but several times, quite willfully, like someone coughing to dislodge something from his throat, or angrily sobbing out the blues.

It didn't work. Nothing worked. So long as the nightmare was *in situ*, nothing could budge it, until its appointed time to leave—at which point nothing could have stopped it from budging. The tyranny of Mood was total, and shockingly new to me; for years now I'd been working my own thermostat, with a little drink here, and a little pill there—here a drink, there a pill, everywhere a drink-pill—but now I could only sit by helpless as forces outside myself played craps to decide exactly what sort of day I should have today, followed by just what sort of night.

By a not disagreeable irony, the one thing I could do really well now was sleep as deeply as my subconscious could burrow. Indeed, my dreams were sometimes so much pleasanter than my wakings that I would dearly have loved to take a pill and keep them going indefinitely (joke). But the aridities of dawn could not be kept at bay forever, and even before my eyes were open, I'd be desperately asking myself what they were sending me *this* time; and then, later on, if my Masters had relented and granted me a "good one," as we all devoutly wish each other every day around here, wondering how long it would last. I remember one quite sublime nine hours or so, complete with lunch by the sea, and a giddy drive home full of song, and nothing wrong so far, until later, while watching something on the VCR, I knew that *it* was back and the fun was over.

I suppose a shrink might want to know what I was watching, but this time it made no difference at all. Once or twice, especially during Nightmare I, movies had bothered me, not for reasons of theme, but because of some sight or sound that had added to my pre-existing confusion. The song "Blue Velvet," for instance, is not something that you want to hear over and over again in such a state, though the movie itself seemed quite innocuous, and the jumpy hilarity of *The Gods Must Be Crazy* seemed maliciously nerve-racking.

Obviously, sense impressions counted for more than subject matter, but why this one and not that one? The theme song of the show *Jeopardy* drove me nuts simply because it had seemed to be playing every minute of the day at Happy Valley, but why on earth did the parking lot outside one of our local supermarkets bring me out in a cold sweat? or the padded elevator in the local shrink's building? However it got there, the list of phobias would grow and grow in the coming months until my head felt like a private zoo. Certain houses began to look homicidally aggressive, they had an "attitude," while some kinds of cars had incurably stupid expressions; and vans across the board needed to lose weight. And on and on. But the worst was always that parking lot, which seemed like the abomination of desolation—I had to summon up all my nerve just to scoot quickly across it. Revisiting it today, I can find no trace of this fear, or clue to it. The place is *bland,* and I don't even know if *Jeopardy* still has a theme song, though I watch it regularly.

It may be typical of the early medieval state of study in this field that no one I talked to about this strange condition seemed to be able to come up with a better word for all this than *depression.* But if depression was the right word for what I had last time, as I sweated out the phenobarbital and fended off suicide, we needed a new one for this, because the one bad thing that this *wasn't* was suicidal—almost to my regret at times. "Would that the Almighty had not fixed his canon against self-slaughter," I would wake up muttering (incorrectly). Although the pressure might be every bit as intolerable as ever, it didn't take me in the direction of death. In fact, on one particularly tense day, when I was just about hanging on to the railings of sanity, I found myself contemplating Ernest Hemingway's suicide and thinking sternly, "I know how you felt, old sport, but you shouldn't have done it; you shouldn't have given in like that." Thus, the intolerance of the barely saved. Who knows what extra pressure may actually have forced poor Papa over the edge? All I knew was that I needed someone that day to lean against and compare myself favorably with, if *one* of us was going to survive. And God knows, Hemingway always liked a good contest.

Once again, it's maddeningly hard to describe the physical symptoms of a neurological ailment, except to say that I was aware at every minute of its physicality, of a body imposing itself on a mind and not just the other way round. But the closest this came to a specific sensation was a very vague sense that my head was clenching itself into a fist that couldn't be prised open by Hercules himself, while inside the fist lurked the purely mental equivalent of the same old foul taste and smell that covered everything. In this condition, I finished off a long piece about J. D. Salinger, thinking "I hope I can finish this before I go crazy." My head was clenched so tight that it felt dizzy, as if it wanted to throw up brains all over the page.

Was there a name for this? Not so far. But when the fist did open briefly, it would often as not release me downward into a kind of desolation that might indeed fairly be called depression. And this was the one mood the battery of shrinks I consulted in my comical search for information *could* talk about—it was a word they knew, one of their categories, and all the other stuff could be swept gratefully into it, the way my bleeding had once been swept into "diverticulosis."

Looking back on this period, nothing puzzles me more than my persistence with these worthy men, long after I realized they had nothing of consequence to tell me. As a child, albeit a sulky one, of our advice-mad society, I simply assumed that I wanted to talk to someone, and talk I did, to my increasing annoyance each time. "Now *you* say something!" I wanted to scream at these dummies, these cigar-store Indians. But when they did, it was usually so tentative and obvious that I wanted to go right on screaming: "Is *that* all you have to say for yourself, my good man?" Since I had already analyzed my situation at coruscating length, I don't really know what they *could* have added, except possibly some fresh physiological news, which they manifestly didn't have. "I believe people who dry out undergo severe chemical changes," I said to one of them, passing on the sum total of information I'd been able to glean. "Is that right?" he said. "I hadn't heard that."

The next one I talked to had heard about my chemical revolution, all right, but had no idea of what the chemicals were or what they were doing in there now that took so long. "We're pushing at the envelope of knowledge here," he would say in reference to this, and to all other scientific questions that came up, and to prove it, he supplied me, at my urgent request, with reams and reams of undigested findings, still in their original code of jargon, to show just where the envelope was these days.

He was an extreme case—and an interesting study in laziness for a connoisseur like myself. But the others, who really cared about their patients, ransacked the shelves for me in search of useful information, and couldn't come up with anything either. As at Happy Valley, everywhere you turned you got the same lecture on the evils of addiction and a list of approved ways— always the same ones—to combat addiction, "and if you have any other questions, don't hesitate to call."

So the impasse continued through the summer and into the fall, with me repeating over and over the stuff I had already said to myself *ad nauseam*, and the shrinks nodding away, waiting for me to cure myself, I supposed. "You're awfully hard on yourself," said one, and this was true. "I'm only talking like this because I wouldn't take it from anyone else," I told him. For all my blistering self-analysis, I remained as touchy about outside criticism as ever, because I at least half believed all of it, however far-fetched; and even if I didn't believe it, it still hurt. But Uncle Fergus, the old Scotsman in my head who, incidentally, hadn't stopped talking since Happy Valley, regularly flayed me alive for my sins and pretensions, and I didn't mind it that much; I was used to Uncle Fergus.

What puzzles me even more than my faith in witch doctors is the length of time it took me to realize that I didn't really want to talk about myself to *anyone* anymore; I'd *done* myself and was ready to move on, but couldn't. I was trapped in my own head, paper the walls of it as I might to make it look cheerful, until, as winter came on, I felt as if I'd never see the sun again.

The summer of 1988 had been a great time to get out of one's head for a few hours. There was a quite macabre election going on, which seemed almost as strange as I felt. To find a modern election being fought over the Pledge of Allegiance—that's entertainment. And when one wearied of this form of nonsense, there were the Olympics and a great pennant race in the National League East (i.e., the Mets won), and great play-offs and World Series too, and I felt a sense of loss as each of these ended, releasing a few more hours into the day to be filled somehow. I had never before considered the twenty-four-hour day a problem—but without a drink or a smoke it suddenly seemed to stretch forever, like a desert in the movies across which the hero must crawl all day, before starting over from scratch the next morning.

The only landmark remaining, now that the pre-lunch drink and the after-lunch cigar and the cocktail hour and the nightcap were all gone, was the clock itself. In this new demonology, the morning hours were the good guys, if there were going to be any at all today. Unlike most topers, I'd never had any quarrel with morning, as long as people kept their voices down. But the era of goodwill expired sometime between twelve-thirty and one-fifteen, to be replaced by the worst hours of the day, led by two P.M., which was the famous Afternoon Devil incarnate. After that three-fifteen wasn't bad, and six was surprisingly good. Seven-thirty was awful, and anything after ten was gravy. By then most of the middle-aged population had had its fun for the day and was deciding whether to stay up for Johnny Carson. *I wasn't missing anything.*

Stepping back to look at the big picture—*November* was now the enemy. The shortening of the days had begun to seem ominous as early as Labor Day, when we had some people over for drinks, and the fringe of the lawn turned dark and cold at least an hour before I'd expected, as if I'd only just noticed the change, and the guests began to leave early for the city, where the lights were always on. But now there was blackness over the face of Long Island, and my last companion of summer, the election, pulled out too, leaving a vacuum yawning all the way through the newspaper, from front page to back, and positively howling through my beloved sports pages.

In this condition, you soon learn to sort out which pleasures come with booze and which don't, and I was quite shocked to find my old friend football standing on the wrong side of the divide at first (by February, I would miss it to distraction as usual). I suppose I had counted on this sport to lead me gently into winter as it had as a child, but I hadn't taken in how much support it had been receiving lately from that fan of fans, John

Barleycorn. When the sky had gotten dark in recent years, it was no big deal, because off in the distance, toward the second half of the second game, glimmered the first golden drink of the evening, and winter would seem cozy and safe.

Now when you came to that point in the game, you would drop off a cliff instead, into the usual bottomless pit. A year later, I would learn that one's own vitality fills the pit to bursting, and I would find winter cozier than ever, a fascinating little season, in fact. But while the chemical moving men are still hurling things around, you can't even imagine this, and you may well suppose that alcohol is the only thing on earth that could rescue these moments and make the winter human again. Alcohol is the classic best friend turned worst enemy for denizens of the frozen north, and for what it was worth, I now had me a hell of an insight into Scandinavian drinking patterns. American ones too, come to think of it, because AA meetings take on a new urgency in the winter, as the members tramp in from the frosty battlefield, fresh from their latest skirmish with their former ally. Old Mr. Barleycorn still stands in the doorway of saloons and smiles and offers his hand before he tries to kill them, and in winter he offers them warmth and light too, which the meetings then have to try to match. The fact that they're at the meeting at all means that they've won one, and maybe they can suck up enough strength in the next hour to win another and add another day at a time to the string.

But there's always an edge of uncertainty as they step into the night, which makes the meetings exciting places to be in the winter and, incidentally, the perfect answer to the football second-half blues. These people are *about* something, and they don't waste time on small talk. Yet the talk is constant, as close in texture to the punctured hum of a good saloon as a bunch of old drunks can make it: which is to say, it is alternately boring beyond words and rivetingly interesting. Under the drone of booze-talk, which has its wearisome side, I heard more useful tips about life in general at these meetings than from all my shrinks laid end to end, because this stuff was hot from the furnace. There was no theory about it: you're fighting for your life, and this helps and that doesn't. King alcohol is waiting outside to reclaim your soul so you have to think fast and well. Until yesterday, booze had been these people's whole universe and through its infernal haze, real jobs, mates, children were still being lost and found; despair was wrestled with and hope was savored, and the most humdrum of episodes were relived again and again with a blinding intensity because *nothing* could be taken for granted anymore, everything had to be concentrated on. These people were *serious,* not in the sense of humorless but in the sense of absolutely no bullshit, not even, at times, the Higher Bullshit of the AA theorists. Compared with Happy Valley, it was like stepping off a plane in New York after a year in a rain forest.

The meetings also satisfied, as the shrinks could not, a contradictory state of mind that I imagine a lot of people experience in the Twilight Zone, to wit, one craves company and one can't stand company. At meetings, you are semi-invisible, so you don't have to worry about appearances—there is always someone in worse shape than you anyway. And yet you're not *just* an audience either, disconnected from the show. You get to put in your own two cents at some stage, and maybe somebody will pick it up and run with it or maybe not (none of the meetings I attended had as much interplay as I'd have expected, and some had none). By the end you feel as if you've actually done something today, and there aren't many things that can do that for you right now.

Certainly not in my own case, anyway. In the middle of September, I and two perfectly healthy colleagues lost our jobs at the book club, which is a story for another time perhaps. But I learned a couple of useful lessons from it, the first being that work, any work, is absolutely the best thing you can be doing right now—partly because it's probably the one thing you still *can* do well (since my phenobarb clearance, I'd had no trouble with it), and largely because leisure is so full of regrets and unhappy comparisons, while work hasn't changed that much, it was never that hot to begin with. Indeed, it may actually have become a lot better now that it has no competition.

The second lesson is that you might be advised to keep any pink clouds that come your way under your hat until you know what their plans are. Obviously, in my pink period, I looked quite recovered enough to be fired. Yet on the day I got the news, the cloud was someplace over Australia, and my head tasted worse than ever and the words I was hearing seemed *ugly* like hideous paintings set to John Cage music. For the next few days, the outside and inside of my head actually matched each other in unpleasantness, so there was nowhere to turn for relief. (Well—at least the outside world was registering this time— under phenobarbital I would barely have noticed I'd been fired, but might have killed myself anyway for the hell of it.)

Since I was still spinning downward, there is no need to assume cause and effect in what followed, but from that day on I was unable to write a publishable word for several interminable months, which meant, as far as I then knew, forever. No sooner would I launch into a dependent clause than my head would clench and fog up and I'd have to take another day off before the frustration became unbearable.

After taking a week to write a full page for a prospective piece about (don't ask me why) women sports fans, I finally, to look on the bright side, had to abandon it, along with any further attempt to write for a living. I felt as if that whole part of my brain had been closed off indefinitely, and the work crew had gone home, and the only sign of life was the attack dogs guarding the site.

So I decided to keep a journal, the last refuge of the brain dead, in which I would simply write everything down without calculation, and maybe start the machine up that way. The result is a curious document, now that I can bring myself to read it—for two years, even the cover made me wince—dense with calculation and, like many historical documents, even less reliable than memory in many places. As a literal record, it is almost worthless because it is clearly an effort to (1) get my brain going again and (2) feel as good as I possibly can. It is an exercise book in the most literal sense, and at a certain point I give the game away completely by stating that confession doesn't seem to be good for my soul at all, but just makes everything worse. So obviously I was not going to try it myself, and I find the diary skipping blithely over miles of good swampland to perch in branches that can barely support my weight.

What's strange now as I look back on it is that for once, my usual practice of remembering good things better than bad is completely reversed, and the upbeat tone of the journal seems to me completely phony. Face the facts, you cowardly bugger, I say to it: but yet, as I turn the pages and my eyes get used to the light, I can see the bad parts all right, shining through the cover-up, so that reading the shabby old exercise book still shakes me to the foundations.

Although the diary's style is, to my eye and with my memories, no more convincing than the paint on a clown, it also surprises me with its quite genuine liveliness in places. Although the pen can hardly seem to drag itself across some of the pages, and presumably dropped from my hand at journey's end that day, it fairly skitters across others in an obvious attempt to lighten things up around here. If energy were all it took, I probably would have succeeded, too. Clearly the problem is the sheer *heaviness* and stillness of depression—but a clinically depressed man could not have written those pages at all.

Neurologically speaking, I had come a long way from the doldrums of phenobarbital, when I could scarcely hold a pencil straight, and was by now obviously bursting my britches to come further. But my unhappiness must have heated up too, because I distinctly remember lying in bed some mornings trembling uncontrollably, as if I were plugged into a live socket, and knowing that this *right here* was Hell, a word we don't use lightly in my tradition; it was simply not in Nature to feel worse than this, and I remember asking around frantically about shock therapy and hypnosis, and anything under the sun short of lobotomies and suicide—always short of suicide—to relieve this unbelievable pressure, which I report now, not in the interest of laying on the agony, but simply to demonstrate how dark it can get just before total dawn, and how hard the last minutes of labor can seem when you're delivering a devil. In my waking dreams I would occasionally imagine myself just a few feet away from a pearly pristine beach, from which the current would then viciously suck me away at the last moment, or else a huge wave would imperiously bar me, but I was so *close,* and maybe next time.

For want of any hard information from my experts, the pearly beach was the best I could do by way of a scientific estimate of my chances—that and another dream I had of marching up the steps of the local library chuckling (that's all—just chuckling, up the steps). Maybe. Sometime.

For a while, I also had hopes of my latest shrink, who believed that chemistry was the key to a great many psychic disturbances, and who energetically set to work determining the perfect pill, the dose made in heaven, for me. But for all his brave talk, it turned out that the science of cerebrochemistry, or whatever, was still at the twig-gathering stage. Since it seemed that Desyrel was still the only kind of antidepressant that didn't mime acute prostasis, and since I was already using it, we had pretty much exhausted the doctor's arsenal before we even got started, except for the wonder drug lithium, which he naturally put great stock in and which effectively put an abrupt end to my interest in this field.

Consulting my feel-good journal on the point, I find the lithium episode consigned to a hasty parenthesis, which means, I deduce, that it was obviously too big to ignore, but that one didn't want to dwell on it—and I remember exactly why. Lithium was a new experience in disasters, just in case I'd missed any, and even though, as usual, I never got beyond the side effects. My notion that this would be just another pill was quickly disabused, when I was told that I would need to have my heart tested in advance, and then at regular intervals, along with God knows what all—kidneys? blood count? I remember wheeling myself from department to department in the local hospital, trolling for tests. Obviously this lithium packed quite a wallop. Even though I had always associated the word itself with calmness and stability, it must use maximum force to achieve these effects, like a peacekeeping force that kills half the populace. And I braced myself for Armageddon, and one more undetermined sentence in Purgatory, before attaining Nirvana.

But this was ridiculous: not Armageddon at all, but more like the fun house at an amusement park. I felt dizzy and became aware of ship's engines rumbling under my feet, as if the earth had decided to up and go somewhere at last. Walking just a few feet was like lurching across a ship's deck in a Joseph Conrad typhoon. For a guy who needed two canes already, this was simply impossible—I had appointments to keep and motions to go through. On lithium, I not only couldn't walk straight—I couldn't even lie still in bed; my insomnia returned with a vengeance, and for the sake of a crucial lunch date, I even took a Librium, which wasn't as daring as it sounds—I'd long since thrown out all of my Happy Valley baggage—but was good for only about three hours of rest, after which the crazy status quo returned and lunch was like a bad meal at the captain's table when I should have stayed in my cabin.

So I dropped lithium before it could hit me again, and dropped the doctor too before he got *another* idea. If he had known anything at all about the chemical upheavals subsequent to sedation-addiction, he would simply have left well enough alone and talked, as I prefer my doctors to, about the Super Bowl, and spared me and my churning chemicals this last ferocious shake. At that point, I was a mere two months away from complete relief, and I believe now that I would have got there with or without assistance of any kind.

Not knowing that, I returned to my humble Desyrel pills and to the mysteries of cause and effect. I would take a pill and feel better, and I would take another and feel worse. If pills could talk, I'm sure they would have taken credit for the good stuff and washed their hands of the bad; "We tried; it would have been much worse without us." And the funny thing is, I still assumed they were right.

I also used this time to perfect my panic control, once again breaking it down into moments and not letting the moments coalesce. As noted earlier, panic jabs at you repeatedly, but it needs your help to string the jabs together into a major attack. This is not a magic formula—panic remains an intensely disagreeable experience. But I found it helps a lot if you regard it as a strictly physical phenomenon, with a natural time span. Don't worry about its psychological origins, or about whatever current problems you think may be causing the latest one. Just wait until your nerves have jangled to a halt—there's plenty of time to think about that other stuff later.

And don't think about it then either, just concentrate on feeling better. I went to a couple of Zen meetings with this in mind, but got the giggles when they began to chant—my fault, not theirs. Like AA meetings, Zen is not for every temperament, but the basic exercise of counting one's breaths continued to work occasionally, releasing me from my head and into clear air for precious minutes. Going to early-morning Mass, and watching the local small fry trying to stay on their best behavior, was soothing too, and the best medicine for me in particular, taking me back to a sweeter, prechemical time.

But it would be misleading to say that any of these things helps very much, except to pass the time. What a person in this plight really needs to know is simply that it *does* end, and probably soon if you're thinking this clearly about it. Almost the worst thing about a panic attack is fear of the next one and the one after that. And these fears can spill over and blight the interregnum as well, the truce between storms when you should be getting a little R&R. How can you enjoy this perfect day when you may wake up shaking and trembling tomorrow?

To which my working answer is a simile drawn from the game in season, football, where they give you credit for something called "forward progress." No matter how far the enemy pushes you back after they've landed on you, you are legally entitled to every yard you've gained so far. And rereading the journal, I see that this is much truer than it felt like, as I lay there in the mud with the world on top of me. Every inch you have gained really is yours now, and you will return to it shortly to resume your offensive from there.

What I did not know, of course, was even roughly where I *was* on the field, whether I was in my own end zone or near the other one. The next and last shrink I saw—as usual on the strongest possible recommendation from *someone*, I didn't think these guys up on my own—knew at least that there were real chemical changes going on, but he hadn't the foggiest idea how long they were supposed to last: two years, five, eight? Even when I was less than a month away from deliverance, we were still pondering this—as indeed were the friends I discussed it with at AA. As happens more often than it should, the people in the field didn't even know more about it than the professionals, because they hadn't really been listening to each other all that closely (to repeat—ex-drunks don't have to be told to be selfish: they have to have told not to, and to try gazing into someone *else's* pool for a change).

With no better estimates or grounds for hope than that, it seems to me no wonder that so many addicts go back to their comforters—why the hell shouldn't they? It can't be any worse than a lifetime of this. That Christmas, I was quite genuinely surprised to find myself actually tempted to have a drink, though what I meant by the word *tempted* I'm not quite sure. I didn't feel as if I needed a straitjacket or a guardian when I went to parties, or a safety lock on the liquor cabinet when I got home. I didn't miss the taste of booze, because I could barely remember it, and I didn't miss the effects either, because I hadn't yet ceased being bored by the idea of them and depressed by the memory (I'm bored still, come to think of it). What I missed was Christmas itself, the fun, the party. With my nose pressed to the windowpane, I could still see the magic of it: normal, shopworn people would come in, and take off their humdrum galoshes and sad-looking coats, and dip into the waters, and emerge a few minutes later barking with joy, louder and *louder* (the noise drinkers make came as a great shock) until it sounded like the city pound at feeding time. "How do you do it, old buddy? How in the world do you *do* it?" Somebody drapes a sympathetic arm over you—don't ask me how we got inside the house—and someone who doesn't know you hands you a glass, "Whoops, I'm sorry," and yanks it away again, spilling some on your sleeve. His breath smells awful, as does everyone else's—suddenly it's Christmas night at the skunk factory. Can anything that smells that bad really be worth all this fuss? Anyway, you pray as you've never prayed before that they won't start *singing,* or arguing, or telling jokes that last ten minutes and make no sense, and that the clock hands will start whirring around magically like in the movies, and it'll be time for everyone to leave.

Or else you can stay home and imagine the whole thing.

Or, as they might recommend at Happy Valley, you can go into your workshop and make a table or something.

Yet I was so close at this point that I wish I could simply reach through the mist now and hand my floundering self a note saying "Hang in there, old bean—40 days to go, the length of one good Lent. And—you won't believe this part—but next year you'll actually enjoy these things again, and be the last to leave, just like old times."

Physically speaking, things came to some kind of boil the night of December 27, which happens to be my birthday. I went to bed, well content, after dinner with my son and his wife, but found I couldn't sleep, which was okay with me. If you're not working, who needs sleep?

But insomnia was never just insomnia in those days, it always devolved into something worse, and never more so than that night. As my diary describes it, "my head was not preparing for sleep at all, but dizzy and light; I didn't feel bad, but I cried convulsively anyway and seemed to degenerate into a child. Desyrel kept me almost buoyant throughout, but my head wouldn't work: it was light and fogged in at the same time," and so on through the dreary night, the best hour of which was spent reading on the john, until, sometime around dawn, "I howled uncontrollably, then spoke calmly about it when [my wife] woke up. But the second time, could not control my speech, but said in a pinched way that I was in a bad way. The pill [I can't remember *what* pill] was necessary to keep my bones from flying apart."

Never has my body, which the Happy Valley brigade of shrinks had conspired to treat as a servant of my psyche and theirs, so imperiously called the tunes and written the arrangements for the whole ensemble. Earlier that day, I am startled to find, I had seen someone off at the airport and "felt exhilarated by the bustle . . . felt like playing on the escalators" (good grief!). So I was up someplace near the top of my arc when the bad stuff, the rebellious angels in one's nerves and blood, got to work to bring me down again. And by the time they'd finished hammering I could barely speak. What I delicately describe as a

pinched mouth was closer to an intermittent lockjaw that made
me sound like a beleaguered mouse in a Japanese cartoon.

Sometime during the night I decided to blame the whole thing
on some nonalcoholic beer (which is actually .o5 percent alcohol, and a subject of AA anathemas) I'd had for dinner that
night; and since the whole grim procedure was repeated on a
smaller scale two days later when I tried one more of these
innocuous imitations, I decided to have no more truck with
them, and this turned out to be a minor blessing, because it took
me one further step away from the very idea of alcohol, around
which neighborhood there is no special point in hanging. If
you've had a great romance with booze, there's nothing to be
gained by coming back for a good-night kiss; it's tough enough
that the *girl* won't leave town.

The next day records that I went to a party where one good
thing happened (using *good* in the Happy Valley sense of good
for ME) and one kind of dreary. The hostess, whose name would
astonish you, said what a pity it was I'd quit drinking because I
"was so good at it"—a compliment I would have treasured once
upon a time, but which was worthless at current exchange rates.
I was a "happy drinker," she added, rubbing it in all the way.

More encouraging, in a bleak, midwinter sort of way, was a
conversation I had later on in the evening with an old friend who
was halfway into the bag, and wondering why this kept happening to him. "I'm beginning to worry about it," he said and
told me he knew he should try to quit but was afraid of losing
his "cutting edge." "Old drunks don't have much cutting edge
either," I said, and he agreed that this was probably so—and
just like that, he seemed to give up all hope of keeping his
cutting edge, but went on drinking anyway.

After Christmas, the diary enters a garrulous phase as I pace my
cage faster and faster, shaking the bars and jabbering. On New
Year's Eve, "I drove past a police blockade, and prayed that
they would stop me. A breathalyzer would have made my year
. . . I felt the late night tranquillity that is my only pay-off." But
then, the next morning, I woke "feeling quite naked and un-
armed as if there's nothing between me and the enemy."

And so it would go through the rest of that last turbulent month in the outer boroughs of Hell. On January 3, it seems, I was "jumping out of my skin. Began, in fact, so jumping at four a.m. [and] my hand is [still] jumping with the only energy I have . . . can't concentrate or calm down enough to write," which is the terminus for pill takers; the nerves jangle like telephones in an empty office, but you're too tired to keep your eyes open.

"Jan. 4. I can't believe I felt that bad yesterday." This is a great harbinger: I'd finally had a day so good I couldn't imagine a bad one; but "Jan. 5. Overslept grievously, the joyless sleep of the depressed." "Jan. 7. If anger sees you out of depression, then I'm there."

To judge from these headlines, my fear that sobriety consisted of only one mood repeated ad nauseam was as far off the mark as a fear could be. I was now starting to hit extremes quite alien to the muted world of sedation, which tends to slur everything like the loud pedal in music, and on January 10 would find myself in a definitely staccato mode and abuzz "with a fearful frustration . . . I wanted to punch through a wall, lash a tennis ball, swing a cricket bat, use my goddamn body, which has been rendered inert by my gassy soul, and by circumstance." This past winter, five years later, I would witness a contortionist in Key West writhing and biting his way out of a straitjacket bound with chains, and know exactly how he felt. If he'd been a painting, I'd have called him "January 1989."

To meet at least a minimal need for physical expression (post-polio syndrome had eliminated the maximum ones), I asked the congregation at one of my AA meetings if anyone knew of a pool table around here, but I'd picked the wrong group: these guys were much too ethereal for that kind of talk. It is a widely held superstition that all AA meetings are equally valuable: AA is not a religion, and meetings are not masses, though many members regard them as such and are not noticeably discouraged from doing so (if it helps . . .). But the helplessly discriminating should be warned that, for instance, some groups understand the value of things like pool tables to a drowning man while others would say that shooting pool is just a Band-Aid for your real problems, and a regular no-pain, no-gain placebo to boot.

Right now, with the steam gathering in my head for the final breakout, I was losing patience with the lot of them, and the diary contains several pages of silent heckling as I argued my way back to health. I argued (to myself, always to myself) with the doctrine, and also with the members who were "niggling their way back to unhappiness," and between meetings, this fury would expand magnanimously to take in *all* the advice that rains in on you from every side once you admit to a weakness of any sort. It was like being surrounded by a hundred panting Saint Bernards, all of them carrying flasks full of hot air around their necks as you struggle to your feet. The whole country was suffering from a Polonius complex, with everyone taking turns receiving advice and dispensing it like a twenty-four-hour answering service.

And the recurrent theme of the advice was to go to *more AA meetings,* which had apparently captured the complete trust of people who'd never been within miles of a meeting themselves; and when you got to meetings, you were told to go to more meetings yet, the way you were once advised in the confessional that what you needed was to go to confession more often. I'm here *now! Tell* me something!!

So maybe the psychobabble was right about something at last. Depression really did seem to be anger turned inward, in which case, that January was the month that it all began to turn around for me, like the lining of a jacket, so that the anger faced the right way. Believing in AA obviously helps many alcoholics, and bless them, but criticizing it can be just the ticket for recovering depressives—a service I'm sure it wouldn't mind providing. After meetings I would go home and write reams, not just about AA but about all the psychological debris the chitchat there had shaken loose. I had found meetings, like church services, a great occasion to think about other things, *high-minded* other things.

Rereading the latter part of the diary, I come across days when I could swear from the tone that I must have been in high spirits, if the text didn't keep insisting otherwise. A typical entry begins, "Precarious, baby. Felt desolate in bed, frisky when I got up, and then back and forth till my neck got tired from following the ball." And even on days that start out singing the blues and nothing but the blues, the writing is likely to take off suddenly like a rocket, displaying every symptom of well-being except the thing itself. "The head remains muddled," I write, with a curious mix of grandiosity and chaos, pink cloud and gray. "So I am obliged to fall back on the crutch 'brilliance' with which one can hop anywhere; also I could use some coherence."

If, in short, I only had a brain. But at least I was trying. "I have been tempted at times to think lately that the kindest thing you can say about God is that He doesn't exist" is a genuine attempt at an epigram, though any small French child could do better. And even the blue notes are brisker now. "I don't bother to record the bulletins of despair during the night. They are all, so to speak, the day's work . . . the bottom is removed from everything, and my brain feels pressed together. I expect to see brown thumb prints on it in the morning—nothing special." One picks up the tone of a busy doctor, scrawling his last in-patient report of the day.

"Although I feel as if I can't get out of bed, I know that I really can and just go about my business," I cackle bracingly. Despair had become a routine, and although it was still quite unspeakable, it held no more surprises, and hence no terror. One simply awaited what I call on another page "the insistent rhythm of the seesaw." And the next day, February 4, "one could no longer refer to them as sufferings, only nuisances . . . during the night I worried oppressively about money, noting in passing how a real worry clears the head," an observation that brings on a burst of gallows humor. "With a foggy head, I imagine that everything will be okay once the weather lifts; but on a clear day, things look quite hopeless."

Meanwhile my exterior was racing down the block way ahead of my soul, and people began telling me how well I looked, or even sounded on the phone—which is not my medium—long before I'd noticed any change myself. "You must be feeling good today," my wife would say, and I'd realize that I'd been indulging my vice of car singing—quite joylessly, as if the song was one more chore to be gotten through, but apparently that didn't show. On another occasion, I actually sang along with some friends at a bar and realized with a shock that I was being the life of the party. Although I still felt absolutely nothing, my imitation was getting better by the minute, and I understood perfectly the people who go home and kill themselves after such evenings. "He seemed to be in such good form."

Then at last, the cheerful feeling that goes with the cheerful behavior began to come in, like power coursing into an engine after you've pumped and pumped. The final pages record the last false starts before the motor catches, and the sense of aborted hope each time, but they don't, oddly enough, record the moment of truth. Maybe I knew I'd remember it and wouldn't have to look it up. *Lear's* magazine was throwing itself a huge first anniversary party at the Rainbow Room in Manhattan, and there on the slow, rotating dance floor, and surrounded by insanely cheerful Art Deco, I realized that it was over, and that it wasn't coming back—or that if it was, I could handle it.

Talk about grandiosity: there was not one shadow of doubt about this, from that day till now. Depression is *sui generis* and totally unlike any other feeling, such that in my very last entry, on February 27, I can look over the diary one last time and pronounce it already the work of a stranger, adding that if I tried to make the same sounds as he had, "it would be a fake." Anytime I think I might conceivably be depressed these days, I have only to look at the spine of that notebook to feel not only better but absolutely marvelous.

The next morning we flew down to Puerto Rico, and as I watched the martini cart approaching, I noticed for the first time that it contained other beverages as well—how had I missed that?—and that it was all just a bunch of liquid anyway, going clink and squish down the aisle, the Coca-Cola and the Jack Daniel's alike. That phase was over, and I broke out a brand-new notebook to celebrate, and didn't even bother to report my jubilation in it, because unbridled glee came under the category "introspection," and the whole point of this particular cure is that it releases you from that. The tomb I'd been trapped in these last months suddenly sprouted windows and doors, and now the guard and the cleaning lady were telling me to get out immediately. No problem, ma'am.

So I wrote about the enigma of Puerto Rico or whatever instead, and gazed out the window, and thought what a relief it was not to be the center of the universe for a change: like a celebrity who really *is* tired of attention and isn't just saying it, I was delighted just to sit in the grandstand and observe the scene. What was even better was that I didn't even have to *like* myself or esteem myself or take any position concerning myself whatever, but was free to smell the roses on their merits and meditate on the joys of being alive with or without esteem.

Pink Cloud II has several advantages over the original. In each case, the self-satisfaction takes care of itself, and you can jeer at the self-esteem movement to your heart's content, and still have plenty of the stuff itself. But with PC II you've actually *earned* the satisfaction, you've accomplished something, if only by hanging on, and the euphoria is as solid as a note drawn on the Bank of England and countersigned by Queen Victoria.

The first pink cloud, contrariwise, is strictly on the house, and consists entirely of relief that the chemicals have left your system. As such, it should be Exhibit A in any case against drugs, and if I were a twelve-step program, I would place it at the front of my pitch, because it demonstrates how long and thoroughly you've been conned by your favorite chemicals. Under the guise of making you feel good, these smirking impostors have actually dragged you down so low that just feeling normal again seems like Heaven.

But Pink Cloud I is still just that, a cloud, a parody of happiness, and, God willing, a forerunner. People who return to the sauce or the needle after the cloud sails away are missing the really good part, which in my case was just a year away from the day I quit drinking in February 1988 and is made of granite. A lot of people are stamped and stamp themselves as hopeless addicts because they haven't been fully apprised of this second stage. They've had their standard-issue pink cloud, and they've fallen off it—and then a *long* time passes and nothing seems to get any better, and what precisely are we waiting for *this* time? Happiness, if they can see it at all, still looks impossibly far away; yet if I, logy with pills and sludge and thirty-seven years of heavy-hitting, got there in a year, with time out for one cloud ride and some half-day excursions, I imagine many others making it in less. At any rate, my experience suggests a rational target, which is what one craves.

If during this long, monstrous wait, nobody either tells them about or, better of course, shows them something *worth* waiting for, then a relapse in the manner of a Judy Garland or an Oscar Levant (one picks the names from the air) is not *necessarily* a sign of sickness or of a disordered personality, but a rational choice of intense, intermittent pain over unbroken, unendurable boredom. As every preacher knows, it is never enough just to keep reminding sinners of Hellfire, the fear of which keeps fading like paint; there must also be some hint, some plausible and seductive glimpse of Heaven. And here I find a huge hole in my education. Our guardians at Happy Valley seemed so afraid that we'd misinterpret the least bit of good news, or let down our guards over it, that they refrained from giving us any at all, and I left that strange place never knowing that things do get incredibly, unrecognizably better as you go along.

But another reason many drunks don't get, or take in, the word about PC II resides as much in themselves as in their counselors. The truth is that, no matter how accurately you describe it, sober happiness still doesn't sound like their idea of a good time, but more like a forced retreat into the safety of childhood and childish tastes: sugar over salt, morning over night, waking over dreaming. Since it's hard to imagine states of mind, one is left with the unappetizing surface of things and the pink shiny face of sobriety that had so spooked me once upon a time. And since one apparently has to get brainwashed to attain even this, one may understandably prefer to leave well enough alone and order another round.

But if Pink Cloud I *is* like that, a little too wholesome and hearty like a cruise director rubbing his hands over another wonderful day, what surprises one about PC II is its mellowness and its resemblance in a different key to the well-being of drunkenness. The war is over now, and the safety you suddenly feel is not the least like that of a child holding a grown-up's hand, but more like that of your old self entering a tavern at the peak of your powers and knowing that nothing can harm you tonight.

You've seen the worst and it hasn't killed you, and nothing else that life can throw at you can henceforth hold a candle, or a blowtorch, to what has already happened. Indeed, I had a dream around then in which I was informed I had exactly ten minutes to live and I thought, Okay, at least I won't have to worry about the rent anymore, or the electric bill; and then I thought, But I won't see my wife and children either—these being the one and only Achilles heel you have left, the one thing that *could* hurt you—but things were going so well that I had the answer to that one too, as if an angel had brought it on a tray. "I can believe in the afterlife for ten minutes," I decided, and woke up feeling mighty content to be alive, or dead, as the case might be.

Once the last vapors had trailed off and I had done full justice to the Puerto Rican question, I gave up my second journal too and the whole idea of journals until something bad enough happened to justify another one. Happiness is notoriously hard to write about, and besides it was time to do some real work, which, just like that, became a pleasure again—a rich, velvety pleasure. The only catch was that I wanted to write in celebration of everything—of baseball, of my hometown, of songs and songwriters—and in fact couldn't imagine any other reason for writing. So if anyone should come across a piece of mine that seems to have been written with a golden goose quill dipped in cream, it undoubtedly dates from this period. Lent was over at last and I was living it up like a kid in a soda fountain, rolling the words and sentences around on my tongue—who cared whether anyone else liked them?—and thinking, for positively the last time, who needs woodwork?

The Church undoubtedly knows best about this, but I used to wish as a kid that the Sacrament of Confession was matched by one in which you got to boast with equal fervor about how great you were, so that the Almighty could forgive your pretensions and enjoy a good laugh as well. Ah, well.

Without a diary either to prompt or dispute me, I would say that there was much less self about the satisfaction the second time around—my only hard evidence for this being a note I jotted down around then that said, "Why do people always have to feel good *about themselves*? Isn't it enough just to feel good?"

PC II was much more rational in its mix of extroversion and intro than the cartoon version and, if you will, more housebroken, and there was no more bursting into gas stations demanding service; strangers on checkout lines were relatively safe from my chatter; friends could call up without fear of being tied up all afternoon—though they'd better not be in *too* much of a hurry. Even my old stage fright returned halfway, reassuring me that I hadn't changed beyond recognition and become the shiny, moist-palmed extrovert of my nightmares.

At the height of my troubles, an old friend from way back when had said, "You have the exact same problems you had when you were sixteen," sixteen being indeed my *annus horribilis*, as Her Majesty Q.E. II would put it. If so, I was now *seventeen* again, and swooning over the Roman Forum once more and dancing, bad leg and all, at the Olympic Ball in London, and enjoying by every means available the fact that I was over the last hurdle to adulthood. Nothing as bad as sixteen would ever happen again—well, I was wrong about that. But some wonderful years followed seventeen, rendered all the sweeter by the memory of my trek through the fever swamps of adolescence. At late fourteen/early fifteen, I'd rejoiced at stretching what remained of my legs from polio, but now I seemed to be stretching everything. Nineteen forty-eight was one sweet beautiful year. Ditto 1989.

The image of a second or third youth, of another go-round, returned to me more than once, as I listened for the last few times to the tales of the alcoholics at AA, and realized that many of these poor souls had never *had* a seventeen, a year when they felt their absolute best without the assistance of chemicals. So they had no "role model" year, no specimen of the sober life to steer by or look forward to. And this, I believe, makes an enormous, sometimes crucial difference in one's odds of recovery. Scott Fitzgerald pushed the dates further back, but made the same point. "Drunk at 20, wrecked at 30, dead at 40/drunk at 21, human at 31, mellow at 41, died at 51," which in those days would have been considered a respectable age for it—not good, but respectable. But the worst cases I was hearing now had been drunk as early as seven or eight, and were ready to die at twenty-five.

After we got back from Puerto Rico, I went to a few more meetings for old times' sake and because I *liked* these people, but it was becoming a strain because with the departure of the blues went the last vestige of interest in booze as a subject of conversation. At a meeting in April, I told a fellow-member that I found these things wonderfully entertaining, and she said, "That's a peculiar attitude," and I knew that time was up. But not so long before that, the entertainment element of AA had done much to save my sanity. The Christmastime entries in my journal suggest that I believed myself to be in some kind of death grapple with John Barleycorn because of all the fun I was missing, and I still recall my murderous gloom at foreign movies as late as January, still trying to imagine Rome without wine, Dublin without whiskey and London without a pint in my hand. Although I'd lost almost all taste for it, booze still occupied a corner of my imagination as stoutly as ever, holding whole civilizations hostage in there: "Get rid of me, and you'll never see Paris again!" So AA became a substitute for the movies.

Yet when a physically good day came along even then, booze flew obligingly out the window, as if the two tyrants were inextricably entwined, booze and blues, blues and booze, linked together in a dance of death. From which I deduce that at least some of what passes for alcoholism *is* depression and should be treated as such, without this constant prattle about drinking, drinking, drinking, which in itself is profoundly depressing.

At Happy Valley they told us we were in mourning for alcohol, and undoubtedly booze and its associations did come first among my sorrows, but one year is a sufficient period of mourning for almost anything and I'd had quite enough of it by the late winter, early spring of 1989. It was now, as they say in B movies, "payback time." I was on a modified high that would last me from that day to this, reimbursing me "one day at a time" for the inconveniences of the previous fifteen months— killer inconveniences, to be sure, but let bygones be bygones.

"Will my son be able to play the violin after the operation?" goes the old joke. "I expect so," says the doc. "That's nice," says Momma, "because he never could play it before." And that's how it is now with a number of things. I can't remember ever loving nature before, for instance (and I'm still not *interested* in it, which would take a real miracle), but I suddenly couldn't get enough of it, and would look out the window again and again as one steals glances at a fine painting or a beautiful face, with delight but no specific curiosity. What I could see was plenty for me, and knowing the name of it in botanical Latin would have added nothing.

That spring and every spring since, I have felt the same arterial gurgle as first the daffodils and then the forsythia (now there's a name) and then, hot damn, the dogwood come bop-bopping along, and the trees get out the spring finery, the light greens that hit the recovering eye more agreeably than the dark heavy stuff that comes down on everything in August—not that there isn't a lot to be said for August, too. That year I would even discover something good about winter—a fascinating little season in its own way, quite indispensable in fact.

My God, what's happening here? I would apologize to my old self for these coltish effusions and the calendar poetry they come in, except that they sound sort of *like* my old self—after he'd had a few drinks. In many respects one is probably more like one's old self in this phase than one has been for years, like an old building that's just been scraped clean. But be prepared for surprises. Much of what had passed for maturity and wisdom may turn out to have been simply the side effects of sedation—it's awfully easy for a drunk, or an opiumhead, to seem wise. Drunk as an owl, wise as an owl, it looks and sounds pretty much the same. Ditto serenity. In the philosophical sense of this word that AA members pray for, you will very likely have all you want of it from now on; but don't count on it to behave itself. Your endorphins have been down a long time, and they're ready to play now. In my first months of freedom, I was delighted to hear that I looked younger but alarmed to find myself generating enthusiasms like unto a teenager's for things like sports and music in my case, who knows what? in yours, and generating bursts of genial indignation over the world's silliness that collapsed into sheer simpleminded happiness. Even losing one's temper became a positive pleasure, and for the first time I understood the loving families who scream at each other all day and fall into each other's arms at night, still screaming.

But at this moment of victory, individual testimonies part company. There is obviously no universal style of feeling good, nor can I guarantee that everyone who takes this trip will end up in the same place. Capacities for happiness vary with each customer. But I doubt I was alone in finding a particular pleasure in regaining some small control of my own moods, after years of first happy and later abject slavery, to the point where I could say to myself "Calm down" and get at least *some* result, or even "Be happy, boy" and tap for a second into the reserve of mental well-being that goes with just being alive. On what looks like being a bad day, I still recommend lying back and trying to let the pulse of things take over, the rhythm of the universe. *Sometimes* it works.

Although we're not talking about one of the great animal acts of all time, if you've ever had no vote at all in how you feel, this much say-so is intoxicating. And depression veterans have the extra advantage that they *know* when they're happy, it doesn't slip past them, because they've been to the other place. The world of menacing cars and haunted parking lots has turned into a garden of wonders, and just the sight of a bright red barn or of a pond packed with Canada geese discussing their flight plans is enough to make me back up the car and drink my fill of it.

Was it worth it? Did the outcome make up for the pain of getting there? If you'd asked me this at the time I was in midtravail, I would have said "Hell, no," and I would say it again now to anyone who thinks, "I think *I'll* try that myself: drink and pill for thirty-five years or more, grit my teeth for one or two lousy ones, and sail off into the sunset on my pink cloud." Outside of the odds against getting away with it for even half, or even a quarter, that long, and outside of the well-known difficulties of renunciation when the time comes, the grief itself is simply not worth it, not worth any imaginable reward, in fact, while you're actually going through it.

However. Once you *have* been through it, it becomes, like Greek irregular verbs or Marine boot camp, a point of pride, an experience you wouldn't have missed—once you're absolutely sure it's over. Indeed, you may even feel that an important part of your life would be missing without it. At the start of the odyssey, I remember thinking that I would now have to find out what was in me, whether I liked it or not, and this is one promise that sobriety always keeps, for better or worse. Some old barflies turn out to be even duller deep down than they were on the surface, quite awesomely so, in fact, but with any luck it won't seem dull to them. Or if it does they'll blame it on temperance. And some people are bored by sobriety simply because they expect to be. Having spent so many years overrating booze, they can't imagine having fun without it and continue to crouch in the dark while the parade passes by outside.

Norman Mailer summed up the negative neatly when he said that sobriety knocks out all the little "capillaries of bonhomie." As it happens, I'd be willing to match my capillaries of bonhomie against any capillaries in the house. And I suspect that if other *nouveaux* teetotalers would pay a bit more attention to what their senses are actually telling them, they would find their capillaries blooming too, in the midst of a carnival of color and sound worthy of Rio itself. To put it another way—how can you see better and hear better and taste things better and *not* enjoy yourself? And if this orgy of sensuality (much of which, incidentally, can be enjoyed in a monastery) seems too jarring and flashy, there is always the greatest of all gifts to enjoy, a thrilling lucidity that sorts through the impressions and holds them to the light—or decides it prefers the dark. If you have a morbid turn of mind, you can actually go further with it now without fear of falling off the edge into insanity.

And one last bonus: whatever it is that causes people to believe that saving a human life is the noblest thing one can do becomes clear, perhaps for the first time. So many lives seem hardly worth saving. Yet if one put each of them up for auction item for item, bone by bone, one might begin to get a dim idea of their real value. "What am I bid for this pair of legs—two genuine, functioning legs, barely used. They walk, they run, they even go into reverse—we'll start at a million for those, shall we?" (Believe me, if you don't have a pair already, you'll find the money somehow!) "Now we come to eyes—evolution's little masterpieces—20/20 or correcteds, whichever you can afford. Both kinds bring you shapes, colors, sunsets, art galleries, and, above all, surprises." For these the bidding should probably start with all the tea in China, except that you may want to save a little something for ears, so you can hear Mozart and Gershwin and birds outside the window, and we haven't even eaten yet. Wait till you hear about *that* one.

Mourning bells are tolled every time someone loses any one of his senses, and I imagine many of us have had twinges of terror at the very thought of it. Yet people who have magically been handed the whole package, a complete set of both limbs *and* senses, have been known to mope around the house as if they're still missing something, and to worry themselves sick about happiness. An old polio hand is likely to lose patience with these people perhaps too quickly—"Why don't you just shut up and go dancing, or play softball, or just wave your legs in the air?" you feel like snarling. And I suppose you'd lose patience even more if you were blind and everyone else could see. How can *anyone* be unhappy with a pair of good eyes? And why, I was now obliged to ask myself, had I ever considered a pill or a drink necessary to these delights? (Not that drinking isn't fun too, if you can get away with it. But *necessary*?) Anyway, now that you've known depression, you can see beyond the eyes and ears and arms and legs of happiness to the thing itself, the heart of the matter. As I'll relate in the final chapter, my physical losses weren't quite complete yet—a small army of scares was waiting around the corner for me, and a couple of shabby little realities, and perhaps the best tribute I can pay to Pink Cloud II and the value of waiting for it through thick and thin is to say that all subsequent troubles have seemed like nuisances, not tragedies. The shivering wreck who feared being flung out on the street without a tongue simply doesn't exist anymore—perhaps he wasn't a person anyway, but an assemblage of rotten, festering ganglia that have since healed or been replaced—who knows what happens to old ganglia?

So one of the several gifts that nobody so much as hinted at down in Happy Valley has turned out to be the best of all, namely the gift of gifts—the ability to face sickness and death with something like equanimity. This was another instrument I'd never played before, and I'd say it was worth the price of admission, although it was a ridiculous price, and if you can get there by just imagining it, I would recommend trying that first—starting perhaps with the lost souls, the Garlands and Levants, the Kurt Cobains and River Phoenixes, who went through all the misery but never got to the other side of it. If you can imagine even half the horror of that, I believe there is little left to fear in life, and a lot more to celebrate than I would have thought remotely possible when this story began.

9

Cancer: The Disease with the Terrifying Name

During all this blissful time, not one peep had been heard from the macguffin, the white patch on my tongue that had set the whole story in motion. Every few weeks, and then months, I would haul it over to the cancer hospital to have my doctor peer at it suspiciously, presumably trying to remember what it had looked like last time: cells are busy rascals and it's hard to draw boundaries that stay put, especially around ones like mine that are neither quite good nor quite bad, but are forever waiting to jump. As I attempted to say "e" for the man, which cannot be said in these circumstances, he would squint over his tiny spatula and pronounce the magic words: "Your voice box seems to be all right."

And that was the ball game each time. Nothing else in my mouth had changed either, but that was incidental: as I had learned on that night of terror long ago, losing my voice was far and away what scared me most. As I left the building after the benediction, I would pass the occasional celebrating face, on somebody else who had just had good news, and the occasional look of blind apprehension, on a newcomer who wasn't into the cancer groove yet, but foresaw all the horrors at once.

Mostly, however, they looked like just another day at the

doctor's office: whatever happened was not going to happen in a hurry. The doctors would probably be chipping away at them and radiating them until they died of old age. Meanwhile, they'd have plenty of time to finish their newspapers. Parts of faces might be missing, or voices, but the patients involved had already made prodigious accommodations to this, and the sickest patients seemed by no means the unhappiest, any more than they had in my polio days.

It's a sobering building from top to bottom, the kind of place the Spanish buried their kings in, but it was always hard not to break out in smiles as one hugged one's latest reprieve. Not that one felt exactly superior, merely one of the chosen, the favored ones, which I guess comes to the same thing. This was as close as I ever wanted to get to cancer, and I only hoped it could teach whatever lessons it had for me at this safe distance.

After three years, I felt well and truly safe. I had kept my end of the bargain, walking over hot coals to do so, and cancer seemed to be keeping its. And as with all such rescues, I had come to place an inordinate value on the thing saved: talking and eating, what more could a man ask of life? The sound of my own voice, which had always grated horribly when I made the mistake of hearing it, now sounded, at least from the inside, somewhat like Paul Robeson imitating Charles Kuralt, or vice versa, and even my singing, which has never been more than functional—useful mostly for delivering the words to people who didn't know them—didn't sound quite as bad as before (delusion could go no further than that: on my worst day, it never actually sounded good). But chiefly, one rejoiced at just being able to do these things, and I did an extravagant amount of both.

Food, properly considered, proved more than capable of filling, to overflowing, the chief psychological hole left by wine, as something perennially to look forward to. At my age there is no more attractive image than walking into a great restaurant on a sunny day with three courses before you. And never mind that, like the perfect bottle of wine, the image was a nine-tenths mirage. Three courses, indeed! Once you start to feel full, someplace in the middle of the entree, you might as well be chewing a bag of oats. But, again as with booze, one's dreams of food could take a lot of beating by reality and come back fresh as paint the next day.

As you will perceive, I was setting myself up in the classical manner for a truly ferocious kick in the teeth. At the peak of my hubris, I'm sure I would even have maintained that the tongue, with its songs and whispers and, as Archie Bunker used to say, "whatever," was a much more suitable symbol for Valentine's Day than the heart, whose repertoire seemed to consist entirely of beating faster and standing still. What kind of courtship is that, compared with say, reciting Ronsard or Shakespeare's sonnets? "Shall I compare thee to a summer's day?" "Thump, thump." "Thou art more lovely and more temperate." Silence. "Are you all right, dear?"

But for a maximum letdown, it is not enough to be smug; one must also be lazy. In the late summer of 1990, my doctor gave me six months' leave from inspection, the longest so far, and I reacted like Charlie Brown on a Friday afternoon. Eternity stretched before me, and I suppose I must have felt completely free from worry for the first time in three years. At any rate I stretched the doctor's prescription to eight months, the first time I had stretched it so much as a day; and my wife threw me the mother of all sixtieth birthday parties, although I felt about three years old at the time, and we hied ourselves off to Key West, partly because we were sick of hearing about the place and wanted to see for ourselves, but mainly just to wallow in what had returned to being a pretty great life after all. And when we got back, the roof fell in.

Or part of it. The supreme advantage of early detection is that they can still pick the offending cells off one at a time like snipers. Once the damage has proliferated, they can never be quite sure where the buggers have got to, and all surgery is exploratory, in the widest sense; e.g., you don't know whether you even needed it until you've actually had it and they've analyzed what they've done. But thanks to early detection, this couldn't happen to me, could it? *Could* it? (Cancer patients habitually look for the most optimistic reading of their situations they can get, and I never met one in any but the very last stage who didn't think in his heart that he had this thing licked.)

Anyway, it's heigh-ho, back from Key West and trying to smother my yawns as I wait eternally for the doctor, who is always running late, always overworked, always, miraculously, on his toes, like a good outfielder who hasn't seen a fly ball all afternoon but has been ready on every pitch. On days when he isn't performing the most exacting form of surgery, Dr. X. spends up to nine hours at a stretch staring into mouths, trying to read cell clusters as different from each other as snowflakes or fingerprints—and, just as he's getting ready to pack it in, he'll finally spot something: an irregularity in the weave, a malign new presence, the face of a serpent among the lines.

And that's pretty much how it went with me. "Something looks different," he said at day's end. And I realized the absolute necessity of sticking to the same doctor throughout this thing. A stranger might well have noticed that the tongue looked suspicious, because that neighborhood *always* looked suspicious, a nest of possible troublemakers and double agents. That's why we were all here. But it took an old friend to notice that it looked *differently* suspicious.

How he remembered what it was supposed to look like after all these months and a thousand patients after my last visit, I couldn't imagine. And I was still ignorant enough to be skeptical—though not skeptical enough to keep fear from getting a foot in the door. If you've had one bad biopsy report, you'll never read another one calmly, and I went home edgy and deflated, barely able to remember why I'd felt so good for the last eight months.

Waiting doesn't improve this condition, but when I got safely to Friday night without bad news, I thought, well, at least this gives me a weekend to dream what I like before facing the music. But even as I was thinking it, the phone rang, and I *knew*. It was a bad ring, a sarcastic ring.

"I'm sorry to tell you," began Dr. X., and my heart gave that usual strange leap of satisfaction it saves for bad tidings. "Carcinoma . . . operate . . . soon as possible." I don't know *what* all he said: nobody hears much after "carcinoma." He could have said, "I love you, let's get married tonight," and I would still have said, "What do you mean, carcinoma?" It's not quite the dread word, but it's awfully close. All the same, I did rally slightly when he said, "We think it's *in situ*." I knew what *that* meant. Six years of education had finally coughed up something useful. *In situ* means "We've cut them off at the pass"; it is the difference between life and death.

I did my darnedest to see the sun shine through the gaps between his sentences—so they snip out the carcinoma (who's afraid of a big, bad word?), which can't be much bigger than a pimple yet, and I live happily ever after, no? I could easily have slept quite peacefully on that, if Dr. X. had stopped talking; but he plowed on conscientiously, as if I positively *must* hear the worst before retiring. "I'm afraid you will certainly have a speech impediment," he said, and that did it. Not "almost certainly," as I immediately tried to get him to say, but the whole stammering, stuttering thing. Without a doubt.

After that, there was nothing left to do but spend the rest of the night remembering all the various lisps and grunts and whistles I had heard over a lifetime, all of which I would soon start producing myself. People would look at me expecting something normal and out would come this weird gallimaufry of sounds, lacking nothing but a foghorn and a cowbell. My precious tongue, my Valentine's Day special. "You should be able to start eating normally quite soon," he had said, "but we'll have to reshape your tongue." Reshape it! As I lay in bed trying not to think about it, images of hedges being pruned to look like peacocks gave way in my dreams to the strange shapes people wish on their swimming pools: a pancreas-shaped tongue might be just the thing this year, or maybe a spleen, whatever that looks like. I can't remember the particular thoughts, only a fever of images, a miasma. Compared with the drug-induced terrors of three years ago, this was Disneyland: but Disneyland can get pretty rough.

I awoke muttering "Second opinion, second opinion" and called a doctor friend who comforted me as best he could with tales of faulty diagnoses he had known and also with the name of another specialist, who, he said, was something of a maverick with a reassuringly low view of most of the doctors at my hospital, most of whom resorted to the knife much too glibly in his opinion, and so on. Comfort for the sake of comfort, just a little of which got through to warm my bones till Monday.

My second-opinion man was himself a comfortable, unofficial kind of guy with an office that seemed more like a workshop or artist's studio than the white on white of mainstream medicine. Fortunately I had my friend's word for it—backed, out of left field, by my dentist's—that he was also one of the two or three most respected men in the business, because his style is that of a character actor playing a mad scientist: you probably have to be very good indeed to carry off such a style.

Anyway, Doctor Q.'s way of putting me at my ease was to show me pictures of several truly gruesome-looking tongues, next to which mine was an English lawn, and to repeat after each, "And this person talks okay now" or words to that effect. Most of these cases had also started out with patches on their tongues, but lush, herbaceous ones, not chaste little dabs of white like mine. "So you shouldn't have any trouble," he assured me, "so long as they don't cut into muscle."

Cut into muscle? What was he saying? Was that the kind of thing they could do by mistake? "How do I keep them from doing that?" I squawked, my tiny structure of reassurance in ruins. "I'll call your doctor and see what they're planning," he said. "Who did you say was your doctor?" "*Herbert X.* [let's call him]," said I, and he said, "That's fine, he's one of the good ones."

So there went any hopes I might have had that Dr. Q. would shower Dr. X. and his diagnosis with scorn. Then and later, Q.'s value as a second opinion would be seriously diluted by his enormous respect for his colleague X. "If it's good enough for Herbert, it's good enough for me" seemed to be his stance—and I suppose this was reassuring in its own way. If there was no getting out of my bad dream, I'd better start trusting totally in Dr. X. myself, instead of the 90 percent his stock had fallen to since that phone call.

From where I sat I could just hear the two doctors chatting

away on the phone. And they seemed to be talking, as doctors have since the dawn of time, about their golf games, or the equivalent—about, to be precise, conferences that they did or did not plan to attend, at which they might or might not run into each other. Who can tell about these things? Patients seemed to be just faint blips on their screens, like students on the screens of Harvard professors, something to while away the time between conferences.

Not really. My medicine men had already discussed their business, and the fact that this had taken only a couple of sentences didn't mean that it wasn't important. "You're not going to cut into muscle, are you?" asked Q. And after a pause, said, "Well, *I* don't think you'll have to. And it's important to Mr. Sheed's livelihood that you don't." (Damn right.) But there was no argument about it, and I sensed that the small talk that ensued immediately was a means of establishing that the two men were of one mind about absolutely everything, of which my tongue was just one small detail. There was something very English about this and calming. You're a sound man, I'm a sound man. And away we go.

When I got outside, Park Avenue looked quite sensational in the April sunshine, which was a good sign. I had just cut myself the best deal I could possibly get, and first indications were that I could live with it contentedly enough (otherwise, Park Avenue would have just looked rich and insolent as usual). The terms were that Dr. X. would not rescind his threat to my powers of speech, but that he didn't expect to cut into muscle either, which would have truly gummed things up in there; and over against that, I had, and would treasure to my bosom for the next two weeks as I awaited surgery, the memory of Dr. Q.'s tongues, all lined up for parade like Lord Wellington's troops, "the scum of the earth," but all I had—tongues bloated and scabrous and almost too horrible to look at, and surely the strangest source of consolation and good cheer that anyone has ever had to resort to. If the poor bastards responsible for those objects could talk, at least well enough for Dr. Q.—who, I had to admit, didn't seem like the world's best listener—then I certainly could.

Especially if I had no choice.

* * *

Thus I found myself checking into a hospital for the second time in some forty-five years. After a small lifetime of visiting friends and relatives in these places, and feeling each time that slight involuntary lift of the heart that says "You're here, and I'm not; you're sick, but I got over mine," I was back on line myself. And the next time I went to Dr. X.'s clinic, I would be on the other side of the great divide, sitting with the slightly impaired, the people who had "been there" and would be there again.

It occurs to me now, and only now, that if ever the Great Depression was going to come back, this was logically the time. But real depression was simply not in my range anymore; and besides, I knew from experience that depression has only the most glancing relationship with the facts. This was *action* we were getting into now, change, and however grim these things may seem, they are seldom depressing; the pulse is racing too fast to sag or droop. I was now on the far side of the map from that, in the Kingdom of Anxiety, but moving too swiftly to remain even there for long. By the time I checked into the Escorial for real, *curiosity* would turn out to be the overwhelming emotion, capped by a burning itch to peek at the end of the book and see what happens next.

It wasn't until I was actually on the inside that I first decided to take some notes, to see how precisely I could record this experience while it was in process and while I did *not* know at any moment what happens next. What follows was mostly scrawled on a yellow legal pad as I strove fruitlessly by raising the head—no? let's try lowering the knees—to get comfortable in a hospital bed and strove more seriously both to forget and to remember exactly whatever was on my mind at that particular instant.

10.

OPERATION I: TONGUE

[Interesting clash between heightened confidence and heightened capacity for embarrassment.] As they wheeled me into the operating room I felt *almost* totally calm—the one reservation being that calmness seemed unlucky, so that each time I thought "how calm I am," I'd feel quite shaky about thinking it; also I remembered my days of depression and my feeling then that I could give great advice about this stuff the moment it was safely over.

The operating room was remarkably casual—more like a workshop of some kind, a carpenter's maybe, and quite unworthy of the grand word *theater*, unless you're talking extreme off-Broadway. Having only seen these things in movies, I was expecting something more Wagnerian. As it was it seemed quite natural to swap wisecracks like RAF pilots preparing to take off and give Jerry what for. I tried to say "night night" as I passed out, but was already gone.

Coming to in the recovery room was similarly low key. There was no disorientation—I knew exactly where I was, and with the help of the oxygen mask I also knew exactly who was saying what about what to me—and who was saying what at the adjoining beds too. "Nice and clear at the margins," says one voice. "Good mobility," says another. If that's my tongue they're talking about, it has to be good news, right? Otherwise, it felt like the time of day when the staff is thinking of going home and are trying to figure how to get everyone out of there, but this may have been the constant need for beds, starting with yours, which at every stage somebody else is waiting for. Again, very workaday. The occasional amateurishness of real hospitals can have an unintended relaxing effect—so long as your life is not in danger.

Now two days later I do notice one small change in myself, perhaps temporary. My morbid fear that I would come out of this with a speech impediment is suddenly nowhere to be found. Now that I'm "in action" I take the possibility quite in stride. The doc is pretty sure he got the cancer, and I have all the time in the world to straighten out my speech, which is muddy and monosyllabic at the moment because my tongue hurts so much. It all very much puts me in mind of polio days, when abstract terror gave way to delight in just being alive. In fact, *all* the terror has come in advance, then and now, so there obviously wasn't much point to it in the first place.

Day Four

Setting one's mind at rest is child's play compared with the physical labor of breaking in a new tongue. It came as a shock to find I couldn't swallow a lump of Jell-O, and the fizz of ginger ale made my tongue sore on contact. Offsetting this was the sheer pleasure of *tasting* something, which can be a wonderfully exciting adventure in these rather special circumstances. It has been strange never once having a meal or a drink to look forward to for these last days: I would approach the various meal times armed with reflexive expectations, like a horse circling the track at the Grand National—and find that they've taken the jumps away. The breakfast jump, the tea-time jump. There is not even some remaining point of taste, a tomato juice or cracker, a landmark to remind one that there once *was* a mealtime at this hour.

In a small way, it's liberating. But meanwhile to make it

work, they've been pumping stuff down my throat all the while to make my stomach feel fed. And my mental interest in food dies as I fill up just as surely as if I were tasting the stuff. I feel like a car staring at a gas pump and deciding it's had enough.

Home Thoughts

Came home on a great high. Spring had waited for me, and the leaves were still coming in one by one, like students gradually filling up an auditorium, still a very light bright green at this point (not the students). A couple of days later, the leaves would just be looking like leaves again, and even then I realized it was more mood than leaves that I was celebrating. Still, the ratio between mood and subject matter was much better, and saner, than it was when the mood came from a glass of wine or a highball. Then, by God, I saw epiphanies everywhere—and they were *all* mood, and no substance at all. Now I thrill longer and more particularly. That whole sweep over the Triboro and along the Grand Central Parkway past the bay and Flushing Meadow and Robert Moses' folly, the World's Fair of 1964, seems like a prolonged song with a dozen key changes. The next day, I had the rare experience of materializing like an apparition at a friend's Derby day party, to a general intake of breath "What are *you* doing here? I thought you were supposed to be in the hospital. Are you all right?" The urge to strut is tempered only by the fear that so much naked showing off may be more than people can stomach. I imagine Lazarus himself may have had the same problem at his coming out party. (I also know that if my wife had been married to him, her first words would have been "Lazarus, honey—that winding sheet is a disaster!")

But people seem to get an uncomplicated pleasure from such a rude assertion of health from one of their own species and one feels a glow in return at just being the carrier of good news to these people: messengers don't *always* get killed—sometimes they get hugged and given a paper crown.

I am complimented on how clearly I'm speaking, but I already know from experience that a few days hence these same people will be saying "boy, your speaking has improved. I couldn't make out a word the other night." Someone refers to "reassuring baritone sounds" issuing from me, and I think, a split second too late, of saying "well it wasn't a sex-change operation." By the time I have decided whether this is *worth* saying out loud, it is well and truly too late. On the actual state of my tongue, I accept two opinions as more reliable than the rest, my daughter's that I sound like a kid with braces on his teeth and Ed Tivnan's that I still sound better than Tom Brokaw. The rest is flattery, and very welcome anyway. You can't really get sore at friends who want to please you.

Flattening Out

After such high-flying, you're lucky if you can find a soft spot to land. By the next morning, I was quite literally running out of fuel, which concealed itself behind irritability as I reached back for extra strength that wasn't there. The tube in my nose had previously kept my tank topped up all day long, and the motor had fairly purred. But now as the nutro-glop sputtered and burped its way into my system, my spirits herked and jerked accordingly and I felt for the first time that I was faking my euphoria.

Yet the fact that the cancer has apparently gone treated me to a pretty good day anyhow, leaving me holding the scales and trying to figure precisely how much good news it takes to outweigh *feeling* rotten. Impossible, of course, because all the elements keep jiggling. On Sunday, drinking soup seems so much easier than it did on Saturday that a whole little packet of pleasure seems to burst open. But this is severely relative, because when the improvement doesn't keep up, drinking soup seems once again like an almighty chore. And meanwhile regular food looks better and better—and more unattainable. Between me and it lies the equivalent of Marine boot camp, with no certainty of graduating at the end. Now, as with polio, the prospect of hard dull work somewhat blunts the pleasure of just being brave and taking bows. Also, I'm disappointed that my talking hasn't improved more: I had already gone as far as I could on native ingenuity, outracing my tongue muscle by plenty. Now I must wait for the muscle to catch up—and, worse than wait, work.

Above all, though, I have to refuel for the big push, as I accelerate from the mode of resignation and of "Thy will be done" to one of *my* will be done, dammit—but obviously, at Thy pace. I can't control *all* the elements.

Tongues and Their Ups and Downs

Just talking like that lifts the spirits. After years of being technically a grown-up, I still know of no greater pleasure than setting up targets and knocking them down, and the speaking targets should be a pleasure—so long as I keep hitting them. Eating is something else, because for one thing it's kind of messy, as one's increasingly sore tongue flails away at the alien stuff that keeps coming into one's mouth, like Hercules cleaning out the Augean stables. Anything that gets under your tongue is out of reach and just sits there until you flush it out with the hose afterwards. The only benefit is for philosophers, if there are any, who've always wanted to know exactly what it was that tongues did during the act of eating. I am decidedly not one of these, but I know the answer anyway, and it is "just about everything," particularly the cleaning up afterward. The trick to the happy eating of even nondescript soup is, of course, to make yourself so hungry that no obstacle seems too great. Disadvantages to this technique are (a) you can get pretty rundown waiting and (b) your longing for *real* food passes all reason. And it still seems like dirty unrewarding work.

It's now two-and-a-half weeks from the operation, and the good and bad news remain the same, in subject matter if not in degree. My talking is way ahead of schedule, but the doctor says he can take no credit for it: medically speaking, I simply shouldn't be talking this well with this particular tongue. It feels too small even to me, and I guess the shape is different too. But if you know how to do it, you can probably talk with any old tongue at all, a toothpick if necessary—though I wouldn't want to try it with less than I've got right now. When the doctor's nurse phoned to advance our appointment, I ran up a scenario immediately in which the doc had found some new horror in the biopsy and was calling me in for another operation. It wasn't too likely, since Dr. X.'s track record suggested he would call me himself in such a case—but likelihood has nothing to do with nightmares, so I had worked out my hypothetical answer before I got there: "nix on any more cutting." This was the tongue I'd been dealt now, a pair of deuces, and I wasn't going to play with anything smaller. Nor was I going to set myself even further back from eating. By chance my case coincides in time with that of Michael Landon, the gallant TV actor, who has hitched his wagon to alternative medicine: I would do the same now, if I had to—caffeine enemas and all—and at least go down talking.

So I marched in, all prepared with my defiant answer, only to find that nothing was amiss and that the doctor had sent for me in order to take some more stitches out and make sure my mouth got a good cleaning, which is hellishly difficult to ensure at home (those stables again. Even on a liquid diet, the crud piles up like a New York sidewalk).

There is nothing like a reprieve, even if you had to invent the scare yourself, and I walked out into the sunny streets around New York Hospital as if I'd just been accepted by them for membership: on this luscious day I was still one of the living. On the way home I celebrated by singing along with the car radio, somehow managing to get my chops around the Dorsey version of "Sunny Side of the Street" ("what a drag old man—getting caught in the shade . . . get hep, don't be afraid—move it on over, you'll be *there* in the *clover*" or words to that effect). It felt as if I were singing through fur, but I like to think that I generally sound better than it feels as if I'm sounding, so maybe it wasn't *too* Mongolian: anyway, I'm glad the window was up. Singing is another of those absolutes, something I have to be able to do if life is to be worth living—and I mustn't sound too pathetic to myself while I do it either. (It's funny—you'd suppose I was any good at it. Not so. It's just like breathing, at which I'm probably nothing special either.) Looking at myself in the mirror as I talk, my lower mouth looks stiff, as if it is guiding the words out, which it is. But perhaps talking always looks funny. And hey—I just looked in there again and either I'm getting used to it, or the mouth is back to its old flapping ways.

11.

INTERMISSION

By now I knew better than to take anything for granted with this illness, but the first words I'd heard as I came out of the ether—"the margins are nice and clear"—were themselves something nice and clear to hang on to; and as spring turned into summer, the ground under my feet began to feel about as firm as it was ever likely to feel again. At every stage of cancer, you will find someone else who has reached exactly this point and stuck there; so why not you? Victims have gone to the very brink of the grave and stopped on a dime, so there were always grounds for hope.

On my next few visits to the morgue, Dr. X. was assuringly perfunctory, flipping my tongue this way and that like a pancake and pronouncing it fine, fine, as if there weren't a cloud in the sky; a quick glance at my throat, like a tourist checking out the Grand Canyon? a cat looking into a mouse hole? (hospitals give you plenty of time to think up metaphors, memorize phone numbers, and recite the alphabet backwards)—and a perfect bill of health at the end of it.

So I was back on the right side of the line, on the outside looking in—and what did I care if the doctor kept us all waiting for up to five hours? (I could write a thesis on a couple of the *New Yorker*s I read in there.) I savored every moment now.

Looked at in a certain light—and one becomes an expert on lighting—I was even better off now than I had been before the operation, when I felt so safe. My tongue was clear for the first time in years, and I was even free to go back to smoking cigars if I liked (fat chance!) or drinking, if I felt like giving up sleep and putting a new spot on my tongue. I had learned my cancer lessons and was still here to tell the tale.

In fact, I was becoming more worried about Dr. X.'s health than my own. He seemed, by the time I got to him at the end of his day, plumb worn out from carrying us all on his back for so long. There were no major symptoms you could point to— maybe a little herky-jerkiness, maybe a little distractedness— but just plain fatigue built up over such a long time that a good night's sleep wouldn't put a scratch on it.

So at first I ascribed it to his fatigue when he said once again that he thought he saw "something different," this time in my neck. For a closer look, he stuffed a tube gratingly through my nose with, I suppose, a magnifying glass or microscope on the other end (what I still don't know about these procedures staggers me); and for a second opinion he asked the latest visiting fireman from the Far East to take a look too.

To my immense relief, the fireman could see nothing. And I hoped that Dr. X. would just give up at that point and start taking his vacation, which was coming up anyway. But X. was nothing if not dogged. "The next step is a CAT scan," he said, as if his suspicions had just been verified. "Where would you like to have it done?"

So a CAT scan it was, just to humor the man, to be administered in a genuine space-age machine in our utterly reputable local hospital. And when the chief radiologist there said, in the course of time, that *he* couldn't see anything wrong with the picture, I thought the case was well and truly closed. But to my amazement, Dr. X. seemed to treat this as yet further confirmation of his conjectures. After another quick look on his own, he said, "I guess what we have to do now is either just go on examining you—which I *don't* advise—or we can radiate the area, or we can cut it out right away. And if we find what I think we will, we'll then have to remove all the lymph glands on that side of your neck"—a root-and-branch operation that reminded me somehow of watching whole strands of Virginia creeper being ripped off our college walls back when I was at Oxford.

Since Dr. X.'s vacation was coming up almost *immediately* now, I would mercifully be granted a reprieve from his preternatural pigheadedness—after which, I trusted, he would come back tanned and rested and fully cured of his callow wish to be different. Meanwhile, we compromised on a needle biopsy performed by himself and aimed directly at the target of his suspicions. Ever the chicken, I failed to call his nurse to find out the results of this before he got back, but when I next saw him, he told me they were negative, and I relaxed all over, all the more relieved for the three weeks of cowardice that had preceded this radiant moment.

But not for long. Because uncannily, this news seemed to bother old X. worse than anything yet. "With 'positive' at least you know where you stand," he muttered; as if sickness were the only thing you could be sure of in life. Again he examined me, most probingly, and his Asian assistant *du jour* also examined me, with the same results as before. The assistant saw nothing, but X. came up, unbelievably, frowning once more. "I wish to God I could say it wasn't still there," he said with genuine feeling. "But I'm afraid I think it is. And in fact, I'm more convinced than ever."

Having that elongated microscope up my nose probably made me even tetchier than I would have been anyway. "How many needle biopsies would it take to convince you otherwise?" I rasped.

His eyes, as he thought about this, looked quite strained and he seemed somehow even tireder than he had before his vacation, as if the first good night's sleep had simply uncapped all the poisons. "I wouldn't believe *three* needle biopsies," he said fanatically.

Or at least I heard it fanatically. While I knew there must be at least one more good argument I could use, I didn't know enough about the subject to imagine what it might be or whether he'd even listen to it. And as always, I was constrained by the same deadly thought—supposing I win the argument, and the doctor turns out to be right anyway?

"I'm surprised" was all I could say, and he said, "I know it isn't what you were hoping to hear."

"No—it isn't what I was *expecting* to hear," I corrected. "Because I've never felt so well in my whole life."

Well *that* was no argument, and he didn't even pause over it on his way out the door: how I felt was neither here nor there. It was an irony that had pursued me all year like a harpy, that I don't suppose I have ever passed a year in better all-round good health or well-being than this, the year of the hospital.

Very soon after that, Dr. X. was indeed sidelined with some mysterious ailment. Although the hospital personnel knew every last detail about us, the patients, they were quite kittenish about what ailed the doctor, as if any news at all would send stocks tumbling. So naturally, we imagined the worst—namely that Dr. X. had somehow, through sheer empathy, caught what we had, like Father Damien and the lepers. (It was nothing like that bad, as I learned independently.) The hush-hush treatment reminded me of the way nuns used to talk about priests. "Doctor," like "Father," wasn't quite like the rest of us, and he didn't have health in the usual sense. So to learn that Dr. X. was sick was like catching the pope in his pajamas.

A wave of consternation swept through Dr. X.'s flock, at least if I was anything to go by, and I found myself in loud agreement with a patient whose throat had been implanted with a boom box, or mechanical voice, that doctors had no business getting sick at all, that sickness was *our* department, not theirs.

More practically speaking, I had to find me another surgeon right away to replace one I had come to consider the best there was. Now that Dr. X. had discovered my pinpoint of possible carcinoma, all the subsequent doctors I auditioned, or who auditioned me, seemed to find it with laughable ease. And I soon wearied of telling them not to be confused by the wayward saliva gland that wandered through that same area and had hurt since I was a child, if you stuck a finger into it. A layman can't last ten seconds in a discussion like that, and even my skeptical friend Dr. Q. soon agreed to finding *something* there after at first thrilling me by saying "You seem all right to me."

So my phantom "something" that didn't show up on CAT scans or needle biopsies had come a very long way in a short while, and opinions now varied only as to its size and urgency, the opinion makers ranging from one guy who seemed to find it as big as a pumpkin and almost beyond saving to good old Q. who felt that a lick of radiation would handle the little fellow nicely.

But even he agreed that they first had to take whatever it was out and look at it. So once again there was really no second opinion to be had. Once a question mark has been sighted with this illness, the doctors close ranks immediately, no one wanting to be the one to say *"Don't* operate." Even my understanding that I had a choice between an operation and radiation proved illusory. If they found a trace of anything in there whatsoever, I would receive both, lickerty-lip, one on top of the other.

On the plus side—and I found it made all the difference—nobody said anything about a speech impediment this time or even its companion in terror, a food impediment. Which meant that the hospital menu I had only been able to stare at longingly the last time I was here was now at my mercy.

And while I was busily collecting silver linings by the armload, I also learned that the operation in prospect was the commonest (true) and most straightforward of cancer operations and could be performed by your average plumber, although the man I was getting turned out to be considerably better than that, an ace in fact, although I didn't learn this in time for it to help. And as for radiation—it was not, as I supposed, the same thing as chemotherapy, which laid waste in those recent days like a Mongol horde, wrenching out hair and teeth and reducing you to a skeleton, but is a civilized affair that takes just a few minutes a day of your time and leaves you free to work and play to the maximum. A friend of mine, who'd had it, reported that he'd felt a little too weak to eat one day out of the thirty or so. Period. That was it for the side effects.

But perhaps the shiniest of my silver linings came, in a round-about form, from good old Dr. Q., who told me I really should have the radiation anyway, unless I "wanted to come back in six months and repeat the whole thing over again."

The notion of cancer as some kind of nuisance that came back periodically to inconvenience you, boringly, if you didn't take simple precautions was so benign that for a moment I couldn't imagine how the disease had gotten its reputation.

More critically, I had already noted that in Dr. Q.'s world, nobody ever seemed to die or even stay sick for long. For a moment this bothered me, but only a moment. A good silver-lining collector has no trouble processing thoughts like that in double-quick time. From the number of cases I now knew in my own small circle, and from what I'd heard of Dr. Q.'s reputation, I could easily imagine that his world really was like that, a place where good news drowned out bad every time, and where you didn't have to soft-soap the customers *too* heavily to give every one of them grounds for hope.

All this, plus my unfailing mantra, "early detection," was enough to guarantee a smooth sail over the next few weeks, right up to the moment I entered the house of jitters, or panic zone—i.e., the period of mixed and heightened emotions that comes just before a major event and immediately imposes its own rules and thought patterns regardless of who you are and what you know: the coolest of athletes will suddenly throw up when he's in this zone, and the jumpiest will experience moments of icy calm—too soon to do him any good, poor chap, but it should go on record that he was cool once. The supreme example of the panic zone is, of course, Jesus Christ's agony in Gethsemane the night before his crucifixion, which remains an inexhaustible in-spiration to anyone on the brink of undergoing anything. To even a momentary believer, the story says that God has been there Himself and is with you now.

Once again, I reached for my yellow pad and my pencil, but this time I decided just to keep on writing until I reached the end of the road, or some other logical stopping place. A sickness is as good as a grant from an arts council, and it provides a subject as well. A long health "condition" that doesn't either kill you or preoccupy you with pain can give off as many reflections as Walden Pond—and who knows? perhaps in some corner of the mind, I also felt that as long as I kept on writing, and dancing in my red shoes, I wouldn't die. (This superstition never strikes me as absurd until I've thought about it for a moment.)

Although there's nothing you can really do about it, I would find having cancer far from the passive experience I'd expected. Until the very end of my particular road, you will not be a particularly sick person, but more like a healthy one with termites and the sense of a murderous, if vague, fight on your hands. And everything you've got goes into the fight, all your interests and excitements and loves, like the French piling into taxis to fight the battle of Verdun. Although it's never clear who or even how you're fighting. You are in fact answering the cancer with life itself, and if you can't beat back the bad cells, they'll still have to drag you out of this party by your heels.

The details of any illness are too tedious and repetitive to occupy you for more than part of the time and what you do with the rest is critically important in this case, as you bet your whole self against death. A friend called Joe Hagerty probably lived more vividly during his doomed three years of cancer than during the rest of his life put together and died, while I was actually working on this journal, a happy man, consoling his loved ones to the end with squeezes of the hand. As if to say "I've been on this incredible journey, and now I want to rest awhile." Or as George "the Gipper" is alleged (I forget by whom) to have said to Knute Rockne in the real version of the story, "Dying ain't so bad, Coach."

But if this seems to remystify cancer and put a throb in its throat, it shouldn't. Cancer remains for most of its span just a nuisance—a deadly nuisance, but that's all. The interesting part is all provided by you, an average citizen and image of God, finding out for probably the first time what's been in you all along.

At least you find this out if the worst happens. What I was hoping for as I started this chronicle and what I hope for still is that I'll be allowed to continue on my shallow way for quite a while longer and not find out till I'm at least ninety any more about what's in me than I absolutely have to.

Still, if you *must* find out sooner, it's nice to know that the recovery machine still functions and that the same forces that gather round to help you fight something as specific as polio will still show up for work when there's nothing much doing except getting through the next day and the one after.

12.

Operation II: Neck

The Eve of Battle. This is actually a period of about seventy-two hours. Monday was full of reluctant agitation—there always seems to be one such day, or night, as you absorb what's about to happen to you, and if you have a skeptical streak, your own Uncle Fergus, to imagine all the worst possibilities. I answer with my best garbled Shakespeare, "The coward dies a thousand deaths, the brave man dies just once." But imagining deaths isn't necessarily cowardly. It's just that you shouldn't do it on certain days, this one for instance.

Right now, you are neither fish nor fowl, not a sick man yet, but not a healthy one either, not *carefree*, which is the pith and essence of health. So—are you really serene about death, or is that just on days when it seems a million miles away? An unfair question on these in-between days when you're not serene about anything. But perhaps it's true that you have to be very near to it or very far, feeling great or feeling lousy, to accept death.

Meanwhile, though, the next day has come along, and I feel just swell again. Death isn't a factor just yet, only the fear of a receding series of scenes with doctors—in offices, on phones, at bedside. "I'm afraid your biopsy . . ." What's spooky is that you always seem to be feeling particularly well that particular day. If one really could fight back against cancer with positive thinking and "attitude" you'd be at your absolute best today. But now, the docs are planning to attack you again anyway, with knives and heat and chemicals, leaving you feeling like God knows what. *That*, I realize, was the real anxiety yesterday, as I stood shivering in my shorts. Supposing my "attitude" is help-ing the bad cells and not the good ones? Mightn't it be better if *everything* just stopped growing in there for a while?

But the next day, you're back on stage checking into the hospital, and everything is cool again. So perhaps the agitation was just opening night jitters, waiting for the show to start.

November 8th

The morning of the operation, I felt calm but flat. My tongue operation had gone so smoothly that there was no fear left of the unknown—the bad dreams of ether, the horrors of waking—and I was left meditating on the power of a bad night's sleep and a sinus headache to dominate one's more spiritual, high-toned side, and also marveling at the crotchets of even the best hospitals.

The guy in the next bed can't talk, yet every time he presses his button for help, they insist on interrogating him over the inter-com at the tops of their voices. Then they come round and fling on all the lights in our joint room and pepper him with more ques-tions, which I suppose he answers with sign language which at least gives them some dim notion of what he wants. The situation is aggravated by the fact that his signalling button seems to go off of its own volition from time to time, setting the whole rigmarole in motion again and again. And when this finally abates early in the morning, the next shift arrives with a crash, greeting their col-leagues like old school chums whom they haven't seen in years—or so it sounds to the sensitive ears of half-sleep.

All such airy meditations are swept into insignificance by the arrival of real pain in the afternoon. My tongue caper had misled me into thinking that pain isn't so bad if it's in the general area of the face where you're on top of it: the neck as it happens is a *terrible* place to hurt, and so probably is anywhere else where you happen to be hurting right now. But it's all in the hands of the technicians. Today's anesthesiologist had laid on his wares with a heavy hand, so I woke in an ugly fog (clarity is infinitely better when you're in pain); and after I came to, I heard someone say "I'll get the morphine," as if my awakening after three hours had come as an incalculable surprise. The glad cries of celebration—"that was a completely successful operation!"—sounded quite hollow this time, and I began to wonder how badly they would have to botch one of these things *not* to celebrate it (on second, more 1990s' thought, the real sub-text may have been "please don't sue us—it could have been worse"). The story within the story was that they'd found *some*thing in there. Which meant that the modest *in situ* carcinoma on my tongue was now *in situ* in my neck—and where else?

So Dr. X. was right, and if one good thing has come out of this, it is that I will never doubt him again, even if he talks feverishly and seems to make no sense at all. Dr. P. gave me a jolt the next day, by referring to the something in my neck, by name, as cancer cells, and I realized how much comfort even an old word-hand had gotten out of euphemisms. I had gotten this far without ever quite using the phrase "I've got cancer," with all its medieval connotations of pain and death. Up to now, I had seen the situation as quite fluid—which is correct too. Cancer lights here, lights there—you chase it off your neck and it lands in your ear, like a bug. Only towards the end do you begin actually to "have" it.

Anyway, I have a least a month to live. The doctor, with his godlike ability to move the game along, just came by again and announced that radiation doesn't start till next month. The bad news is that radiation when it comes can affect your teeth and jawbone—he got away before I could ask him precisely how. He just told me to see a dentist and make sure everything is battened down. Meanwhile—would I rather lose my face, or my voice, or my taste buds? Although I would once have voted overwhelmingly to keep my voice, everyday experience now tells me to hang onto the taste buds: they're the only one of the three that can make life worth living all on its own—even if you were down to one crumpet and marmalade at bedtime every night. Looks and voice matter only insofar as they affect your dealings with the outside world. So I supposed I'd see fewer people and write more letters and eat much more marmalade. But thank God, writing survives *everything*.

You get a good chance to comparison-shop in the halls of the cancer factory: different pieces of face are missing, or skewed, and when one of the patients is spoken to, you feel a thrill of relief if he answers in a normal voice. Yet in this wing they at least retain the rest of their physical dignity, which can seem all the more imposing when you consider the fight that that particular upright body is putting up against death. A referee would halt the bout at this point, because the guy won't go down on his own.

November 13th

Out again. The story of this operation has been a story of anesthetics. In truth I was too woozy to write down most of what happened in the hospital, and remain woozy to this day. Sickness is an excuse from the gods to be lazy and I don't have to be asked twice. But I'm treading a narrow line about this. If I felt any better than I do, I would also lose my excuse not to work; yet I am determined to feel that well as soon as possible.

To be precise, I have an assignment, and each morning, I address it for a few moments. And if I see fog forming at the edges or feel a slight pressure on top of my head, then I'm off the hook for another day. The ideal is to feel quite up to smartchat and crosswords and problem movies, but not quite up to creative work (and all work is creative. See Hannah Arendt). Perfect. Another nice day rolls out in front of me. Tomorrow is soon enough: you wouldn't want Godot to see the house in *this* condition.

What makes today's nice day possible is actually the report from the lab, which is not the best—a clean bill of health and a large gift of money—but is far from the worst. The cancer cells were there all right but in only one of the eleven lymph (what, glands? nodes? I always miss a key word) that they removed, and it is reasonable to suppose that they are just an extension of what they found on my tongue—which leaves them relatively *in situ.* At any rate, they are not raging like a forest fire. And a jolt of radiation should clear out the area for good. (By way of further encouragement, the doc only *recommended* radiation, he did not absolutely insist on it. Now what does *that* mean? one wonders.)

So the vague feelings of malaise in my chin that swarmed around while the situation was in doubt can recede for the time being (everyone feels an occasional twinge in his chin, does he not? Damn right). What hasn't quite receded yet, though it may be on its way, is the numbness in my left ear that makes it feel like a raw cabbage leaf, or the patchier numbness on the whole side of my face, where it lingers like the remains of a local anesthetic, making eating a chore, and eating and talking together quite chaotic. Also my left shoulder hurts like a tennis elbow when I try to do anything strenuous with it.

13.

RADIATION

Nothing could better illustrate the chasm between the grim outside of an ailment and the tedious, anticlimactic inside than radiation. As usual, the worst part of *both* sides comes at the beginning when they first tell you about it, and you're still in no-man's-land between inside and outside yourself, and you realize that *every minute of this* still lies ahead of you. Welcome to Alcatraz. As the radiologist reads off the list of possible side- and after-effects, to run concurrently and forever, it's awfully hard to remember that this guy is supposed to be on your side. There he is, about to kill off thousands of your favorite cells, adding up to a large tract of the body that has brought you this far, and they call this man a healer! Talk about bombing villages in order to liberate them; talk about napalming whole forests on suspicion. For all anyone knew, I might not even *have* cancer at this stage. But bomb we must. One can't be too careful.

It may have been my imagination, but the radiologist seemed a trifle sheepish as he reeled off the damage he planned to inflict on me, and my heart went out an inch or so to any doctor forced to practice medicine sheepishly. Otherwise I remember mostly being torn between wanting to get the whole thing started and over with as soon as possible and a desire to cram in a few last joyless banquets—because among the side effects, along with the stiff shoulder and the neck that wouldn't swivel, goes a probable loss of spit; and if I thought eating was difficult with my stub of a tongue, I could just imagine trying it with artificial saliva.

That last, slightly sickening phrase was the absolute low point, from which the slow climb uphill began almost immediately. I recall also one spasm, not of fear but of utter disorientation, as I walked past a sign that said "Danger—radiation." What the hell am *I* doing here? I thought. This is indeed a primitive form of medication and will surely go the way of leeches someday. But meanwhile, it reminded me bizarrely of the root and branch therapy of Happy Valley which commonly burns away more than it needs to, leveling whole personalities at times. And *that* reminded me of how cheerfully we take to wasting things over here.

And other deep thoughts of that nature. Radiation, as I experienced it, actually turned out to be one long search for something to think about next. Otherwise there isn't that much *to* radiation. The movie *Doctor* makes the biggest possible production out of the prepping procedure, in which they stretch the patient taut, and draw and quarter him with a magic marker to define their target. But even this is nothing like as interesting or fraught with emotion as it looks. What it actually is is your first exercise in boredom, and far and away your longest, thank the Lord: I ran through a *lot* of ball players beginning with B that day, and cities starting with C too.

After that, the routine becomes as humdrum as anything in the annals of medicine, the equivalent of being popped into the microwave for fifteen minutes a day: "one session down and thirty-four to go," you say to yourself, "two down," etc. Some place around ten down, my tongue got so sore battling a piece of roast beef that I didn't mind too much, around twelve or so, when I lost my taste buds as well. I was eating sashimi at the time, and suddenly couldn't tell which fish was which—now *that* is a weird experience, feeling your food without tasting it. But the doctor assured me the buds would come back, and hey—we were killing cancer cells!

This thought would not merely take the curse off all the inconveniences to follow but would positively canonize them, the way clergymen used to bless the guns of war. From now on, the more I hurt, the more bad cells I would be killing. By two thirds of the way through, my tongue got so beat up that they had to give it and me a week off—"one big canker sore" was how they described the little fellow, and I seriously wondered how I was ever going to be able to use it again for either eating *or* talking. "So take that, cancer!" I thought as I jumped back into the fray. "Let's see you get out of this one, you creep."

"Thirty-five down and none to go." "You may feel a little depressed when the treatments stop," said the sheepish radiologist. "The hell I will," I thought. Although radiation leaves you a bit too weak for downright elation, I remember the weeks both during and after treatment as exceptionally *mellow.* I'd been *doing* something about an illness you usually can't do anything about—and as I was assured on the way out, I would continue to smolder quite some time afterward, torching even more of those suspicious cells. So one's spirit soars in inverse proportion to the body's losses and, inevitably, it soon finds something to soar about. My journal records a new and unexpected delight in the old buildings of New York, and in something I'd never given much thought to before—opera singing. There is no telling which of the senses will rush to fill the gap when one of its colleagues falters. But above all, I was now incapable of depression. I'd been there before and it wasn't even along this route. You might run into melancholy around here, but even that looks pretty good next to depression, while physical pain, by drawing such sharp lines around things, may actually remind you of how safe you are now, and how profoundly *un*depressed. I felt as if my euphoria had been road-tested and validated for further use.

A couple of days later, my wife and I left for Key West again and the journal sinks to a level of dailiness every bit as gripping as someone else's home movies. "I think I tasted my soup last night—oops, false alarm." Two themes twine their way around the entries, giving them such point as they have. Twelve days after the bombardment had ceased, my mouth suddenly went dry for keeps (up to then, it had fluctuated like New England weather). I felt as if I'd just been shot after the armistice was signed. They'd gone too far this time. A bullet before the armistice would have been quite acceptable, of course, painful but acceptable—but this was infuriating.

Well, I didn't *know* it was for keeps, though it certainly felt that way. You can live on very little hope for a very long time, and just as I was settling in for a siege, theme two came riding *slowly* to the rescue. After the false alarm with the soup, there was a positive identification of some bananas and cream—the cream, not the bananas—and another of a Carnation strawberry breakfast. Taste was returning, at first in the roof of the mouth, which had been neutral in the hostilities, and then gradually, unmistakably in the tongue too. And simply blew the dry mouth problem away. Another line had been drawn that I could be on the right side of—people without taste buds are the true wretched of the earth (though undoubtedly they're on the right side of some other line).

There follow some excessively home-movie-like entries as I unwrap my new presents one by one and drink in, as if for the first time, the sheer majesty of salt and the *intelligence* of pepper. And do I really like oysters? (Yes, but the buds have to relearn that one.) Tomatoes are angrier than I'd supposed, but crème brûlée is undoubtedly one of the seven wonders of the world. And so on, for private viewing only. After noting earlier that "eating is almost as overrated as drinking," the tune changes to a goofy dithyramb, which I'll spare you. The few pages of journal that follow concern a couple of other subjects germane to this book, and recapture the period, and get one from there to here.

Other People

My tongue being temporarily too sore to speak with, I have temporarily entered the world of muteness, concerning which I divine the following: (1) people come up to you thinking that you will be good, restful company since you can't talk and all, but you won't be. You will very soon frustrate them and make them nervous, after which all the nodding and smiling in China won't keep them around if they're free to leave (my lab was a cocktail party we attended last night). (2) You will, with mixed feelings, cease to think of anything the least interesting or amusing to say because what's the point? This is a relief, until mental atrophy sets in. Quickly. (3) Anything you write down in response to questions will be taken with more weight than it deserves. The person to my right at dinner procured for me a pen and paper, and when I answered her questions with the kind of offhand wisecracks that usually get lost in the crowd roar, she laughed as if she'd just read them in Boswell or Twain. (4) With yourself removed from the competition, you are free to enjoy good conversation more than even before, and I was in luck tonight. Richard Wilbur the poet and Robert Stone the novelist were reminiscing about their days as hoboes in, respectively, the early forties and mid-sixties, and the world they described of dusty rail beds and clanking boxcars, great prison beds and terrible prison breakfasts sounded like the enchanted forest itself.

However, beware if the talk turns dull. It's damnably hard to concentrate and look attentive, which nevertheless seems to be a requirement: even if you can't talk, you're expected to look lively. At least I *think* you are.

The Consolations of Philosophy

Taking the long view—suppose I lose? I have lived through sixty orbits of the globe and can expect maybe another twenty something. If I can squeeze out a few more, I'll settle. Watching the young people romp on the beach, one would like to hang around forever, just to feel the sun and see what's doing today. But the young people will become old people, and you have to move along sometime. There are a lot of already old people around here too, and they seem to enjoy life to the hilt, but enough is enough. When the mind slows and I can't think of the word I want to write next, to hell with what's doing today.

On the other hand, the physical decrepitude of old age seems to bother people surprisingly little. When they were young, the old-timers around here must have dreaded the thought of some-day looking the way they do now, all scales and wattles, but when it comes, it must seem like the only way to look. There may come the occasional shocking day when you notice some-thing missing, but on the whole, old age is the essence of tact. And like all afflictions, old age seems to carry its own remedies, or placebos, within it, and its own mysterious sources of fun—and its own piece of the secret that nothing is ever as bad as it looks from outside. *No* one's life seems tragic from inside.

This last week has coincided with the Winter Olympics in Albertville, France, and the steady contemplation of that no-blest of elements, snow, even on television, goes very well with thoughts of mortality and whatever one means by *im*-mortality. Two nights ago, a young woman from Canada and another from Alaska came hurtling down the most harrowing-looking (and exquisitely photographed) mountains to take first and second prize in the downhill ski run, to the dyspeptic frowns of the European aces who had skied earlier under worse conditions. And the unholy glee on the faces of the two North American rapscallions was enough to make one's heart laugh. This was happiness on the same epic scale as tragedy, and not just the usual slaphappy scale of comedy. And it oc-curred to me that they would probably always be happy be-cause of this moment. Only in fiction do people shrivel after some early triumph: in real life they are usually well pleased with themselves, as if some crucial thing has been settled once and for all.

Unfortunately the losers have to suffer inordinately to pro-duce this effect, but even *losers* seem finally strengthened and in a strange way cheered by the experience, so that when you see Bobby Thomson and Ralph Branca together these days, you'd have a hard time guessing which one hit that ridiculous home run and which one gave it up. At any rate, Branca, the loser, has certainly gotten over it better than I or my friends have, which suggests in comic form a larger and more serious truth: that while suffering may carry its own antidote, watching someone else suffer doesn't necessarily. It is almost always easier to die than to watch a loved one die, and two friends of mine who recently lost their husbands to cancer suffered, palpably, much more than I ever have. (Incidentally, their respective revivals since this was written would have fit very well the theme of Olympian struggle and triumph: it *is* infinitely better to have loved and lost, but it can take a long time to realize it.)

Things Are Tough All Over

After dinner we went looking for music, which is blessedly easy to find in Key West, this time in a largely gay saloon where a woman was playing and singing most wittily to one of those magical keyboards which seem to sound like any instrument you want them to. It was the kind of atmosphere in which for many years I would have felt uncomfortable and foreign, but there wasn't a trace of that tonight. On a recuperation high, all the world is your brother, and as the young guys milled around in their undershirts and whatnot, I found myself appreciating their various interpretations of manhood the way you appreciate a choppy but original play. Some of them seemed completely successful, others touchingly less so. But it occurred to me that so many heterosexual men don't even try to do it differently: masculinity is a narrow formula that you stray from at your peril. This is the way it was written, dummy. Don't try to improve on John Wayne.

However, anything that walked in the door would have been just fine with me tonight: e.g., the one other straight couple, sitting defiantly close to each other, or the two middle-aged ladies who rocked and clapped ecstatically to the music—as did I, mind you. What was interesting about these particular gays was that almost to a one, they were the kind of men who could, and probably did, "pass" the rest of the time. In fact, until recently, and the great closet-opening, I didn't know that guys who looked and moved like that could be homosexual. As it was, I had no trouble imagining that I was roistering right now with a platoon of superbly fit, extravagantly *macho* young Americans with whom I would be going into combat tomorrow. As they greeted each other, I sensed the same kind of sweaty comradeship you might expect among soldiers, and I realized that these youngsters are *always* between battles: tomorrow will be another one, or next week when they have to return to Jersey, or indeed any time they stray from their base. So being completely themselves is something they can only practice on rare and incredibly exciting occasions, and it must seem a bit like putting on fancy dress, strange even to themselves.

Perhaps what particularly prompted these thoughts was a conversation going on right next to me between my wife and a gay we'd met earlier in the evening, who'd recommended the music here and seemed quite delighted to see us again. Or more specifically, to see my wife. Because it was to her ear exclusively that he now confided his thoughts—namely that he feared the straight world despite himself, and wished with all his heart that there were more heteros like her, who seemed so much at ease with him. They hugged over this, and my wife said that there were *lots* more like her and that we weren't all his enemies by any means.

But none of this talk included me. Either my manner still seemed too alien (you can't change the style of a lifetime in one sentimental moment), or else the whole world of heterosexual males was suspect. After all, if we weren't the enemy, who was? At least, it was probably too soon to trust any of us on sight. And, even as I sat there feeling beneficent, a young, all-American-type boy, the kind that grown-ups dote over and have great hopes for, took it upon himself to start smooching wetly with all and sundry like the love-hungry puppy that he was, and I thought about parents and children, and despite myself, about how this boy's parents would feel if they saw him now. And I thought how having sad parents might seem almost as oppressive as having angry ones, but how both kinds, sad and angry, were more likely to be fathers than mothers: this is just so far from what we had planned.

And this is probably what my wife's young friend saw in me, or remembered from elsewhere, and in any event, refused to confide in now. And with that, I decided to add a veritable new army to the ranks of lives worse off than my own.

(And what does this have to do with health? It's about recuperation, that's what, and recuperation is not concerned with sickness, but with everything else under the sun and how much better it seems when you're not sick.)

Mortality

Yesterday, my wife noted that someone we knew seemed to be having a hard and resentful time of it facing the first onset of old age, and it occurred to me that there must be a right way and a wrong way to do this also—to do what George Bush might call "the aging thing." Since old age is written into the blueprints, and is not a vicious interpolation like polio or cancer, or else a trick we hadn't been warned about, it's obviously just a question of finding the key, as it is at every age. Adolescence, for instance, with all its turbulence, had compensations that you'd kill for now: even the melancholy of a teenager, which seems almost too heavy to bear, is rich and creamy with poetry if you know how to go with it. (Tip to parents: *do not try to cheer Junior up.* You'll spoil everything.) I remember turning out the lights and listening to Gershwin and gazing out the window at the London rain, and feeling exquisitely sad, "laugh out loud sad."

Anyway, I'm sure old age offers equivalent pleasures. Do these include the prospects of an afterlife? They include the *possibility* of an afterlife, yes. My conviction hasn't changed that the best of all outcomes would be to expect an afterlife and not get one. But as the tastes come flooding back into one's mouth, it is easy to believe in a generous God. Anyone who took the trouble to implant a different flavor in each of his creations—some of which flavors can provoke ecstasy in his *other* creations, i.e., us—can be counted on to provide whichever is best for us in the end. The God one turns to in sickness, and only in sickness, is, on reflection, a sickly fellow himself, made of slender hopes and corrosive fears, and is easily blown away; but the God of Recovery fairly bursts with confidence—the sages of Happy Valley might even call it grandiosity—and the landscape seems to be littered with His gifts. To put it another way, Evolution winnowing its way among swirling gases from a collapsed supernova, or whatever, might conceivably account for the taste of the crab, but only God could make a lobster.

Is That All There Is to Bad News?
(With apologies, and greetings, to Jerry Lieber)

Yesterday, the other shoe dropped, with considerable force, on my head. "By the way," I asked the oral hygienist casually on the way out of my examination, "what's the prognosis on a dry mouth?" "Oh," she said, suddenly flustered by the need to be kind while informative. "It's usually for life—but you get used to it." As she stumbled on, I waited for it to hit. "Look at those people in the waiting area. They're all drinking water," she said. And so they were, to the tune of "Where will we all be one hundred years from now?" Picture three or four elderly gentlemen in blue hospital gowns taking turns bending over a water cooler like cows at a stream. "That's how it is," she said. "But you get used to it."

I had predicted a lousy day when this happened, and looked forward with some irritability for it to kick in now. But my response to bad news will never cease to baffle me. At least I seem to have gotten over the crazy elation that always used to come first, like a nervous smile; this time I felt nothing at all, followed by a frustrating certainty that the bad part, the brooding part, would be along shortly and absolutely could not be avoided. God, they hand out life sentences lightly around here, I thought. "Will I ever enjoy food as much as I used to?" I asked the kind lady. Obviously, this was a tough one for her. "Well—knowing your interest, you may come close," she said. Which meant nothing, of course.

So out into the sunshine, and wait. The ultracautious northern springtime was finally under way, and Manhattan is the place to be at such a moment, as at most moments. And I waited and waited. Either bad news is sinking in slower or I'm getting used to these things faster. (I finally gave up worrying on account of darkness, and have not resumed it since.)

Journal's End

Dr. X. had to be faced sometime, although I knew that the man was perfectly capable of ruining even spring, as he tried to last year. And I must say, the examination was quite grueling, as if he were teasing me. Doctors are essentially mythical creatures anyway, and it took no great imagination to see in his overflowing benevolence a spirit of pure mischief. As he tooled along twisting my tongue this way and that, he told his apprentice of the day a couple of things he'd never told me, which indicated almost in passing how much he cared about his patients and how heavy his own burden of decision must be: he said (1) they had not simply run my tongue and neck operations together as they usually did in such cases, because the radiation that inevitably follows the combination usually weakens one's shoulders and "this man needs his shoulders" (to walk with), and (2) they were constantly aware that this man also "partially works with his tongue—and I think he has done outstandingly well in that department," i.e., saints be praised that I can still talk.

Saints be praised indeed for that, and for the next part, where he said to me, "Everything looks fine. I'll see you in six weeks."

Appropriately, it was raining like hell when I got outside, and Park Avenue looked just awful. I hadn't realized until he said it how much tension had been building up for this moment, and how sweet his words would seem. Suddenly the last trace of fret about dry mouth, etc., was gone, but so were all my sophistries about cancer not being what it was cracked up to be, and about my own form of it not being so serious—nice try, fellow, but I could tell from the way the corners of my mouth seemed to touch the lobes of my ears that I had taken it a bit more seriously than I had cared to admit.

Here the journal pauses, and although it would resume shortly to record further ups and downs—saliva sightings and ominous twinges that came equally to nothing; a tie, in other words—my relationship to the disease was pretty much established. An ounce of fear stirred into a gallon of habit so you'd hardly notice it. The mixture is different with every illness, but there are family resemblances. You've survived, it could have been worse, and you find yourself with this mysterious pocketful of loose change, the extra adrenaline or whatever that you were given to fight this thing, which you are now free to spend in any way you are still able to, and even without legs or arms, you'll think of something.

14.

REFLECTIONS IN A DENTIST'S CHAIR

When I started writing this book, I actually had visions of posthumous publication, with a wake serving as the ultimate book party, the one that doesn't even wait for the reviews. But here I am, high and dry (still dry, alas), back in the very dentist's chair where this whole saga started—well, not exactly in it, but just out of it—and feeling quite decisively alive.

Which seems like where we came in. Every true story has numerous beginnings and an infinity of endings, but as this particular one began to form a shape in my mind, I kept returning to this primal scene, the one where I'm asking Doctor Omega here if he does biopsies. Everything before that is prologue, to be disposed of in an Elizabethan couplet; what comes next will have to start its own story. I know a good symbol when I see one, and a dentist's chair makes a most attractive one for me right now. Placed in the upright position, this article of furniture could almost pass for a place of execution, but just tilt it back a bit and it becomes its real self, a small-claims operating table, a short-order surgery, with its picks and drills and paper cups arrayed unpretentiously around it the way they were in Grandma's day. You certainly don't come here to die, but to live on indefinitely in straitened but thought-provoking circumstances. Similarly, the kind of cancer I have *can* kill you, but not, I devoutly trust, before it has asked you to open wide and told you to rinse a hundred times.

Today's procedure is a perfect blend of cancer and dentistry, of deadliness and dailiness, which provides absolutely no space for heroic posturing. After all, it's the same old dentist's chair it's always been. My regular dentist, Dr. T., sometimes asks— after he's filled my mouth with cotton and I can't answer—why there has never been a dentist hero in fiction; but I think it's partly the setting. There's something nurserylike about a dentist's office, something that reminds you of your first bad, but harmless, dream, and I dare anyone not to revert to childhood at least a little way on entering one. You don't feel a great big grown-up fear, but you wouldn't get mad if the nurse held your hand.

Not me today, though, for some strange reason. The pleasantries have been exchanged, and the doctor is outlining the worst that can happen, and it's bad all right, but somehow not serious. To be sure, I've heard most of what he's saying before, but it always sounds worse from a few inches away, and when the speaker already has a drill in his hand. And Dr. Omega adds a wrinkle I hadn't taken in before. One of the games oral radiation plays is that, having laid waste to your teeth, it then insists that you hang on to them anyhow, in whatever shape you find them. And this I have apparently failed to do. ("Did you remember to brush your teeth tonight?" my mother asks; the sheets are warm and the floor is cold, and I answer with my first lie.) To my relief, I gather there is nothing I could have done about it anyway. All the brushing in the world would not have helped. These babies have been *napalmed* by radiation, and the enamel long since burned away. Nightly applications of fluoride can only do so much for the survivors. Radiation is, as noted, primitive. It burns and moves on.

And now the doctor is reading me the consequences, some of which could, if I get an infection in the area, turn out to be serious enough even for my taste, the worst of them being that my beat-up old jaw might simply crack under the strain. I can almost hear it do so as he speaks, like the creaking door in *Inner*

Sanctum. But this is old news, and news only gets to scare you once. Was there anything else, Doctor?

Well, yes, as it turns out. The likelihood of my catching an infection is also *far* greater than I thought. Stripped of the technical jargon, which I don't understand anyway, it seems that the radiation target area has acquired the equivalent of an immune-deficiency problem, which means that it will be almost impossible for me *not* to get an infection, even if I seal off all the exits and entrances. The mouth is the Hong Kong of the body, an open port, and some damn thing is going to get in there, trust Omega's word.

So I brace myself for another round of indignities. If the worst does happen, as now seems likely, I'm obviously in for a very bad time—the whole cycle, in fact, as I break in a new affliction: a day or so of utter dismay, a determination to fight back if I can find anything to fight against, and then good cheer on new, more modest terms. Meanwhile, I'm beginning to feel like Croatia, or some other carved-up territory.

However, all this is still in the conditional and it hasn't so much hit me yet as tickled me. "Stop before you scare me to death," I say to the doc, who laughs obligingly. Has he been exaggerating slightly and putting the worst possible face on things in order to get me to rinse thoroughly, etc.? Or perhaps not. What interests me right now, because I'd never realized it before, is this sense that nothing absolutely intolerable or conclusively bad can happen to me so long as I'm safe and sound in a dentist's chair.

Now that's weird. Infinitely worse things have happened to me in these contraptions than anywhere else I've been, including having my teeth drilled without Novocaine, and to this day the collective memory of these atrocities obliges me to grip the chair arms convulsively every time I have my teeth cleaned. Yet perhaps because I've seen the worst they have to offer, and it goes without saying lived, I don't fear dentists' chairs, in the ultimate sense. There are no stricken faces gathered around them and no hushed voices in the next room. So—flinch? yes, every time; cringe, no.

"After all, they're only teeth," I almost said to Dr. T. when he first glimpsed my irradiated molars and saw what "they" had done to his handiwork. My friend loves his subject, his chosen angle on life, and I certainly didn't want to insult it. But if you're born in Great Britain, you spend the first half of your life preparing to lose your teeth, it's almost a birthright, and hey! *it wasn't going to kill me.*

Thus does the ante raise itself in these war games. Recently, I'll admit to getting just a tiny bit bored with my dry mouth, which is obviously here to stay, and with the whole recovery cycle itself, from apprehension to false hopes and trial balloons to, at long last, the weird jubilation at the end of the tunnel. A *steak au poivre avec pommes frites* still looks awfully good, jubilation or no, yet such dishes will remain forever a problem in sewage disposal after the first few magical bites.*

But something always seems to come along to keep life interesting, and suddenly the last two years with nothing but a dry mouth to complain about seem like a golden age. Just let me get through the rest of my life without a broken jaw, Oh Lord, and I'll never be even a little bit bored again, I swear.

But supposing I do get the broken jaw—what will I say the *next* time, when my ears fall off or my skin starts to itch or burn uncontrollably, like the late Dennis Potter's? "Today I consider myself the luckiest man on the face of the earth," said the dying Lou Gehrig, and, objectively speaking, this remark is as crazy as anything in Voltaire's famous satire. But maybe *Candide* isn't a joke: maybe the chap who insists that this is "the best of all possible worlds" in the teeth of the evidence is the natural man facing his grotesque afflictions the way, in fact, most people do.

Gehrig, by chance, makes an excellent witness, because he was generally a stolid man not much given to overstatement, or for that matter statement of any kind: the above words are, to

---

* On the way to learning this, I discovered, to my surprise, that whole volumes have been written on the subject of saliva—and fascinating volumes they must be—but a wonderful friend who was able to run through the high points for me reports that the "saliva literature" all comes up empty on the last page. This slimy, disgusting material, which it can cost you money to eject in the wrong place, e.g., the subway, is harder to replace than gold or uranium.

the best of my knowledge, his only ones to come down to us. So what on earth had gotten into him that day?

For one thing, a stadiumful of fans and a benchful of teammates, all unequivocally on his side for the first time in his or most anyone's life. I remember from polio days the rare pleasure of seeing an enemy, or a guy you weren't quite sure about (he seemed friendly on alternate Tuesdays), smiling uncomplicated encouragement at your bedside: you're sure of him now. And for Gehrig, there was Babe Ruth, the Big Baby himself, with his arm over his old friend's shoulder, their famous feud either forgotten or shrunk to size. Lou wasn't the only lucky man present. All present in Yankee Stadium that day had been given a license to love a fellow human to the limit, without qualification or prenuptial agreement, and to root for that person as ardently as they'd ever rooted for themselves. Granted such a license, people can astonish themselves with how much raw emotion is in the well, some of it blarney, of course, to be forgotten on the way home, but some of it good coin to last a lifetime.

However, I fancy that, for the central figure, all this was just a (most welcome) bonus, a sideshow. If the stadium had emptied out suddenly, and he had been left standing there alone, Gehrig would have felt no less lucky, because the applause merely confirmed what he already knew: that he was having a very good day.

A series of them in fact. Up to now, no one had ever done more than Gehrig to make baseball seem like just another day at the office: he'd never missed a game in all of fourteen-some years, and, as far as anyone could see, had never paused to savor one either (according to legend, his record for rapid postgame showering and locker-room evacuation still stands). But this one, he savored. The Iron Horse, as he was called, was presumably in possession of all his formidable resources that day, lined up in ranks for a fight they couldn't possibly win, a fight they couldn't even *fight*. (Never has "winning is the only thing" seemed an emptier doctrine: Gehrig had been winning for years and it was never this good.) In this heightened, fully mobilized condition, the man knew exactly the value of a moment of human life, and knew that, on this scale, a day like this was worth a thousand of his old ones.

But all this seems a million miles and years away from my sanctuary in Dr. Omega's office. Two months have passed, thanks to the magic of print, since my teeth were plucked from the radiated zone, and much of the time seems to have been spent in this here spot as Dr. Omega, who is a worrier, broods repeatedly over his work. "I guess technically you're healed," he says grudgingly, as if *he* were the one having his teeth pulled, "but I'd like you to stay on the antibiotics anyway."

Done and done. I've been warned that it takes six months to be absolutely sure my jaw won't crack, but this is the kind of danger it's a pleasure to live with: it's like playing Russian roulette with a thousand-barreled pistol. As a danger sport it ranks somewhere between chess and being hit by a flying tiddlywink. A couple of times since the last operation I've had some real old-fashioned scares, and I've felt the same giddy rush that swept over me as I learned each time that the obsessive throb in my neck wasn't going to kill me after all but was probably just the radiation making its slow, graceless departure and taking, I trusted, the pain in my tongue and the twinge in my chin along with it. Great! There is nothing like gambling for your life so long as you keep on winning. Yet for all the wild elation that follows these victories, I can't imagine anyone volunteering for another round. For myself, a low-stakes game of Old Maid with Dr. Omega seems quite rich enough for my blood these days. Once you've been well and truly frightened, all you need is a touch-up to bring it all back.

In other words, when you don't need the strength to fight for your life, you not only find you don't have it anymore, you can't imagine having it. Although it would clearly be wonderful to feel as good as Lou Gehrig felt that day, it's a safe bet that not one soul in the stadium would have changed places with him. There is an unimaginable leap involved, which is why it is always so thrilling to see someone else standing triumphantly on the other side of it.

But of course, one could never do it oneself. Precious few people, perhaps not even Gehrig himself, ever receive the faintest hint of that kind of strength until they absolutely need it. And to compound the mystery, even *after* you've been there, you may have trouble imagining it, which is why I can only stare at the polio years in wonderment and why I still live in the same simmering apprehension of cancer I started out with. Nothing can quite convince me that the next bad news won't overwhelm me. I know better, which helps. But I don't *feel* better, or stronger, or less essentially cowardly. (A hero would have been useless in this experiment anyway.)

One thing, though, you are allowed to bring down from the mountain is the memory of how beautiful everything looked up there. In G. K. Chesterton's novel *Manalive*, the manic hero forces a nihilistic philosopher out onto a window ledge at gunpoint and keeps him there until the latter *sees* some merit in staying alive. And this is when you're going to see it, if ever— while it is outlined brilliantly against its opposite, death, the void. I suspect that people who've returned from the dead have very few complaints afterwards.

Happily for the rest of us, one doesn't have to go to anything like that far to make out the colors of life. Just recovering from a head cold, or a sick stomach, can do it, if you drink in the contrast attentively enough; or else just walking out of the dentist's office, as I recently did, with a reprieve and with a news clipping in one's pocket promising a brand-new saliva pill that really *works* this time. Great balls of fire! Sydney Greenstreet, receiving a tip on the Maltese falcon and girding up for another adventure in its improbable pursuit, could not have felt more pleased with himself or with the universe than I did as I drove home that day through the magnificent streets and incomparable foliage that lie like a carpet of welcome between my house and the dentist's office.

Being sick is the small tax I pay for noticing this gorgeous route and so much else. But please don't hit me again. I don't think I could take it. As usual.